C0-AXD-242

Child Snatching

The Legal Response to the Abduction of Children

SANFORD N. KATZ

Produced by the ABA Press
Copyright © 1981 Sanford N. Katz
ISBN: 0-89707-036-4
Library of Congress Catalog Number: 81-65945

To the Memory
of

Brigitte M. Bodenheimer

Acknowledgments

This book is based on a study prepared for the National Institute of Justice of the United States Department of Justice under P. O. No. 0-0608-JARS. I appreciate the support and guidance given me by Ms. Annesley K. Schmidt of the Institute. Points of view or opinions stated in the book are my own and do not necessarily represent the official position of the United States Department of Justice.

In preparing the study for the National Institute of Justice, I was aided by four Boston College law students: Kenneth H. Ernstoff '81, Todd F. Simon '80, Dianne W. Mills '81, and Madeline Mirabito '80. I should like to thank them for their able assistance. An additional thanks is owed to Kenneth H. Ernstoff who undertook and completed with care and good humor the painstaking task of proofreading galleys with me and to Atty. Patricia M. Hoff, Director of the ABA Project on Child Custody, for sharing with me her materials and views on the Federal Act. I should also like to thank Mrs. Mary Nardone for typing the manuscript and preparing it for publication.

I should like to take this opportunity to express my gratitude to Professor Homer H. Clark, Jr. whose writings on family law, especially *The Law of Domestic Relations in the United States*, have influenced my own research.

During the preparation of this study and in other family law projects I have benefited from the wise counsel of the late Professor Brigitte M. Bodenheimer who died while this manuscript was in progress. It is to her memory that this book is dedicated.

SANFORD N. KATZ

Waban, Massachusetts
May 14, 1981

Contents

I. Introduction

The primary goal of this book is to provide a detached analysis of the problem of parental kidnapping of children in the United States[1] after or during divorce and separation. We focus on the Uniform Child Custody Jurisdiction Act (UCCJA) because it is the most important legal deterrent to kidnapping. The Act itself is analyzed and cases decided under the Act are analyzed, interpreted, and compared with one another. We have aimed for objectivity and believe it has been achieved for the most part by looking into the largest potential pool of cases; it is impossible, however, to assess the effectiveness and weakness of the UCCJA without making projections of judgments, particularly when dealing with sections that have not received close attention from the courts. A projection or judgment is related to the writings of legal scholars in this area of the law, or is based on analogous reasoning from other legal subject areas.

In the final chapter we analyze the remedies available to aggrieved parents in the state courts and discuss the variations in these remedies from state to state. Although a small number of states have hinted in their opinions that violations of the UCCJA may be grounds for a court to make a remedy available, in the vast majority of cases the UCCJA and the question of remedies are strictly separated. The UCCJA itself makes no formal reference to any remedy. State remedies discussed in the book include

---

1. The problem of international kidnapping is beyond the scope of this book. For a discussion of international child abduction, see Bodenheimer, B.M., *The Hague Draft Convention in International Child Abuction*, 14 FAM. L.Q. 99 (1980).It should be noted that the Draft Convention discussed in Professor Bodenheimer's article is the Convention on the Civil Aspects of International Child Abduction. Subsequent to her article, the Convention was unanimously adopted by the member countries (October 6–25, 1980).

criminal kidnapping and interference laws, civil tort liability, civil contempt, and the writ of habeas corpus. We discuss recent attempts at creating and passing federal remedies, but do not analyze potential effect, since the book is limited to existing law.

Through each section, old laws and court cases are compared and contrasted with new ones. This is necessary not only to understand the background that produced the UCCJA and the various state remedies, but also to understand the great changes in legal and judicial reasoning expected under the newer laws. New laws cannot become fully effective until they take center stage in the minds of those who must work with them most regularly. We discuss cases in which either lawyers or judges, or both, appear to have misunderstood applicable law; they are viewed as exceptions that will decrease in numbers as time goes on.

An Overview of the UCCJA

In Chapter II we discuss the Uniform Child Custody Jurisdiction Act and the legal and social pressures that led to its promulgation and eventual enactment in forty-four states. The potential for widespread child snatching had been lying fallow in the system for many years. Although the potential was noted by legal scholars in the late 1950s and early 1960s, public attention was not aroused until there occurred an explosion of child snatchings during the late 1960s and throughout the 1970s. Estimates of incidents (by no means officially documented) run up to 100,000 a year and higher.[2]

The potential for parents to remove their children from one state to another successfully developed as a combination of two major factors. First, the United States Supreme Court gave the Full Faith and Credit Clause of the U.S. Constitution only extremely limited application to child custody decrees. Any state could modify another state's decree. Second, the states developed conflicting or multiple bases for exercising jurisdiction in child custody cases because they were permitted under Supreme Court decisions and because the states believed strongly that flexibility

---

2. Empirical research in this area is extremely difficult to undertake. For a discussion of research possibilities, *see* R. J. Gelles, Research Issues in the Study of Parental Kidnapping (July, 1980). Dr. Gelles prepared his report for the National Institute of Justice of the U.S. Department of Justice.

was necessary to best protect children's interests. Often, however, as a result of easy modification standards and multiple jurisdiction, more than one state would simultaneously conclude that it was best suited to determine the interests of the same child. The problem became more acute as the population became more mobile.

In Chapter II we analyze the major provisions of the UCCJA, beginning with the statement of nine general principles in § 1 of the Act; in close cases, the general principles are meant to help courts make decisions. One state court has concluded that the general principles reflect a continuation of the "best-interests-of-the-child" test, but in a tighter structure.

The most important provision of the UCCJA is § 3 on jurisdiction. Initial jurisdiction to render a custody decree exists in the child's home state, which is considered the state where a child has lived for six months or more. A secondary jurisdictional basis is provided if the home state rule does not apply for "significant connections" between a child, parent, and a given state. Finally, § 3 provides for emergency jurisdiction to be exercised by a court which would otherwise be powerless to act, when a child faces danger in the state. Emergency jurisdiction is a modified continuation of *parens patriae* jurisdiction, which was a chief culprit in opening the courts to easy modifications.

Three other UCCJA provisions, designed to keep a child custody case in one single state court, are considered appropriate under § 3. The doctrine of *forum non conveniens* applies when it appears that two states may have jurisdiction at the same time. In such a case, the state with less contact should defer to the state with greater contact. The time in which an action is brought weighs heavily under the UCCJA; other states must defer when an action has begun in another state. To be certain that both these provisions operate properly, the state courts are urged to make sure that actions are not in process in other states before proceeding.

Section 8 of the UCCJA incorporates the clean-hands doctrine that was used before the Act was passed. Under clean hands, a parent who abducts a child and later seeks to bring an action for modification of a custody decree in a new state is refused jurisdiction and directed back to the original state's court. Properly used, § 8 directly limits incidents of child snatching.

In Chapter II we also discuss recognition, validity, enforcement, and due process provisions of the Act that attempt to overcome the problems presented by the U.S. Supreme Court decisions and the state decisions that followed. The chapter concludes with a discussion of the Act's weaknesses. A major weakness appears to be that the UCCJA places a great amount of discretion with the trial judges in custody cases. A second weakness is that the Act itself provides no direct remedies, and in fact does not require, but only urges, interstate cooperation. Early experience, however, shows that application of the Act in fact reduces the incidence of interstate child custody cases.

Jurisdiction under the UCCJA

A central principle under the UCCJA is that a single state should have primary responsibility for any given custody case and that jurisdiction should shift to a second state only under specifically circumscribed circumstances, if at all. Once a state court issues a custody decree upon proper jurisdictional standards as provided in the UCCJA, the Act requires that all other states in which it is in effect must recognize and enforce rather than modify the decree.

In Chapter III we analyze cases that have construed the jurisdictional requirements—both for initial jurisdiction and for modification jurisdiction—to see how effective the Act's provisions have been and whether a pattern emerges in the various state cases. One notable feature is that the states appear to rely heavily on the Commissioners' Notes that accompany each section of the UCCJA in interpreting the Act.

The home-state provision simplifies the exercise of jurisdiction. The cases show that a child's home state is usually easy to determine and that other states will typically defer to a court in that state. It is not clear, however, that the home state remains as simple a question when a modification action, rather than an initial action, is brought; under such circumstances, two courts may technically qualify for jurisdiction.

Significant connections as a basis for jurisdiction is meant to limit the parens patriae principle under which courts often assumed jurisdiction for no reason except that the child was within the state. The cases show that the provision works. Also, it appears that significant-connections jurisdiction continues with the initial state court after another state has technically become the child's home state. At any rate, preferred jurisdiction remains with the initial state until it is shown that proper jurisdiction lies elsewhere. When concurrent jurisdiction exists, the courts have generally been willing to defer to the court of original jurisdiction before acting.

Emergency jurisdiction appeared to be a major exception to UCCJA, a potential loophole that, if opened, could harm the overall operation of the Act. States use the emergency exception with remarkable restraint, limiting it almost exclusively to situations where a child is likely to suffer physical harm. Although emergency jurisdiction retains the concept of parens patriae, it is a limited retention. The state courts have readily interpreted it as a rejection of the old, comprehensive law of parens patriae that almost automatically opened up the courts to parents. The courts are also devising procedures to distinguish genuine evidence of emergency from mere allegations before taking formal jurisdiction. And, even when emergency jurisdiction is exercised, it is used to provide temporary placements that only remove the child from potential dangers.

The inconvenient-forum provisions also appear to work as intended. The courts are eager to assure that an action is heard in the state most capable of deciding it properly. The use of these provisions, however, rests on the discretion of the judge. No hard-and-fast rules define an inconvenient forum. Because of this discretion, a few inconsistent cases have appeared.

One positive trend in the state court opinions has been that the courts of states which have not enacted the UCCJA often apply its provisions or principles of their own volition, showing that the judiciary is convinced the Act offers the best means of resolving interstate child custody disputes. It also appears that courts in states where the Act has recently become effective—the majority of states where the UCCJA is in effect—are monitoring court decisions from states where the Act was adopted earlier as guides for decision in their own cases. This bodes well for assuring uniformity of results and interstate cooperation in the future.

Full Faith and Credit and Comity

Four U.S. Supreme Court cases, decided from the late 1940s to early 1960s, helped create the legal climate in which child snatching could flourish. The Court held at various times that the Full Faith and Credit Clause of the Constitution applied to child custody decrees, but only to the extent that there had been no changed circumstances, the standard by which most states justify modification of an original child custody decree. This meant that a court need only find changed circumstances—often remarkably easy to find—to modify another state's decree.

In companion cases, the Court held that a state must have *in personam* jurisdiction over the parties to issue a valid custody decree, and that the principles of *res judicata,* which prevent relitigation of issues tried once, may not necessarily apply to child custody decrees. The Supreme Court's jurisdiction cases helped encourage the spread of parens patriae jurisdiction. The res judicata decision, like the modifiability case, granted res judicata effect to custody decrees only to the extent that the same facts were at issue in a second case. Of course, when circumstances changed, the facts were not the same.

The Court did, however, advise the state courts that they were free to grant comity recognition to one another's decrees and noted that it ruled only on what was required by the Constitution; recognition was not required. Comity is a doctrine whereby courts recognize decrees, based on respect for another state's courts. Few states took the advice to heart.

Following the Supreme Court cases, some states granted full faith and credit to custody decrees; others applied full comity principles that often upheld decrees in their entirety. A majority of states adopted a modified comity approach that left open the possibility of modification; a small minority utterly rejected both comity and full faith and credit. The principle of res judicata was similarly scattered.

Since the UCCJA is a state law, it cannot, consistent with the U.S. Constitution, prescribe that full faith and credit be granted to sister-state decrees. One state court, however, which has held that this is just what the Act intends, may be right in principle, but a state law cannot legislate full faith and credit without intruding in the province of the Supreme Court or Congress.

Comity appears to be the goal of the UCCJA, and a majority of courts that have considered the question agree. But it is a strict form of statutory comity, far removed from the vague, discretionary approach of yesterday. Upon proper jurisdiction, recognition and enforcement are required; formerly, it was a question for each judge. The UCCJA, as a uniform state law, may be expected to meet the Supreme Court's suggestion that the states agree if they choose.

Surprisingly, most courts that have recognized and enforced another state's decree have not even mentioned comity or full faith and credit; but then, neither does the Act itself. Since the provisions of the Act are all founded on the question of proper bases of jurisdiction, the courts need only refer to the provisions to uphold a decree. This is a salutary result, since it frees the courts from the confusing string of comity and full faith and credit cases that preceded the Act.

The UCCJA also provides that a decree issued upon proper jurisdiction be entitled to res judicata effect. Of course, changed circumstances may still be shown, but, barring a shift in jurisdiction, only to the court that first heard the case. Both the jurisdiction and res judicata provisions appear to satisfy the demands of U.S. Supreme Court case requirements.

The only exception to the principle of comity recognition is found in the emergency-jurisdiction provision. Although emergency jurisdiction is justified as a retention of parens patriae, it must be noted that the parens patriae concept contributed heavily to much of the lack of recognition prior to the Act. An alternative explanation for overriding the recognition and enforcement provisions might be to argue that, instead of the state-oriented parens patriae approach, the exception offers an approach that stresses paramount rights of children, such as health, safety, education, and similar rights, based on constitutional foundations. The emergency-jurisdiction exception, then, exists to honor rights higher than those held by the custodial parent or the state.

Modification

Standards for deciding which state or states have jurisdiction to modify are discussed primarily in Chapters II and III. Chapter V notes that the UCCJA has no effect upon the states' internal modification laws; they may be strict or loose, as the individual state decides. The Act technically allows a parent to move with a child to a second state and establish modification jurisdiction. In practice, however, parents are virtually unable to choose the least strict forum.

An important issue, developing as a result of the § 14 modification provisions, concerns the circumstances that justify a second state's exercise of modification jurisdiction. The test of the Act appears to allow a modification shift with relative ease. The Commissioners' Notes to § 14 suggest that continuing jurisdiction remains with the initial court until all parties leave that state. Legal scholars urge that the initial state court have continuing jurisdiction until such time as it declines to exercise it and defers to the courts of another state. The cases are also divided. The question of modification jurisdiction may be the most open of all issues posed by the Act. Cases in which two courts hold that they have jurisdiction are fairly common; unless a uniform pattern of decisions develops, the modification jurisdiction provisions could encourage a renewal of interstate competition. Given the strict requirements of §§ 3 and 14, forum shopping would still be far more difficult than before.

Remedies

Except for a few provisions that allow a party to collect fees and costs from a wrongdoer, the UCCJA itself does not specifically provide any remedies. The Act may have an indirect effect, however. Violations of the Act may become useful as evidence in a later remedy action. And the recognition and enforcement sections of the Act appear to have had a salutary effect in returning children to parents entitled to custody more readily. Because the Act is new in most states, it has not widely effected traditional remedies. In Chapter VI, we discuss and analyze the various historical remedies, as well as current remedial approaches.

Attempts to bring criminal sanctions against parents who kidnap their own children have essentially been unsuccessful in this country. If the child was taken before a custody decree was issued, traditional law held that no violation occurred because the parent, as a married person, was still entitled to custody. Most states have simple kidnapping statutes or interference with custodial rights laws designed to prevent child snatching. Although prosecutions under these statutes have increased as the problem has increased, criminal sanctions are still relatively ineffective. Courts are reluctant to imprison parents. When the child is taken out of state, the sanctions are unenforceable. Most important, criminal sanctions do not provide the most efficacious remedy—the return of the child.

Criminal sanctions have been broadened in recent years to apply to relatives and third parties who aid a child abductor. Traditional laws often exempted third parties and parents, even when a third-party abduction was ordered or paid for by a parent.

Tort liability, which in custody cases originally developed from a father's right to his child's services, offers a financial remedy to an aggrieved parent, but again is no guarantee that the child will be returned. A parent is more likely to receive damages on the basis of mental anguish or suffering or violation of a legally recognized right not to have one's child abducted. Relatives and third parties have also been found liable for tort damages. Tort liability promises greater effectiveness than state criminal sanctions, if only because the courts are more willing to assess damages against a parent who has abducted a child than to imprison him or her.

Civil contempt, a limited remedy because it does not prevail outside a court's jurisdiction, is largely ineffective. A parent who violates the provisions of a custody decree may be cited for contempt of court, but it is considered an offense against the power and dignity of the court rather than against the custodial parent who has been deprived of custody. A contempt citation, however, may be strong evidence in a second state proceeding, leading to enforcement of another state's decree. A person who can be subjected to jurisdiction and held in contempt may be fined, forfeit a bond, or even be imprisoned. Contempt, like most remedies, does not effect the direct return of the child. A contempt citation may be most effective when introduced as evidence to convince a second court not to exercise jurisdiction on a clean-hands argument.

The writ of habeas corpus, although direct, has had a checkered history as a remedy for child custody infractions. Such a writ in a custody context requires the wrongdoer to hand over the child. The parent who seeks the writ must merely show a legal right to custody, usually on the basis of an original decree. Historically, however, most courts held that when a custodial parent seeks a writ of habeas corpus, the non-custodial parent is entitled to bring a simultaneous action for modification. Since custody was often transferred as a result of such decisions, custodial parents became cautious about using the habeas corpus remedy, often resorting to child snatching themselves.

Under the U.S. Supreme Court, a habeas corpus case often effectively became a full, new custody trial involving double jeopardy for the parent granted custody in the original action. It is doubtful that the habeas corpus remedy may be so broadened today under the UCCJA, but the Act does not, on its face, apply. The best position, however, would hold that a habeas corpus action, in the absence of an emergency, is a strict enforcement procedure under the Act.

Habeas corpus has created confusion in interstate child custody cases. Full faith and credit, comity, res judicata, and forum non conveniens did not apply under traditional law because, once the custodial parent was lured to the second state to retrieve the child following an abduction, the second state court had full jurisdiction over both parents and the child, a basis for jurisdiction that does not suffice under the UCCJA. Under the Act, jurisdiction may not be conferred by an act of wrongdoing.

Habeas corpus is expected to develop into the primary means of enforcing both domestic and international decrees. Section 23 of the UCCJA provides for recognition of the decrees of other countries.

Federal involvement in this area has been slow in forthcoming. However, President Carter in signing the Pneumococcal Vaccine Bill on December 28, 1980, also enacted the Parental Kidnapping Prevention Act of 1980, which grew out of legislation originally introduced by Senator Malcolm Wallop (R-Wyo.) in January 1979. The Act seeks to encourage cooperation among the states in order to deter parental kidnapping. Compliance with the goals expressed in the provisions of the UCCJA is the immediate objective of the Act. It allows for utilization of the Federal Parent Locator Service to find parents or children who have fled a jurisdiction in defiance of a custody decree. The Act calls for use of the Fugitive Felon Act where it can be shown that a child snatching parent has violated a state statute which defines parental kidnapping as a felony; this in turn would call for FBI involvement in the location and apprehension of the fugitive parent. The Parental Kidnapping Prevention Act of 1980 would serve primarily as a supplement to the UCCJA. Until the federal act undergoes extensive utilization and judicial interpretation, its impact on parental kidnapping is uncertain.

II. The Uniform Act: An Overview

A. Background

The kidnapping of children by their parents has become a problem of national and international concern in the last ten years.[1] A parent who snatches a child is assumed to have one paramount goal—to regain physical custody and the love and affection of the child following a separation or divorce decree. Frequently a child is kidnapped repeatedly from parent to parent. Not all parents who snatch children are anxious only to be with the children; child snatching often becomes a strategy in a long-running war between ex-spouses. The net result is that the child's life is continually disrupted or threatened with disruption as his home, school, friends, and custodial parent change. A completely accurate estimate of the extent of child snatching is unavailable; but estimates (and they are only estimates) indicate that it occurs at least 25,000 times a year,[2] probably 100,000 times a year,[3] and quite possibly more, since parents who abduct their children do not advertise that information.

Until recently, one of the major reasons for the spate of interstate custody disputes within the legal system, and for child snatchings outside the legal system, was the ease with which a parent could find a second court in a second state that refused to give effect to the custody decree of the original court, or that was willing to modify the original decree. The lack of uniformity

---

1. Bodenheimer, *Progress under the Uniform Child Custody Jurisdiction Act and Remaining Problems: Punitive Decrees, Joint Custody and Excessive Modification*, 65 Calif. L. Rev. 978, 980 (1977). [Hereinafter referred to as Bodenheimer, *Progress.*]

2. M. McCoy, Parental Kidnapping, Issue Brief #1B77117, Library of Congress, Congressional Research Service, March 16, 1979.

3. 6 Fam. L. Rep. 2294 (1978).

11

among states stemmed from three basic factors. First, the Full Faith and Credit Clause of the U. S. Constitution[4] does not offer full faith and credit to custody decrees (see Chapter IV). A state simply had no legal obligation under federal and constitutional law to honor the decree of a sister state. Many state courts exercised restraint by using the concept of comity (see Chapter IV), by which one court offers to another court's judgment or decree the respect and recognition it would like to have accorded its own decrees and judgments. Equitable theories, such as clean hands, forum non conveniens, and habeas corpus were also used by some courts to prevent child custody issues from being relitigated. But there was no consistent, uniform approach to the question. A parent could kidnap a child from one state and then appear before a second state's court with a petition that custody be modified. The second state could, consistent with the U.S. Constitution, exercise jurisdiction over the case and modify the decree.

Second, there have historically been several different ways in which a court might assume jurisdiction of a child custody case, namely, if:

- the child involved in the custody dispute is physically present within the state;
- the child's domicile is within the state;
- one or both of the child's parents are domiciled in the state; or,
- the state court issued the original custody or divorce decree.[5]

One result of the jurisdictional guidelines was that an almost limitless number of states could have jurisdiction over the same custody case at the same time. A parent could lose in custody proceedings in a first state, then relitigate the question in a second. Two courts could and have made simultaneous awards of custody to both parents.[6]

Another jurisdictional problem was that courts in custody cases reversed the usual order of the issues before them. Normally, a court must establish that it has jurisdiction before moving on to any factual issues.[7] But in child custody cases, if the court felt that

---

4. U.S. Const. art. IV, § 1.

5. H. Clark, The Law of Domestic Relations in the United States § 11.5 (1968).

6. See discussion in Chapter III.

7. Leflar, American Conflicts Law, ch. 3 (3d ed. 1977).

the child's welfare required that it hear the case and render a decree, the court did so, resting its exercise of jurisdiction precisely on the facts pleaded by one of the parents.[8] As a matter of law, however, it was typically held that jurisdiction rested on whatever contacts might have existed in the case between the child, parents, and state. If the court felt that exercising jurisdiction was necessary *for the child,* and believed it could issue a decree that would be effective, it did.

Domicile of the child was the original, and for a time the only, ground for a court to exercise jurisdiction in a child custody case. Of all the bases for jurisdiction then or today, domicile was the strictest because it required the greatest degree of permanence. The child's domicile is considered that of his parents or, after divorce, that of the parent with custody. Parents were less eager to look for a more sympathetic court in a state that recognized only domicile ("domicile state") as the basis for a custody determination.[9] But as the population became more mobile, it became apparent that a parent who had snatched a child and moved to a "domicile state" without establishing domicile was beyond the reach of the state's courts. The courts eventually concluded that the welfare of children demanded greater flexibility, and other grounds for custody jurisdiction were developed.[10]

The third factor that encouraged inconsistency in interstate custody disputes is the uncertain status of custody decrees. They are never final, and remain freely modifiable in the state that renders the decree.[11] If the non-custodial parent can show that there are substantially changed circumstances, the decree may be modified in the original state (see Chapter V) if the court agrees that a change of custody is in the child's best interests. It was just a short step from allowing modification in the original state to allowing modification in a second, or third, state. A second state's court, with the child before it, often reasoned that it had a better, or at least as good, opportunity to make a decision in the child's interest as any other state.

Child snatching and interstate custody cases fall into four major patterns:

---

8. The leading American case discussing the law of parens patriae jurisdiction as used in child custody cases is Finlay v. Finlay, 240 N.Y. 429, 148 N.E. 624 (1925).

9. CLARK, *supra* note 5, § 4.1.

10. LEFLAR, *supra* note 7, § 243.

11. CLARK, *supra* note 5, § 17.7.

· Before a divorce is final, one parent may leave the state with a child without informing the other parent or the court of his destination, to prevent the other parent from obtaining custody.

· After a divorce and custody decree have been issued, the non-custodial parent may kidnap a child, and seek modification of the decree in another state.

· After a divorce, the parent who has been granted custody may disappear with a child in order to deprive the non-custodial parent of visitation rights, or to prevent the non-custodial parent from effectively bringing a modification action.

· Conflicting custody awards may have been made in separate states.

Relitigation has been encouraged by two other factors. Many of the inconsistencies and conflicts in this area of law are the result of judges' struggles to adapt old, rigid concepts of jurisdiction and parental rights to a modern society characterized by an extremely mobile population.[12] The rising divorce and separation rates have compounded the problem.

Another reason for the growing numbers of interstate custody and child snatching cases is that, until recently, the states have not offered effective remedies for the parent who is wrongfully deprived of custody. Nor have the states sought effective sanctions to discourage child snatching in the first place (see Chapter VI).

The major effort to curb child snatching and create order in this area of law is the Uniform Child Custody Jurisdiction Act (UCCJA).[13] The Act changes the law of jurisdiction and provides—in most cases—that only one court may exercise jurisdiction over any given custody case. Jurisdiction may be exercised in a second state only when it is clear that the first state cannot or will not exercise it.

The UCCJA also legislates the problem of denial of full faith and credit to custody decrees, although it cannot completely solve it (see discussion *infra* and in Chapter IV). Excessive modification is discouraged, not only by the Act's strict jurisdictional requirements, but also by a system of recording, reporting, and

---

12. Bodenheimer, *Progress, supra* note 1.

13. Uniform Child Custody Jurisdiction Act, 9 UNIFORM LAWS ANN. 116 (1977) (hereinafter cited as UCCJA) (see appendix for the complete text of the Act).

disseminating custody decrees and information about custody cases among the various states.

B. The Act

1. *Purposes*

The Uniform Child Custody Jurisdiction Act was drafted to solve the problem of competing jurisdiction over child custody cases—and the related problem of child snatching. The UCCJA was approved by the National Conference of Commissioners on Uniform State Laws in 1968. It has gradually been adopted by forty-six states,[14] only a few at first, the vast majority in the last three years. As a result, almost all interpretations under the UCCJA are quite recent.

The Act, created to ensure that only one state assumes jurisdiction over a single child custody case at a time, has nine general purposes:

1. to avoid jurisdictional competition and conflict between states in child custody matters;
2. to promote cooperation between courts of various states;
3. to assure that litigation concerning the custody of the child takes place in the state with which the child and his family have the closest connection;
4. to discourage continuing litigation over child custody;
5. to deter abductions of children by their parents;
6. to avoid litigation of a case in other states;
7. to facilitate the enforcement of custody decrees;
8. to promote the exchange of information and mutual assistance between states;
9. to make the laws of the states which adopt the Act uniform.[15]

Courts that are to interpret the Act are urged to resolve doubts by referring to the elaborately stated principles above.[16] At least one court has decided that the predominant guiding factor when making a custody decision under the Act is the best interests of

---

14. *See* Appendix A.
15. UCCJA § 9.
16. Commissioners' Notes to § 1.

the child. In *Matter of Marriage of Settle*,[17] the father had been granted custody in Indiana. The mother abducted the children and fled to Oregon, where they remained for many years. The father finally brought an action in Oregon to regain custody, but the Oregon Court of Appeals decided that the children's best interests would *not* be served by enforcing the original decree and returning them to the father. Too much time had passed, the children were entrenched in Oregon, and Oregon had available the best evidence for making a custody decision at the time. There are several possible justifications for the position taken in this case, but the court stressed the best-interests point. It did note, however, that the facts of the cases were peculiar; in most cases, the Oregon courts will not ratify the illegal action of an abducting parent after the fact. The case holds out little hope for those parents who seek new decrees after only a short time has passed.

The Colorado Supreme Court expressed succinctly its view of the Act's effect, at least in that state:

> The underlying policy of the Act is to prevent the desperate shifting from one state to another of thousands of innocent children by interested parties seeking to gain custody or rights in one state even though denied these rights by the decree of another state.[18]

This case has been most frequently cited by other courts that face the UCCJA for the first time. Although a statement of principle only, the case has been used as a cue that courts should use the various sections of the Act to effect the principles.

2. *Jurisdictional Provisions*

The Act attempts to end the multiple litigation that has often surrounded a custody decree by designating one state court alone as the custody court for a particular case. The custody court has the greatest contact with the child and maximum access to any evidence that may be needed to make a determination. It is assumed that the custody court will be able to render a decree in the best interests of the child. The jurisdictional provisions of the Act effectively codify the notion that stability is the most important fac-

---

17. 25 Or. App. 579, 550 P.2d 445, *rev'd on other grounds*, 276 Or. 759, 556 P.2d 962 (1976).

18. Fry v. Ball, 190 Colo. 128, 131, 544 P.2d 402, 405 (1975).

tor in the best-interests doctrine.[19] It makes the question of jurisdiction child-centered—dependent on the location and status of the child at the time the case begins—rather than parent-centered, as it had been under most old jurisdictional approaches.

Section 3 of the UCCJA describes four criteria to be used in determining whether a state court is the custody court and entitled to exercise jurisdiction over a particular case. If two or more states satisfy the four criteria and therefore have technical concurrent jurisdiction, processes required by §§ 6 through 8 determine which state should actually exercise jurisdiction, and which should decline. Once the original custody court has issued a decree, other states in which the UCCJA is in effect are required to recognize and enforce the decree.[20] By use of this structure and analysis of jurisdiction, the Act denies jurisdiction to parents who kidnap their children and seek modification of a custody decree in another state. Once it becomes clear to these parents that their case will not be heard, much of the legal incentive for child snatching will fade. The effectiveness of the Act, therefore, increases as more states adopt it. It is most effective when courts in those states that have adopted it also interpret it consistently.

According to § 3 (a) (1), the child's home state, the one in which the child has lived for at least six consecutive months prior to the court proceeding,[21] is the preferred custody court. Section 3 (a) (1) (ii), according to the Commissioners' Note to § 3, allows a parent to commence proceedings in the home state even if the child is not physically present within it or if the child's absence is caused by a kidnapping by the other parent. However, the parent must act within six months of the child's removal from the state in order to gain the benefits of the provision.

The Commissioners' Notes represent the drafters' intentions and analyses of how the Act is meant to work, but are not binding upon the courts. Since the Act is relatively new, the Notes carry a great deal of influence.

Section 3 (a) (2) provides a second basis for a court to exercise jurisdiction when the home-state test cannot be met or is irrele-

---

19. Graham, *The UCCJA in Idaho: Purposes, Application and Problems*, 15 IDAHO L. REV. 305, 308 (1979).

20. UCCJA §§ 6, 7, 8.

21. UCCJA § 2(5).

vant. The home-state test is not met, for example, when the child has not stayed in any state for the necessary length of time. The test is irrelevant in many cases, as when the parent entitled to custody follows the abducting parent to the new state, planning to regain custody, and does not retain or intend to keep residence in the actual home state. The second jurisdictional basis is "strong contacts"—a child and his family must have strong contacts with the state before jurisdiction will be exercised. The state must also have access to relevant information concerning the child and family. The Commissioners' Notes stress that there must be "maximum rather than minimum contact of the child with the state," and that the exercise of jurisdiction appears to be in the child's interest. This language, on its face, seems vague enough to allow courts to continue past patterns. But most important, the section precludes parents from conferring jurisdiction upon a court simply by agreeing to it. The mere presence of the child, the child and one parent, or the child and both parents will not alone suffice to create jurisdiction. Several courts have adopted this interpretation of § 3(a) (2).[22] These courts, and others persuaded by their opinions, will not exercise jurisdiction when a parent kidnaps his child from one state and appears in a second seeking a modification of the original custody decree.

The Arizona Supreme Court[23] refused to exercise jurisdiction after a mother kidnapped her child from the home state of Washington and moved to Arizona, ruling that the child's strongest contacts were in Washington, and therefore only a Washington court could modify the custody decree. In a similar case[24] a Pennsylvania court held that a child's visit to his non-custodial parent in Pennsylvania did not create sufficient contact between the child and the state to allow that court to assume jurisdiction. These cases indicate that it is fruitless for a parent to kidnap his child, run to states that have adopted the Act, and immediately bring an action for modification.

Section 3(a) (3) codifies the principle of parens patriae, at the same time limiting it. Under older cases, parens patriae became almost synonymous with the child's welfare, and courts would ex-

---

22. See discussion in Chapter III, *infra.*

23. Both v. Superior Court, 121 Ariz. 381, 590 P.2d 920 (1979).

24. *In re* Sagan, 261 Pa. Super. Ct. 384, 396 A.2d 450 (1979); see discussion in text surrounding note 22, *supra.*

ercise jurisdiction on that basis whenever they felt it was good for the child. (For more discussion of parens patriae, see Chapter VI.) Under § 3(a) (3), a state may assume jurisdiction on an emergency basis if a child is physically present within the state and has been abandoned, threatened, mistreated, or abused. A state may assume jurisdiction and temporarily modify a custody decree under this section even if the parent who brings the action has kidnapped the child, if the court feels that the child may be harmed if he is returned to an abusive or dangerous parent. The section is also meant to provide jurisdiction in the event of the death of one or both parents.

Emergency jurisdiction could provide a major loophole in the Act for a parent seeking modification of a custody decree. The Commissioners' Notes therefore stress that it should be strictly construed and used only in extraordinary circumstances, a recommendation the courts appear to be following. A 1969 New York Supreme Court case[25] anticipated the emergency provisions of the UCCJA. That state adopted the UCCJA in 1977; it took effect in 1978. The court refused to exercise jurisdiction when a child had been neglected, but not abandoned or abused. One implicit interpretation is that the home-state court would be preferred for hearing neglect, as opposed to abuse or abandonment, cases.

More recently, the Michigan Appeals Court[26] explicitly applied § 3(a) (3) as anticipated by the Act. While a child was visiting his father in Michigan, the father brought an action for modification, claiming that the mother, who had been granted custody by the original Illinois court, had been abusing the child. The court, finding strong enough evidence of abuse, justified its jurisdiction through the emergency situation that allowed it to intervene and modify the decree, granting custody to the father, to protect the child.

The final jurisdictional basis under the Act is a last-chance type. Under § 3(a) (4), if no other state is able or willing to assume jurisdiction under the first three jurisdictional provisions, a second state's court is allowed to assume jurisdiction, assuring that a child custody case will be heard somewhere. Since the other jurisdictional provisions urge restraint in exercising jurisdiction and encourage deferring to one another, there is a chance that the courts might prevent the case from being heard in any forum.

25. Application of Lang, 9 App. Div. 2d 401, 193 N.Y.S.2d 763 (1969).
26. Breneman v. Breneman, 92 Mich. App. 336, 284 N.W.2d 804 (1979).

3. *Forum Non Conveniens and Concurrent Jurisdiction*

As at common law, § 3 of the UCCJA provides that several states may meet jurisdictional requirements for a custody case at the same time. Mere jurisdictional provisions cannot ensure that child custody litigation will proceed in the continuous, uniform fashion that the Act assumes is required to assure that the child's best interests are protected. Each state court, after determining whether it can technically exercise jurisdiction, is required to inquire further. Sections 6, 7, and 8 of the Act provide guidelines and methods to assure that only one state actually exercises jurisdiction in a particular case.

Section 6 provides that a state could decline jurisdiction and stay the action if a proceeding concerning the child's custody is pending in another state.[27] The consideration is designed to prevent multiple litigation by granting priority to the court action instituted first; since the Act assumes that all state courts take jurisdiction under requirements similar or identical to those of the Act, this priority provision, in effect, assumes that the court with priority has properly taken jurisdiction. Timing the filing of a petition to begin a custody case could become very important. The state in which a petition is filed can be expected to, and probably should, proceed with the case.[28]

Priority is examined in a Washington Supreme Court case[29] decided just before the UCCJA became effective in that state. The court held that a Maryland custody decree was not entitled to recognition because custody had been granted by decree of a Washington Superior Court in an action commenced before the action in Maryland. This result held despite the fact that the Maryland decree was actually issued first and that the children's home state, under the UCCJA, would have been Maryland. The case was complicated by the fact that both parents had engaged in multiple child snatchings, and the court appears to have found that because both had acted illegally, both had equally unclean hands, and were therefore not protected by the clean-hands doctrine.

Under the priority provisions of § 6, courts are expected to take

---

27. UCCJA § 6.

28. Comment, *Jurisdictional Guidelines in Matters of Child Custody: Kansas Adopts the UCCJA*, 27 U. Kan. L. Rev. 469, 475 (1979).

29. *In re* Marriage of Verbin, 92 Wash. 2d 171, 595 P.2d 905 (1979).

an active part in seeking out information concerning possible actions about the same child or children, pending or completed, in other states. In addition, § 6(b) requires that a court consult its state's child custody registry—provided for in § 16—to learn of proceedings or decrees concerning a child before hearing any part of a parent's petition.

Several decisions have strictly construed a court's duty under § 6. The Maryland Court of Appeals,[30] for example, held that the court should make this determination on its own motion even if the issue was not raised by the parties. The Oregon Court of Appeals[31] indicated that a court must go through a process with several steps when determining whether it should exercise jurisdiction:

> It first must ascertain whether it has jurisdiction under the terms of the Act and then must determine whether there is a custody proceeding pending or a decree in another state which presently has jurisdiction, and, if so, must decline to exercise jurisdiction.

A court should also decline to exercise jurisdiction if it is, as spelled out in § 7, an inconvenient forum, namely, if:

1. another state is or was recently the child's home state;
2. another state has a closer connection with the child and his family;
3. substantial evidence concerning the child's family relationship is more readily available in another state; and/or
4. the parties have agreed on another forum which is appropriate.[32]

The Commissioners' Notes explain that the purpose of § 7 overall is to encourage judicial restraint in exercising or not exercising, as the case may be, jurisdiction when another state is better able to make a best-interests determination of custody. Doctrines of judicial restraint and forum non conveniens have been used by some state courts for quite a while (see Chapters III, IV, and VI), but the Act attempts to codify the doctrines and foster uniformity.[33]

---

30. Paltrow v. Paltrow, 37 Md. App. 191, 376 A.2d 1134 (1977); *see also,* Vanneck v. Vanneck, 49 N.Y.2d 602, 427 N.Y.S.2d 735 (1980).

31. Carson v. Carson, 29 Or. App. 861, 565 P.2d 763, aff'd, 282 Or. 469, 579 P.2d 846 (1977).

32. UCCJA § 7(c).

33. Restatement (Second) of Conflict of Laws § 84 (1967).

The California Court of Appeals[34] declined jurisdiction on the grounds of inconvenient forum, even though that state had rendered the initial custody decree and technically met the jurisdictional requirements of the UCCJA for hearing the mother's modification arguments. Instead the court decided that California should defer to Wyoming courts because the children had lived there with their father for five years; Wyoming had become the children's home state and had superior access to current information about the children's family and school life.

Section 7(e) provides that a court which determines that it is an inconvenient forum may either dismiss the case or stay the proceedings, but always on the condition that another custody proceeding is promptly initiated in another, more proper state. The ability to choose between staying the proceedings and dismissing them outright is very important. In some states, a dismissal serves to bar a later action; therefore, a stay is needed to ensure that jurisdiction will remain if another action is not brought in another state.[35] When a court decides that it is an inconvenient forum, § 7(h) requires that it notify the other state's court that, in its opinion, it is more appropriate for the latter to hear the case.

Section 7(e) provides that a court which determines that it is an inconvenient forum may either dismiss the case or stay the proceedings, but always on the condition that another custody proceeding is promptly initiated in another, more proper state. The ability to choose between staying the proceedings and dismissing them outright is very important. In some states, a dismissal serves to bar a later action; therefore, a stay is needed to ensure that jurisdiction will remain if another action is not brought in another state.[35] When a court decides that it is an inconvenient forum, § 7(h) requires that it notify the other state's court that, in its opinion, it is more appropriate for the latter to hear the case.

Section 7(g) provides something of an enforcement mechanism to prevent parents from bringing a custody action in an inconvenient forum at all. If the court asked to hear a case is found to be "clearly an inappropriate forum," that court can require the parent bringing the action to pay all fees, including attorney, travel, and court costs. Designed to prevent parents from bringing

---

34. Schlumph v. Superior Court, 79 Cal. App. 3d 892, 145 Cal. Rptr. 190 (1978).

35. Commissioners' Notes to UCCJA § 7.

frivolous cases, Section 7(g) may also intend to place a burden upon attorneys representing parents in interstate child custody
cases; they too will become reluctant to encourage an action that
may be considered frivolous.

A court may also decline to exercise jurisdiction under the
clean-hands provision of § 8, which codifies an equitable remedy.
A court refuses to exercise jurisdiction when a party has violated
the law or committed a moral wrong (*i.e.*, child snatching), and
that transgression in turn forms all or part of the basis for the asserted jurisdiction. For example, under the old criteria, a state
could exercise parens patriae jurisdiction whenever the child was
before it; the clean-hands doctrine existed to allow courts to decline jurisdiction in cases where the only reason the child was before it was that he or she had been kidnapped.[36]

Section 8 applies to parents who seek a custody decree or a
modification after "wrongfully taking the child from another state
or engaging in other reprehensible conduct." A court may exercise jurisdiction if it is clearly in the best interests of the child, as
in an emergency, but generally should not, particularly when the
non-custodial parent has taken the child from the parent entitled
to custody in violation of the custody decree. Therefore, this section also makes it unprofitable for a parent to engage in child
snatching, through allowing the court, under § 8(c), to charge expenses against the abducting parent.

Section 8(a) expands the clean-hands doctrine to include cases
in which a custody decree has not yet been rendered in any state.
The Commissioners' Notes point out that in such a case "wrongfully taking" does not necessarily anticipate that a legal wrong
must be committed.[37] Technically, both parents retain an equal
right to have custody of a child (see Chapter VI) until a permanent custody decree is made by a competent court. The wrong
anticipated is moral rather than legal. It means that:

> one party's conduct is so objectionable that a court in the exercise of
> its inherent equity powers cannot in good conscience permit that party
> access to its jurisdiction.[38]

---

36. Ehrenzweig, *Interstate Recognition of Custody Decrees*, 51 MICH. L. REV.
345 (1953).

37. Commissioners' Notes to UCCJA § 8.

38. *Id.*

4. *Recognition and Enforcement Provisions*

The Full Faith and Credit Clause of the United States Constitution, as interpreted by the U.S. Supreme Court (see Chapter IV), allows a state to accept or reject a sister-state's custody decree. The UCCJA is designed to curtail the use of that freedom by the various state courts.[39] Once a decree has been issued by a proper custody court, the recognition and enforcement provisions of the UCCJA will prevent relitigation of the decree in the courts of another state—if the recognition and enforcement provisions are applied as intended by the drafters of the Act.[40] Section 13 declares that the custody decrees of sister states, when issued on the basis of jurisdictional requirements identical to or very similar to those of the Act, must be recognized and enforced as a matter of law in any state that has adopted the UCCJA. Recognition is even more routine if the initial decree was issued in a sister state that has also adopted the Act.

The courts that have considered § 13 have generally followed its provisions in cases where a party has sought modification of a decree rendered by another state. Section 13 requires recognition only of child custody decrees that meet the standards expressed in § 12, which gives binding force and effect of res judicata on any custody decree rendered under §§ 3 and 5, or under a process substantially similar to that provided in §§ 3 and 5. Section 23 validates the custody decrees rendered by courts of foreign nations, so long as the custody jurisdiction and determination standards are essentially similar to those of United States' courts.[41] At least one writer has suggested that § 23 operates too strongly in favor of English and other common law tradition courts much like our own, but operates strongly against those countries whose legal systems are far different.[42] Some cases imply that recognition of a foreign nation's custody decrees may turn as much on that country's political system or cultural traditions as on jurisdictional standards (see Chapters IV and VI).

Several courts have recognized and enforced other states'

---

39. Note, *New York Adopts the Uniform Child Custody Jurisdiction Act*, 45 BROOKLYN L. REV. 89, 115 (1978).

40. Commissioners' Notes to UCCJA § 13.

41. UCCJA § 23.

42. R. Crouch, Interstate and International Custody Disputes in the 1980s — Something Can Be Done 16 (unpublished manuscript, 1980).

courts' decrees although the decree-issuing state had not adopted the UCCJA. The North Dakota Supreme Court[43] enforced a decree issued by a court in the District of Columbia because the latter had, in its opinion, assumed jurisdiction under district statutory provisions substantially similar to those of the Act. The North Dakota courts have had a great deal of experience in interpreting the UCCJA, since that state, in 1969, was the first to adopt the Act.

In contrast, a New York court[44] refused to enforce a decree issued by a Puerto Rico court. The court took notice of the fact that Puerto Rico had not enacted the UCCJA and held that statutory jurisdictional provisions did not accord sufficiently with those of the Act. Both cases indicate that a court retains some discretion in determining whether to enforce a decree rendered by a state that has not adopted the Act. This is a potential loophole that has been tightened as more states have adopted the Act. Today, only a handful of states have not enacted the UCCJA; serving to urge passage in those remaining states lest they become havens for child snatchers, as some were once divorce mills.

Perhaps the most important aspect of the recognition and enforcement provisions is the attempt in § 13 to put the confusion created by U.S. Supreme Court decisions concerning the noneffect of the Full Faith and Credit Clause to rest (see Chapter IV). In addition, the intention of the Act is to avoid problems that stemmed from that court's decision that the impropriety of child custody jurisdiction in another state is a matter for each state to decide alone. Section 13 mandates that state courts, where the UCCJA is in effect, adopt a policy of comity toward the decrees of all other states where the Act is in effect or where custody has been decided along similar lines. The section is careful to stress comity, because only the U.S. Supreme Court can require that full faith and credit be accorded to custody decrees. The distinction is probably important only for purposes of balance between federal constitutional law and state statutory law; in practice, comity and full faith and credit should produce the same result.

Courts in many states have carved out an exception to § 13; they will not recognize or enforce punitive decrees of sister states,[45] a possibility foreseen in the Commissioners' Note to § 13.

---

43. Bergstrom v. Bergstrom, 271 N.W.2d 546 (N.D. 1978).
44. Fernandez v. Rodriquez, 97 Misc. 2d 353, 411 N.Y.S.2d 134 (1978).
45. Bodenheimer, *Progress, supra* note 1, at 1002.

They suggested that such decrees, most often issued when one parent repeatedly foils the other's attempts at court-ordered visitation, could be avoided if the parent entitled to but denied a legal right under the decree would directly take the question of enforcement to a second state's court under § 15.[46] Although this approach might well work,[47] it perhaps expects too much of parents, who have continued the pattern of recent pre-UCCJA years by bringing actions for modification. As a result, the exception that prevents recognition and enforcement of punitive decrees continues in many states.

The exception is based on the belief that such decrees are issued merely to punish a parent who has disobeyed and, more typically, flouted the orders of a court, and that the punitive decree is therefore not necessarily in the child's best interests. In addition, a punitive decree is felt to be contrary to the spirit of the Act,[48] which places the child's right to a proper life above the technical rights of parents. Courts, however, may have disagreements and differences over just what constitutes a punitive decree, possibly resulting in inconsistent applications.

Many states consider a decree punitive if it is clear that a court awarded or changed custody merely because a parent disregarded the court's authority. The Oregon Court of Appeals[49] refused to enforce a Montana court's modification of a custody decree. That court, which had issued the original decree, had changed custody from the mother to the father only because the mother had moved to Oregon without its permission. The Colorado Supreme Court[50] refused to recognize a modification of a decree that had been rendered by an Illinois court. The latter had changed custody from the father to the mother because the father had moved to Colorado, making it difficult for the mother to exercise her rights to visit with their children. (See also the decision of an Alaska Court.[51]) The difficulty in these cases is that when a court

---

46. Commissioners' Notes to UCCJA § 13.

47. *See, e.g., In re* Marriage of Steiner, 89 Cal. App. 3d 363, 152 Cal. Rptr. 612 (1979).

48. Bodenheimer, *Progress, supra* note 1, at 1002.

49. Brooks v. Brooks, 20 Or. App. 43, 530 P.2d 547 (1975).

50. Wheeler v. District Court, 188 Colo. 218, 526 P.2d 658 (1974).

51. DeHart v. Layman, 536 P.2d 789 (Alaska 1975), *aff'd on repeal from remand,* 560 P.2d 1206 (Alaska 1977).

decides it is being asked to enforce another state's punitive decree, it has dealt with only part of the overall question. Punitive decrees, for one thing, have a long history as a means by which courts enforce their decrees. When an arguably punitive decree is not enforced in a second state, the latter state's court is still faced with the problem of enforcing the custody decree as originally issued or, even more confusing, the problem of making a custody determination on its own. A court, by naming a decree punitive, effectively says that the first court, which issued the decree, has abused its jurisdiction—even if that jurisdiction was proper under the Act!

Punitive decrees are most often issued when the parent legally entitled to custody moves from a state in violation of a valid custody decree in order to remarry, take a new job, or prevent the non-custodial parent from seeing the children.[52] Since many of these cases concern visiting rights, a number of state courts have held that visitation is to be treated as a "custody matter" under the Act.[53]

Section 14 deals with the modification of custody decrees. It attempts to limit the scope of a U.S. Supreme Court decision,[54] which held that custody decrees, since they are by state statutory terms not final but modifiable, need be granted full faith and credit in a second state only to the extent that the original decree is effective in the original state court. To a great extent, the state courts decided that custody decrees might as well be modified in their state as another. According to § 14, a state generally may *not* modify a decree issued by a court in another state, but must defer to the continuing jurisdiction of the original court to maintain the stability of custody arrangements and to avoid forum shopping. This was the interpretation of § 14 promulgated by a Colorado court.[55]

A second state may assume jurisdiction and modify the original decree in only three circumstances:

1. if the state that issued the original decree declines to exercise jurisdiction for a modification;

---

52. *Id.*

53. *See, e.g.*, Smith v. Superior Court, 68 Cal. App. 3d 457, 137 Cal. Rptr. 348 (1977).

54. People *ex rel.* Halvey v. Halvey, 330 U.S. 610 (1947).

55. Brown v. District Court, 192 Colo. 93, 557 P.2d 384 (1976).

2. if the state that issued the original decree no longer has jurisdiction to make the change; and
3. if it is necessary to make an emergency modification under § 3(3) in order to protect the child from harm.[56]

Unless these strict conditions are met, a court in a state where the UCCJA has been enacted must decline to exercise jurisdiction for modifying the decree of another state's court and assume that the original court exercises continuing jurisdiction over that particular custody dispute.

Section 15 provides a convenient, simple, and potentially efficient method for enforcing out-of-state decrees in a second state's courts, under which a certified copy of a decree may be filed in the court of any other state. The decree then should, according to the Commissioners' Note, become in effect one of the state in which it has been filed and be enforced by any method available in the second state. Sections 16 and 17, which provide for a registry of out-of-state decrees in states where the Act has been adopted and for certification of copies of custody decrees, respectively, act as aids to the purposes of § 15. Again, § 15 provides that costs may be assessed against a wrongdoer in any enforcement action. As a result, a parent who is legally entitled to custody in West Virginia can reasonably expect to recoup the costs of traveling to Utah to regain custody from a parent who has abducted the child. This financial incentive alone should help encourage parents to use the Act to enforce valid, existing decrees, as, with other sections of the Act, it provides a comprehensive approach. Decrees may be had in only one court—the custody court—*but* once a custody decree has been properly rendered, it may be enforced in any state's courts. The Act, however, does not explicitly deal with the specific remedies. Aggrieved parents and legal guardians are expected to use the legal sanctions and remedies already available in the various states.

5. Due Process Requirements

A child custody decree, to be enforceable,[57] must be issued in accordance with the procedural safeguards mandated by the Due Process Clause of the United States Constitution, as interpreted

---

56. UCCJA § 14.
57. Commissioners' Notes to UCCJA § 4.

by the U.S. Supreme Court. If due process requirements are not observed, the jurisdiction exercised is improper because a party who has not received due process cannot be bound by the subsequent decree. Section 4 provides for appropriate due process requirements, requiring that each and every party to a custody proceeding receive both a notice and an opportunity to be heard in the case. Individuals who live inside the state where the action has been brought are notified according to the law of that state. In most states, some sort of personal or guaranteed notice is required. Individuals who live outside the state are notified in accordance with the provisions of § 5 of the Act. Failure to comply with either § 4 or § 5, or both, is likely to be fatal to a decree's validity. Notice is not required if a person voluntarily submits to the jurisdiction of the court, according to § 5(d).

The Commissioners' Note to § 4 emphasizes the importance of the due process requirements. The note argues that "strict compliance with sections 4 and 5 is essential for the validity of a custody decree within the state and its recognition and enforcement in other states." Section 12 provides that a decree that has been issued in accordance with the Act's due process requirements will be conclusive in a later action as to all issues of law and of fact and will be binding upon all who were parties to the action.

The due process requirements are a response to more than just the requirements posed by the U.S. Constitution for rendering an enforceable decree. Under the old jurisdictional criteria for child custody cases—which were neither approved nor disapproved by the U.S. Supreme Court—jurisdiction could be and was exercised in *ex parte* cases—when only one parent was before the court. For example, an ex parte divorce could often include a child custody determination under the former criteria. An ex parte divorce may still be possible today, but an ex parte custody decree will not be allowed under the Act. The due process provisions, then, also serve to prevent the relitigation of child custody questions at the behest of only one parent.

6. *Procedural Aspects*

The UCCJA emphasizes the need for, and encourages methods of providing, cooperation among courts of all states. Such cooperation includes an exchange of information about the child and his parents from one court to another. The ability to get the most pertinent information, no matter where it may be located, is crucial to a court in making a custody decision in the best interests of the child. Sections 9 and 10 provide mechanisms for the collection of pertinent information in child custody cases that involve more than one state.

Section 9 requires that every person who is a party to the custody proceeding give certain information, under oath, to the court. At a minimum, the following information must be provided: the child's present address and addresses for the past five years, the names and addresses of the persons with whom the child has resided for the previous five years, and details of other custody proceedings concerning the child.[58]

If the initial information a court receives from the pleadings in a case indicates that a party necessary to the proceeding to make it enforceable has not been included in the action, § 10 requires the court to join that party to the case. The person joined must be given notice and an opportunity to be heard in accordance with the statutory requirements of §§ 4 and 5. The Commissioners' Note to § 10 indicates that the requirement of joining a necessary party who was not initially before the court was drafted and included to prevent relitigation by the necessary party seeking modification of the resulting nonenforceable custody decree at a later date. In the interest of promoting the purposes of the due process requirements and of § 10, the courts have a duty to take an active role in seeking out necessary information and ensuring that all necessary parties are brought into the litigation.[59] The due process requirements and necessary joinder of parties provision, while enacted to further the primary goal of working for the best interests of children by providing finality to cases, also furthers the goal of making courts that consider custody decrees more efficient. This dual effect must have a persuasive and attractive aura for judges who do not want to hear the same cases again—in their court or another.

C. Weaknesses of the Act

The UCCJA has already had a beneficial effect in the problem areas of child snatching and interesting custody disputes. The late Professor Brigitte Bodenheimer, co-drafter of the Act has concluded that, "Initial experience with the operation of the UCCJA has, on the whole, been positive and promising. The Act is begin-

---

58. UCCJA §§ 9(a), 9(c).

59. Comment, *Child Custody Jurisdiction in Ohio—Implementing the UCCJA*, 12 Akron L. Rev. 121, 139 (1978).

ning to have a detrimental effect on child snatching."[60] Since Professor Bodenheimer reached this conclusion in 1977, when the UCCJA was still not in effect in a majority of states, it seems safe to assume that the deterrence of child snatching is more pronounced today. The Act's emphasis on interstate cooperation and the inclusion of elaborate guidelines governing jurisdiction have reduced the multiple litigation of custody decrees.[61] The UCCJA has also helped reduce the number of child snatchings by parents.[62] The exact extent to which the Act has been achieving its purposes cannot be assessed for three reasons. First, it is designed to prevent multiple litigation by stopping the cause at its source —courts will not exercise jurisdiction except when authorized by the Act. Since it is impossible to count the number of cases not brought because of the UCCJA, it is difficult to assess the Act's effectiveness in preventing them. Second, the reduction in the number of child snatchings cannot be conclusively proved; perhaps parents, aware of the Act, are simply abducting their children and remaining hidden because they know that a modification action is not likely to succeed. Third, the bulk of the states have only recently enacted the UCCJA. Chances are that parents, lawyers, and judges in those states where the Act is freshest have not yet adjusted to it, and as a result the number of interstate custody cases has not yet dwindled. Once all the states' courts have had the opportunity to interpret the Act's provisions at length, as states such as California and Colorado have done, any decline in the number of interstate cases may be carefully documented. Despite the evidence that the Act has been successful in many ways in attempting to achieve its goals, it does have several weaknesses that threaten to undermine it, and several potential loopholes that threaten to prevent the enforcement of decrees rendered under it.

1. *Judicial Discretion*

One major weakness is that the Act relies too much on judicial discretion.[63] Several actions are written in vague language; as a

---

60. Bodenheimer, *Progress, supra* note 1, at 1014; Professor Bodenheimer repeated this optimism in her last article on the UCCJA. *See,* Bodenheimer, *Interstate Custody: Initial Jurisdiction and Continuing Jurisdiction under UCCJA,* 14 FAM. L. Q. 203, 226 (1981). [Hereinafter referred to as Bodenheimer, *Interstate Custody.*]

61. 45 BROOKLYN L. REV. at 123.

62. Bodenheimer, *Progress, supra* note 1, at 985-87.

63. 45 BROOKLYN L. REV. at 123.

result, they are capable of several interpretations, depending on the court. For example, the "significant connections" rule of § 3(2) may allow a state to exercise jurisdiction over a case when the spirit of the Act suggests it should not.[64] Similarly, the emergency jurisdiction provided for in § 3(3) could be more clearly defined in the Act. A number of courts have used the emergency provision sparingly, as suggested in the Commissioners' Note to the section; but others have decided that it allows parens patriae jurisdiction to operate as before (see Chapter III).

The Act's versions of the clean-hands and forum non conveniens doctrines are other sections that allow a court to make a discretionary decision whether to exercise jurisdiction in a given case.[65] As a result, the use of both clean hands and forum non conveniens is likely to depend on the development of a set of fact patterns in a state's cases rather than upon the actual jurisdictional posture of the cases. Because of vague and discretionary provisions, a court may fail to exercise jurisdiction when it should, or exercise when it should not, undermining the effectiveness of the Act in either event.[66]

The recognition and enforcement sections also pose a potential source of discretionary abuse. Section 13 does not and cannot require states to accord full faith and credit to all sister-state custody decrees. Recognition and enforcement are assured only for decrees issued in accordance with the Act's provisions. But, to decide if a previous court, even in a state where the UCCJA is in effect, has complied with its provisions, a judge must exercise discretion.

2. Lack of Force behind the Act

The lack of force behind the Act may be another weakness. Interstate cooperation is made desirable, not mandatory, and a court

---

64. For proper application of the rule, *see,* Marriage of Ben Yehoshua, 91 Cal. App. 3d 259, 154 Cal. Rptr. 80 (1979); Bacon v. Bacon, 6 Fam. L. Rep. 2709 (Mich. App. 1980); and Custody of Holman, 77 Ill. App. 3d 732; 396 N.E.2d 331 (1979) where the California, Michigan, and Illinois courts properly refused to apply the "significant connections" rule. *But see,* Weinstein v. Weinstein, 6 Fam. L. Rep. 3075 (Ill. App. 1980) where an Illinois court accepted jurisdiction in a pre-decree child snatching case when Montana should have been the proper forum. These cases are discussed in Bodenheimer, *Interstate Custody, supra* note 60.

65. Bodenheimer, *Progress, supra* note 1, at 992-993.

66. 45 Brooklyn L. Rev. at 124.

remains powerless to endorce a decree in another state if that state refuses to cooperate. More important, the Act cannot be completely effective until all the states and territories have adopted it. While the number of states where modification may be available to a child snatcher is dwindling, parents may still be able, at least in theory, to find a state willing to relitigate custody decrees.

Another lack of force is that its provisions are not tied to any specific enforcement provisions, sanctions, or parent-oriented remedies (see Chapter VI). Parents who have had their children abducted are expected to place their faith in a system for stabilizing custody litigation that is grounded in a highly abstract area of law—jurisdiction. The costs that may be assessed against a wrongdoer may be expected to have some deterrent effect, but since the Act relies on the legal theories of jurisdiction, it relies most heavily on the decisions of judges and advice given to parents by lawyers.

More direct sanctions are needed to deter child snatching and any direct sanction, such as a criminal penalty or tort recovery (see Chapter VI), should be applied uniformly throughout the country. While only speculation, it may be that parents determined to abduct their child may deliberately choose to relocate in states where the likelihood of apprehension and punishment are slightest. Efforts to bring about a national law that makes child snatching a crime have finally occurred at the federal level, even though there has been a long-standing tradition that family law issues have been matters for the states rather than the federal government. These issues are discussed in Chapter IV and reappear in Chapter VI.

III. Jurisdiction

A. Jurisdiction Prior to the UCCJA

Until recently, one of the major reasons for interstate custody disputes and child snatchings was the ease with which a parent unhappy with a custody decree could find an out-of-state court that would either refuse to give effect to the original decree or modify it freely. Although the flood of interstate child custody cases and child snatchings may be attributed directly to decisions by both the U.S. Supreme Court and the state courts that did not grant full faith and credit or comity recognition to original custody decrees (see Chapter IV), it is also certain that the problems in this area of law would not have become as pronounced had it not been for the laxity of the various states' jurisdictional standards in child custody cases.

Before the promulgation of the UCCJA in a majority of the states, the trend for over fifty years had been in the direction of allowing custody claimants to sue in the courts of almost any state, no matter how miniscule the contact of the child, parents, or family with that state. The normal rules of conflict of laws did not usually apply to interstate child custody cases.[1] The courts of the various states acted in isolation; at times they appeared to be in competition.

The UCCJA was developed as a response to the interstate child custody problem (see Chapter II). Rather than deal with the legal theories that encouraged a multiplicity of jurisdictional bases[2] in the first place, the UCCJA simply restricts the availability of jurisdiction. Consequently, while the UCCJA may result in cases

---

1. LEFLAR, AMERICAN CONFLICTS LAW §§ 243, 244 (3d ed. 1977).
2. RESTATEMENT (SECOND) OF CONFLICT OF LAWS § 79 (1971).

where a court grants what amounts to comity recognition to another state's decree (see Chapter IV), the court need not, under the UCCJA, mention comity.

B. Jurisdiction under the UCCJA

The UCCJA requires the courts of a state that adopts the Act to recognize and enforce the custody decrees of another state if that state had proper jurisdiction—either under the Act or under similar provisions—to render the decree. The UCCJA, then, makes the critical factor in a custody decree's future validity, recognition, and enforcement the original jurisdiction it was based upon.

Under the UCCJA, initial jurisdiction is vested in the courts in the child's "home state," which is defined as the

> state in which the child immediately preceding the time involved [*i.e.*, the time an action was filed] lived with his parents, a parent, or a person acting as parent, for at least six consecutive months,[3]

with allowances for temporary absences and a child under the age of six months.[4] The home state retains paramount jurisdiction for at least six months after the child's removal or departure.[5] The importance of the original state's grant of continuing jurisdiction for six months or more is of particular importance when a child disappears or is removed from the state prior to a proper child custody adjudication. By this provision, the abductor is prevented from establishing jurisdiction in a second state.[6] This is true even if that second state may technically qualify as the child's home simply because the child has been there for a considerable time.

A secondary basis for jurisdiction is contained in § 3(a) (2). It provides that a court may exercise initial jurisdiction if the child and at least one of the persons contesting custody—normally a parent—has a significant connection with the state and there is within the state a body of information relevant to the court's duty in determining custody. The significant connection also allows jurisdiction to continue with the original state's court for six months or more. Significant connections jurisdiction, however, is not to be the normal form; it is secondary to home-state jurisdiction and is meant to be exercised when, for whatever reason, a child does

---

3. UCCJA § 2(5).
4. *Id.*
5. UCCJA § 14.
6. Commissioners' Notes to UCCJA § 3.

not appear to have a home state,[7] for example, when the parent the child lives with moves more often than every six months.

The question of both continuing jurisdiction under the § 14 modification provisions and of a better court to decide under the § 7 inconvenient-forum rules, however, may turn on significant connections when the child has been away from the home state for a sufficient time to have acquired a new one. The original state may continue to have such significant connections when, for example, the child and one parent move to a second state, but the other parent, perhaps other children, the extended family, and all original court records remain in the first state.

The importance of allowing an extension of six months or more on original jurisdiction and possibly unlimited continuing jurisdiction is especially critical in preventing child snatching. Any other reading would subvert this purpose of the UCCJA by permitting an abductor to go into hiding for six months and then seek modification or by encouraging a parent who has been visiting his child according to the terms of a previous custody decree to prolong the periods of visitation, with or without consent of the parent entitled to custody, to seek modification in the state where the children are visiting. The drafters of the UCCJA offer an example:

> If custody was awarded to the father in state 1 where he continued to live with the children for two years and thereafter his wife kept the children in state 2 for 6½ months (3½ months beyond her visitation privileges) with or without permission of the husband, state 1 has preferred jurisdiction to modify the decree despite the fact that state 2 has in the meantime become the "home state" of that child. If, however, the father also moved away from state 1, that state loses modification jurisdiction interstate, whether or not its jurisdiction continues under local law.[8]

The reasoning in this example influenced the Kentucky Court of Appeals[9] in a case decided before the UCCJA was adopted in that state. The mother had been awarded custody of a child in a Kentucky decree. She and the child later moved to Indiana, where both became residents. The mother later permitted the father to take the child to Kentucky for a two-week visit. During the visit, the father filed a motion in a Kentucky court to modify the original decree and grant custody of the child to him. The mother entered the Kentucky case, seeking a writ of prohibition

---

7. *Id. See also,* Chapter II of this book, note 64, *supra.*
8. Commissioners' Notes to UCCJA § 14.
9. Turley v. Griffin, 508 S.W.2d 764 (Ky. 1974).

to prevent the trial court from exercising jurisdiction over the case. The Court of Appeals held that "the provisions of the Act (UCCJA) clearly provide that, six months after JoAnn and the child moved to Indiana, this state was divested of jurisdiction to make a child custody determination as to the home state."

The New York Supreme Court, Appellate Division,[10] was faced with the problem of determining a child's home state in the first case to interpret the home-state provisions after adoption of the UCCJA in that state. The father had been awarded custody of a child in Massachusetts, where he lived. The mother took the child, and they lived together in New York. She brought an action requesting modification of the original Massachusetts decree. The father entered the case and urged the New York court to decline to exercise jurisdiction, and also moved for an order dismissing the proceeding under the UCCJA. The New York court refused to exercise jurisdiction and ordered the mother to return the child to the father. The mother had based her claim for modification largely on the fact that she and the child had not been separated since the child was born, but that the child *had* been separated from the father; in other words, the mother claimed essentially that the Massachusetts custody determination was wrong. The New York court also declined to consider this argument. It reasoned that the Massachusetts court had faced the same facts and arguments in the original action that had been concluded just three months before the New York action. The New York court hewed to the policies of the UCCJA: it avoided jurisdictional competition with courts in another state and discouraged continued controversy and litigation over a custody decision. It is noteworthy that Massachusetts had not enacted the UCCJA. The New York court, to enforce the Massachusetts decree, must therefore have concluded that the original Massachusetts court had based its jurisdiction on criteria substantially similar to those of the Act. New York, incidentially, technically remains one of a few states that confers jurisdiction to determine custody on its courts on no more than the physical presence of the child.[11] This rule, however, is based on a pre-UCCJA case and may be subject to revision in the future.

---

10. Application of Bacon, 97 Misc. 2d 688, 412 N.Y.S.2d 282 (1978).

11. Nehra v. Uhlar, 43 N.Y.2d 242, 372 N.E.2d 4 (1977). *See also*, Chapter II of this book, note 64, *supra*.

Similar reasoning was used in a Maryland Court of Special Appeals.[12] Custody had originally been granted to the mother by a Georgia court. The child had lived with the mother and a stepfather in Maryland for more than eleven months. The mother was killed in an accident, and a Maryland court granted custody to the stepfather. The natural father appealed this decision, contending that the Maryland courts should defer to the continuing jurisdiction of the Georgia courts. The Maryland court held that Maryland had become the child's home state, and that the Georgia courts had no continuing jurisdiction. The case, however, was remanded to the trial court because the appeals court was not convinced that the trial record supported the custody determination. In a move not emulated by many other courts, the court also announced that, under the UCCJA, any prior opinions that were inconsistent with the case were no longer valid; by this action, Maryland burned its bridges on interstate child custody jurisdiction and became irrevocably committed to the UCCJA alone. The same court later held that the Act does not automatically confer jurisdiction upon a second state that has technically become a child's home state,[13] and that the second state should still defer, at least at first, to the court that issued the original decree. Only compelling circumstances, which apparently the case had, justify an exception.

In the recent past, the inclination of courts to grant jurisdiction upon mere physical presence, and sometimes upon almost insignificant connections, coupled with state courts' tendencies to favor local petitioners, encouraged forum shopping by parents who abducted their children. As an example, custody had been awarded to the father by a Puerto Rico court.[14] When the children were visiting the mother in Philadelphia, she brought an action for modification. The Pennsylvania court exercised its jurisdiction, even though the children had been in the state for only thirteen days. The willingness to accept such a meager basis for jurisdiction, grounded on the concept of the state's parens patriae powers, was emphasized by Justice Cardozo in the most famous such case.

---

12. Howard v. Gish, 36 Md. App. 446, 373 A.2d 1280 (1977).
13. Paltrow v. Paltrow, 37 Md. App. 191, 376 A.2d 1134 (1977).
14. *In re* Irizarry's Custody, 195 Pa. Super. Ct. 104, 169 A.2d 307 (1961).

He [the chancellor] acts as parens patriae to do what is best for the interest of the child. He is to put himself in the position of a "wise, affectionate, and careful parent," and make provision for the child accordingly.[15]

The parens patriae approach to jurisdiction, as noted, was a major cause of multiple child custody adjudications. The UCCJA mainly attempts to stop its use. Even before the Act, some states invoked the parens patriae power only in emergencies, and the doctrine found its way into the UCCJA through this long-established emergency exception. Section 3(a)(3) retains and reaffirms parens patriae jurisdiction, usually exercised by a juvenile court, which a state must assume when a child requires emergency protection. To qualify for this exception to the home-state and significant-connections provisions, presence of the child is the major prerequisite. The other requirement is that the exception is meant to be used sparingly and in extraordinary circumstances.[16] (See discussion in subsection C, *infra*.)

Parens patriae should be distinguished from a state's ultimate interest in a child's welfare, however. Most states that have adopted the UCCJA have interpreted it as a reflection of the best-interests-of-the-child doctrine in a particular form; the Act represents a legislative, and in some states judicial, conclusion that stability is a child's primary need and that it serves a child's best interests.[17] It is possible, on occasion, that the action in a child's best interests is inconsistent with or in actual opposition to the provisions of the Act. The Oregon Supreme Court grappled with this problem.[18] Because of the unique facts in the case, the court determined that it must disregard another state's custody decree and grant custody to a mother who had abducted her child and moved to Oregon years before. It was, the court said, a direct conflict between the Act's goal of deterring child abductions and the state's goal (and the Act's) of protecting the child's best interests. When the two were evenly matched in conflict, the best in-

---

15. Finlay v. Finlay, 240 N.Y. 429, 433, 148 N.E. 624, 626 (1925).

16. *See, e.g.*, Neal v. Superior Court, 84 Cal. App. 3d 847, 148 Cal. Rptr. 841 (1978).

17. Bodenheimer, *The Uniform Child Custody Jurisdiction Act: A Legislative Remedy for Children Caught in the Conflict of Laws*, 22 Vand. L. Rev. 1207, 1209 (1969).

18. Matter of Marriage of Settle, 276 Or. 759, 556 P.2d 962 (1976).

terests of the child was predominant; to attempt to meet both purposes would be "schizophrenic." The court recognized that its result might be read as placing a premium upon abducting children, but stressed that the decision was to be limited to the particular facts in the case. There is no evidence that the rationale given has been used either in Oregon or other states as a wedge with which to forge a broad or general exception.

The majority of the jurisdictional cases that have been decided in states after they enacted the UCCJA have reached similar results with similar rationales. Uniformity in interpretation is demonstrating that the UCCJA is capable of achieving one of its most basic goals—perhaps its major one—of providing standard guidelines for determining jurisdiction that result in a consistent strand of predictable results and stable decrees in interstate child custody cases. A few examples of the Act in action follow.

In a Colorado case,[19] jurisdiction was denied in a second state court. The mother was granted custody under an original Kansas decree; she and the child continued to live in Kansas. The father, meanwhile, had moved to Colorado, and arrangements were made to have the child visit him there each summer. During the second summer visit, the father brought an action in a Colorado court to modify the Kansas decree. The mother entered the action, countering with a motion to dismiss the case because the Colorado court lacked jurisdiction under the UCCJA, and filed a petition for a writ of habeas corpus. The Colorado court agreed with her and held that continuing jurisdiction was vested in the Kansas courts. The child was returned to the mother after little delay and nominal expense.

Another Colorado case[20] ultimately reached the same result but was delayed by the trial court's lack of familiarity with the UCCJA. Over a year passed before the child was returned. The parents had been divorced in California, and the mother awarded custody. She took the child to visit the father in Colorado, where he had relocated. When she telephoned ten weeks later to arrange the child's return, the father refused to return the child and immediately instituted proceedings in Colorado to modify the original decree and secure custody of the child for himself.

---

19. *In re* Custody of Thomas, 36 Colo. App. 96, 537 P.2d 1095 (1975).
20. Custody of Glass, 36 Colo. App. 91, 537 P.2d 1092 (1975).

The trial court awarded custody to the father and the court of appeals reversed, holding that California retained continuing jurisdiction and that the Colorado courts lacked the power, under § 14 of the UCCJA, to modify the existing California decree. The Court of Appeals told the father that any modification request should be addressed to the California court.

Under the UCCJA, many of the previous jurisdiction problems virtually disappear and the interstate enforcement of custody decrees may be expected to help innumerable children who, under the older, traditional law, were lost every year. The effects of the UCCJA may indeed be impossible to enumerate because it works best when interstate actions that may have been brought formerly are no longer brought at all.

When a situation arises in which grounds for exercising jurisdiction to modify a decree exist in two or more states, the UCCJA provides a method for resolving the question by conferring exclusive jurisdiction upon the court in which the matter was first raised.[21] The California version of the UCCJA also offers the alternative of a court's using the more appropriate forum rule.[22]

A recent U.S. Supreme Court case[23] is believed to have altered the federal due process jurisdictional requirements. If applied to custody actions that involve status determinations then according to this case, such actions are not subject to the minimum-contacts rule generally used as the standard for jurisdiction. That rule, so far as custody cases were concerned, had acted to justify the in personam jurisdiction pattern that had evolved after *May v. Anderson*[24] (see Chapter IV). The later case held that status determinations should instead be governed by "particularized rules" of their own that apply specifically to the type of status in question. The UCCJA is a good example of just such a set of particularized rules; the requirements of subject-matter jurisdiction and of notice and an opportunity to be heard that are used in the Act should be upheld under the standard. According to a paper by the late Professor Bodenheimer:

21. CAL. CIV. CODE § 5150 (West 1977).
22. *Id.* § 5156; UCCJA § 7.
23. Shaffer v. Heitner, 433 U.S. 186 (1977).
24. 345 U.S. 528 (1953).

If the law were otherwise, in many situations no court in the country could render a binding custody judgment. For example, if prior to divorce both spouses had left the state of matrimonial domicile, one moving to Florida and the other to Indiana, states with which the other spouse had no contacts, neither Florida nor Indiana could render a binding custody judgment in case of non-appearance, despite proper jurisdiction out of state.[25]

Some caution may be in order, however. The case itself did not directly address the question of jurisdictional requirements in child custody cases. The only such case[26] dealt with the question of child support rather than child custody, holding that California had no jurisdiction concerning child support over a father who lived in New York. California's jurisdiction over child custody issues were not questioned, however.

C. Emergency Jurisdiction

One of the basic tenets of the UCCJA is that the physical presence of a child in a second state does not confer upon that state jurisdiction to modify custody if another state has initial or continuing jurisdiction.[27] The exception to this general purpose occurs in a situation where, but for the occurrence of an emergency condition threatening a child, no jurisdiction of any type could be exercised. An emergency justifies a second state court in assuming jurisdiction for the limited purpose of taking measures to protect a child from a threatening situation. On occasion, the threat may be so malevolent that a second state court could find itself required to make a custody determination as well as to institute protective measures.

The emergency exception is meant to be granted in extremely few cases. Under the UCCJA, only when a child is stranded, as by the death of its parent or parents, or when there is abandonment, mistreatment, abuse, or neglect that severely and immediately threatens the child's well-being, may a second state, where the child is present, institute protective measures.[28] As can be

---

25. Bodenheimer, Curbing Child Snatching on Three Fronts, State, National, and International, and the Uniform Child Custody Jurisdiction Act 12 (May 29, 1980) (unpublished manuscript).

26. Kulko v. Kulko, 436 U.S. 84 (1978).

27. Note, *The Interstate Child Custody Problem Revisited*, 16 ABA Fam. L. Newsletter 1, 11 (1975).

28. Commissioners' Notes to UCCJA § 3.

seen, then, the presence of the child within the state is the only prerequisite to a court's exercise of emergency jurisdiction.[29] When there is child neglect without emergency or abandonment, jurisdiction cannot be so based.[30]

One unfortunate result of including the flexibility of emergency jurisdiction within the UCCJA is that, although it was meant to be used seldomly, there has been established a pattern of repeated attempts by parents who are not legally entitled to custody to "shout fire" in any conceivable situation. A claim that emergency jurisdiction should be exercised apparently has become standard procedure in parents' interstate disputes.[31] Because of the potential for abuse by parents, judges and lawyers must become extremely sensitive to misuse to prevent the exception from undermining the essential purposes of the UCCJA. What may be done about lawyers who cooperate with parents in bringing frivolous emergency claims is an open question. In other contexts, courts have required lawyers who refused to disclose the whereabouts of their client's children to do so;[32] but no cases of an attorney deliberately misusing the UCCJA, and being required to face up to it, have been found.

The Louisiana Supreme Court[33] denied jurisdiction when a father claimed that his children, who were visiting with him in Louisiana, had been living in an "injurious environment" in New York with the mother who had custody. "Barring an emergency and clear statutory authority," the court held that jurisdiction cannot lie in the state where the children are living temporarily. The Louisiana court used the policies of the UCCJA to reach its decision, although that state had not adopted the Act at the time.

There have been very few legitimate instances of emergency jurisdiction, which alone may indicate that the exception is being kept narrow, as intended.[34] For the most part, emergency jurisdiction provisions have been used only in cases that involve life-

---

29. UCCJA § 3 (a)(3).

30. *See, e.g.,* Application of Lang, 9 App. Div. 2d 401, 193 N.Y.S.2d 763 (1959).

31. *See, e.g., In re* Marriage of Schwander, 79 Cal. App. 3d 1013, 145 Cal. Rptr. 325 (1978).

32. Bodenheimer, *supra* note 25, at 36.

33. State *ex rel.* King v. King, 310 So. 2d 614 (La. 1975).

34. Bodenheimer, *supra* note 25 at 27.

or-death situations. For example, if a child's parents are killed in an accident while the family is away from home, a court in the state where the accident occurred has jurisdiction to place the child in a temporary home or otherwise arrange for its care.[35]

Another instance in which emergency jurisdiction might be invoked occurs when a parent legally entitled to custody travels to a state where a child is visiting the other parent, then threatens the other parent or the child, or both, with violence. California has accepted this type of fact pattern, which has been broadened to say an emergency exists if, prior to a custody adjudication in any state, a parent takes a child to a second state and the other parent follows to claim the child. Since there has been no adjudication, both parents technically have an equal legal right to the child (see Chapter VI). In such a situation, the child is considered to have no parent who is capable of exercising effective parental control. The dispute between the parents is thought to create a danger of neglect; in addition, the dispute is considered fraught with danger for the child. In such a situation, the state in which the emergency is perceived may award temporary custody to the parent who will return the child to his home state for permanent adjudication of custody.[36] This analysis is based upon two cases, the Colorado Supreme Court's decision in *Ball v. Fry,*[37] and the Wisconsin Supreme Court's decision in *Zillmer v. Zillmer.*[38]

In *Ball,* a child's natural parents filed a petition in a California court seeking termination of a guardianship held by the child's grandmother. The California court entered a decree that returned custody to the parents. The grandparents, however, secured an ex parte order in Colorado, restoring custody to them. The parents countered by instituting a proceeding in a Colorado Superior Court to enjoin the Colorado trial court from exercising jurisdiction to make a final custody determination. The Colorao Supreme Court held that, under the UCCJA, the trial court should have recognized the parents' California decree and should have refrained from modifying it.

The case did not end there, however. The parents had started a scuffle with the grandparents after arriving in Colorado to pick up

---

35. Commissioners' Notes to UCCJA § 3.
36. CAL. CIV. CODE § 5152 (West 1977).
37. 190 Colo. 28, 544 P.2d 402 (1975).
38. 8 Wis. 2d 657, 101 N.W.2d 703 (1960).

the child. The parents were arrested, and assault charges were brought against them. The Colorado Supreme Court then exercised emergency jurisdiction, which it denominated an equitable power, to permit the child to remain in the temporary custody of the grandmother pending the disposition of a petition by the grandparents to the California court asking that court to modify the decree it had issued granting custody to the parents. The Colorado court was concerned that the evidence of violence might justify an inference that the child's well-being was in jeopardy.

Ball illustrates the emergency doctrine at work as intended. The Colorado Supreme Court recognized the validity of the California decree, but also felt sufficiently concerned with a possible danger to the child that it would not immediately transfer custody. All parties were required to return to California for a permanent disposition. The grant of temporary custody to the grandparents was explicitly limited.

The Wisconsin Supreme Court, in *Zillmer,* reached a similar conclusion long before the UCCJA was enacted. The children were in the custody of their grandparents in Wisconsin. The mother, who lived in Kansas, was granted a return of custody by a Kansas court and brought a petition for a writ of habeas corpus in Wisconsin to retrieve the child. The grandmother worried over returning the child; she thought the child's well-being was threatened by a return to the mother, who had been undergoing treatment for mental illness. As in *Ball,* the *Zillmer* court gave overriding importance to the perceived danger and granted emergency jurisdiction. The child was temporarily left with the grandmother. Both the mother and grandmother, however, were told to return to the Kansas court because it was a more appropriate forum.

More often, a second state's court is faced with a case where a parent or contestant claims that an emergency exists as a technical or tactical maneuver. The Court of Appeals of Arizona[39] faced such a maneuver. Although the UCCJA was not then in effect in Arizona, the court refused to exercise jurisdiction after a mother had abducted her children from Alabama, where they resided with a grandmother, and claimed before an Arizona trial court that she feared for the children's welfare if they were left with the grandmother.

---

39. Stuard v. Bean, 27 Ariz. App. 350, 554 P.2d 1293 (1975).

It was a drawn-out case, with many levels of activity. The grandmother had originally been granted custody of the children by an Alabama court. The mother took the children to Arizona, without permission, for a weekend visit; the grandmother followed and took them back to Alabama. A few weeks later, four people in hoods jumped the fence around the grandmother's house, physically restrained her, and took the children. Shortly thereafter, the children were in Arizona. The grandmother again returned to Arizona, this time with a writ of habeas corpus issued by an Alabama court.

At a hearing to enforce the writ, the Arizona trial court declined to act on the issue of whether it had jurisdiction to direct a change of custody and ordered instead that the children remain in Arizona under supervision of juvenile authorities pending a determination elsewhere. The Court of Appeals held that the trial court had failed to act as required by law. The court said that case law provided that it was improper for the real parties in interest in a custody case to attempt to invoke the jurisdiction of Arizona courts after having brought the children to Arizona by abducting them. This rule eliminated the mother's claims of jurisdiction. It appears that the Arizona courts may also have been able to invoke emergency jurisdiction, if necessary, on the grandmother's behalf, based on the child snatching at her home.

The parties in a child custody case when emergency jurisdiction is invoked have attempted to rely on occasion on the duration of the child's stay in the second state. In *Ball,* for example, the child had been in Colorado eight months before the action was brought; nevertheless, Colorado limited its emergency action to a temporary order and deferred to the continuing jurisdiction of California. A Maryland Supreme Court[40] in 1975 refused emergency jurisdiction and sent the parties back to the state with continuing jurisdiction; the child had lived in Maryland for twenty months.

Courts insist upon competent proof that an emergency situation actually exists. Conclusory assertions do not suffice. The need to produce a credible record for a court to exercise emergency jurisdiction is based on the Act[41] and on the California Supreme Court's decision in *Ferreira v. Ferreira*[42] which established

---

40. Wakefield v. Little Weight, 276 Md. 333, 228 A.2d 847 (1975).
41. UCCJA § 3(a)3; Commissioners' Notes to UCCJA § 3.
42. 9 Cal. 3d 824, 109 Cal. Rptr. 80, 512 P.2d 304 (1973).

that a court should substantiate allegations of danger before taking emergency actions. If a parent makes a presentation that initially convinces the court that a danger to the child is likely, a temporary placement pending a final determination, either in the second state or an original state with continuing jurisdiction, is allowed.

Most important for a court's decision whether to use its emergency jurisdiction is the substantiation of charges. A court may expect substantiation from the parent or custodian alleging emergency, but often this will not be enough. In most states, the court may request evidence to substantiate charges from sources such as the state's probation department or other custody investigation units to obtain an expeditious, on-the-spot investigation and report. If necessary, out-of-court entities may quickly obtain information located in another state, if the danger is said to exist in that other state. Other sources that may be used include police departments, public defenders' offices, licensed welfare agencies, and members of the medical profession or clergy.[43]

An important distinction to make is that the mere allegation of an emergency vests the court initially with an extremely limited form of jurisdiction, according to *Ferreira*. At this stage, the court's jurisdiction is limited to holding a hearing geared to discovery of the gravity or frivolity of the charges. Once the allegations are established, the petitioner may bring further action for a temporary placement, and in some cases may persevere toward a permanent placement.

In an example of limited initial jurisdiction emergency, a father asked a Florida trial court[44] to exercise emergency jurisdiction after his children had run away from their mother. The father said the children claimed they had been beaten by their mother in Georgia. The trial court, however, enforced the mother's rights under the original North Carolina decree and told the father to hand over the children. On appeal, the Florida Court of Appeal said the trial court had erred in not exercising jurisdiction to determine the gravity of the father's allegations. Upon receipt of investigative information and whatever other evidence may be available, the court will either dismiss the case for lack of jurisdic-

---

43. Cal. Civ. Code § 5168 (West 1977); Wheeler v. Wheeler, 34 Cal. App. 3d 239, 101 Cal. Rptr. 782 (1973).

44. Moser v. Davis, 364 So. 2d 521 (Fla. App. 1978).

tion—emergency or otherwise—or, if the evidence supports allegations of possible harm to the child, may proceed with any of the alternatives available to that particular court.

Interpretation of the emergency-jurisdiction provision of the Act, even when consistent, cannot always achieve the results desired. For example, in California a grandfather petitioned the court to make a change of custody to him on the basis of an asserted emergency.[45] The parents had been divorced by an Illinois court, with custody originally granted to the father; later, the same court modified the decree and awarded custody to the mother. While the modification action was pending, the father sent the children to the grandparents in California; they, in turn, refused to return the children to the mother, and the grandfather brought the action.

The California court refused to exercise jurisdiction as requested by the grandfather because under the UCCJA it was obliged to recognize and enforce the Illinois decree. The grandfather's allegations of emergency were considered frivolous, and he was verbally thrashed by the court. The court of appeals upheld the trial court's decision, and ordered that the children be returned. While the California case was being litigated, however, the grandmother went into hiding with the children. By the time the appeal was argued in court, the grandmother and the children were still missing, a year and a half after the trial court had ordered the children returned to the mother.

The result is neither failure of the emergency provisions nor of the Act in general. It merely serves to remind that any law cannot achieve its results when the parties deliberately take themselves outside the legal system. (A fuller discussion of the problem is found in Chapter VI.) Had the children been returned, the case would actually serve as a model of proper emergency-jurisdiction reasoning.

A basic concern as research on this book began was that the emergency-jurisdiction exception would become misused and broad, leading to the same trail of interstate disputes and competition. The reported cases, however, indicate that states where the UCCJA has been enacted have applied and interpreted the emergency exception with remarkable restraint, as intended by

---

45. *In re* Marriage of Schwander, 79 Cal. App. 3d 1013, 145 Cal. Rptr. 325 (1978).

the authors. As with other provisions of the Act, cases interpreting emergency jurisdiction are found for the most part in those states that passed the Act in the early and middle 1970s; whether the majority of states that have enacted the UCCJA in the last three years will follow the lead of these early courts on the emergency question remains to be seen. The popularity of the UCCJA's provisions and principles as guides for decision making with courts in states where the Act has not been passed indicates that they will follow this lead.

D. Inconvenient Forum

A primary rule, as noted, of the UCCJA is that the temporary presence of a child in a state does not confer jurisdiction on that state. This rule may encounter problems, however, when the parent who is entitled to custody moves with the child to another state, and the parent and child live in the second state long enough for it to qualify technically as the child's home state; the non-custodial parent continues to live in the state of continuing original jurisdiction. It can be expected that the child on occasion will return to the original state for visits; non-custodial parents have attempted to obtain custody in this situation. Section 7 of the UCCJA is designed, among other things, to prevent a non-custodial parent from using the continuing jurisdiction of the original court to obtain a forum in which to seek modification. If § 7 does not work as hoped, there could be a continuation of the problem of states favoring the local parent, and competition between states would again be encouraged. Fortunately,

> it is the prevailing view in states which have encountered such cases that the state of continuing jurisdiction should, as a rule, decline to exercise its jurisdiction in favor of the new home state of the child in such cases. In other words, the non-custodial parent would be directed to seek modification in the new state.[46]

Under § 7, a court may, upon its own motion or a motion made by a party, decline to exercise its jurisdiction if it finds that the other state is a more appropriate forum. It may be required to inquire into the location of substantial evidence concerning the child's care and personal relationships; whether the other state is the child's home state; and whether the exercise of jurisdiction

---

46. Bodenheimer, *supra* note 25, at 22.

by the forum state would contravene any of the purposes posted in § 1 of the Act.[47]

It must be stressed that the inconvenient-forum provisions are not rules of jurisdiction as such. Technically, both states have the power to exercise jurisdiction. The question, somewhat simplified, is: Which court has the greater right or ability to exercise jurisdiction in the child's best interests? The provisions, then, are just guides representing the need for cooperation among courts.

The inconvenient-forum rule was applied recently in a California Court of Appeals case.[48] The parents had been divorced in California, with custody granted to the mother. She and the child moved to Montana, where they lived for thirty months. The father brought an action in California for modification, and the mother sought a rule from the court of appeals to force the trial court to stay custody proceedings pending the outcome of custody proceedings (yet to be filed) in Montana.

The court held that the California trial court had jurisdiction, but added that the court with jurisdiction under the Act to make an initial or modification decree may decline to exercise that jurisdiction any time before using a decree if it finds that it is an inconvenient forum for making the custody determination under the circumstances of the case. If another state appears to be a more appropriate forum, the parties should be directed to the courts of that state. Since Montana had been the home state for thirty months, the court of appeals concluded that the child had closer connections with Montana than California, and that evidence concerning the child's present and future care, protection, training, and personal relationships was more readily available there. If California had exercised its jurisdiction, the court said, it might very well have contravened the general purposes of the UCCJA. As a result, the California courts in such a case should exercise their discretion to issue a stay of proceedings until an action is brought and a determination made in Montana.

This case does not purport to give strict rules to California trial courts in deciding inconvenient forum questions; it does, however, make the principles of the Act primary guides for decision,

---

47. Commissioners' Notes to UCCJA § 7.
48. Bosse v. Superior Court, 87 Cal. App. 3d 440, 152 Cal. Rptr. 665 (1975).

thereby limiting the discretion of trial judges in such cases. It is also important that the action be stayed rather than dismissed outright, as a dismissal might bar renewal of the action in that state. After determining that it is an inconvenient forum, a court should notify the state court it considers appropriate of the decision it has reached;[49] if, however, the other state, in this case Montana, also declines to exercise jurisdiction, a stay allows the case to be reactivated.

The inconvenient-forum provisions of the UCCJA may be useful in cases where it is both in the child's best interests and in furtherance of stability to pass the jurisdiction power along to a new state. For example, the Oregon Court of Appeals[50] used the inconvenient forum doctrine to encourage just results.

An Oregon trial court had ratified a juvenile court order that placed a child with its paternal grandmother. Several months later, custody was transferred to the father, who moved with the child to Washington. Two years after the move, the father agreed to an order in a Washington proceeding that granted the mother visitation rights. The child went to visit the mother in Oregon, and the mother refused to return the child. The father brought an action to enforce his original rights under the Oregon decree; in the meantime, the Oregon trial court had heard and granted the mother's modification request.

The Oregon Court of Appeals noted that it had the power to exercise jurisdiction as the court of continuing jurisdiction under the UCCJA, but that Oregon was in no way required to exercise its power in all circumstances. It said that under the UCCJA the trial court that changed custody to the mother should have declined jurisdiction "for a reasonable period . . . to allow the institution of an appropriate custodial proceeding by either parent in Washington." The exercise of jurisdiction in Oregon was held inappropriate despite the fact that no Washington action had been instituted and that Washington had not then enacted the UCCJA. However, the mother's case was dismissed rather than stayed, possibly because of the mother's previous appeal to the Washington courts when she obtained visitation rights; she was in effect estopped from saying that Oregon still had jurisdiction.

49. UCCJA § 7; Comissioners' Notes to UCCJA § 7.
50. Moore v. Moore, 24 Or. App. 673, 546 P.2d 1104 (1976).

The inconvenient-forum approach may at times result in inconsistent decisions because the provision is intended to add flexibility to the Act's more rigid rules. Although it too is designed to stop jurisdictional conflict,[51] it may occasionally be unavoidable in a close case, as occurred in California.[52]

The parents had been divorced in North Dakota, and custody granted to the mother. She and a child moved to California and lived there for over six months, long enough for California technically to become the child's home state. The father brought an action in North Dakota to modify the original decree. The mother, in turn, brought an action in California to have the California court declare that the North Dakota court lacked jurisdiction to modify. The California Court of Appeals said that it felt North Dakota should find itself an inconvenient forum and defer to California's jurisdiction, but North Dakota would not. The court said it would defer had the parents been divorced in California and the custodial parent then moved to North Dakota. In this situation, the California court held reluctantly that North Dakota had continuing jurisdiction and the right to use it, showing that the question of inconvenient forum must be a judgment call. The North Dakota trial court apparently felt that it still was the most appropriate forum because more relevant evidence was available there.

The overriding principle of forum non conveniens as used in the UCCJA is that the doctrine will best promote cooperation between states if a custody decree is issued in the state best able to decide the case in the child's interests. The cases discussed show that, largely, this goal is being achieved.

E. Submission to Proceedings

Under the Act, and under some pre-UCCJA cases, a state acquires subject-matter jurisdiction only if it meets the home-state or significant-connection requirements of § 3. Once acquired, this jurisdiction continues technically until all parties have left the state. Subject-matter jurisdiction cannot, however, be acquired by a party's mere appearance in and acquiescence to the proceeding.[53]

---

51. Bodenheimer, *Progress under the Uniform Child Custody Jurisdiction Act and Remaining Problems: Punitive Decrees, Joint Custody, and Excessive Modifications*, 65 CALIF. L. REV. 978, 987 (1977).

52. Palm v. Superior Court, 197 Cal. App. 3d 456, 158 Cal. Rptr. 786 (1979).

53. *See, e.g.*, Sampsell v. Superior Court, 32 Cal. 2d 763, 197 P.2d 739 (1948).

The authors of the Act took efforts to guard against making the courts too easily accessible to forum shoppers and child snatchers who would achieve their purposes, as in the past, by luring a concerned parent into submitting to a second state's jurisdiction, then hope that the forum court would adopt a restrictive approach to the question of subject-matter jurisdiction. Neither personal jurisdiction over the contestants nor submission by them to a court's jurisdiction are among the bases enumerated in the Act.[54] The former rule that conferred jurisdiction upon mere submission to proceedings[55] was intentionally rejected by the Commissioners on Uniform State Laws when the Act was written.

As an example of the new rules in action, a New York court[56] granted a mother's motion to dismiss her action. It held that her mere submission to jurisdiction in that state for purposes of challenging jurisdiction in an action brought by the father was an insufficient basis for a trial court's use of her appearance as the justification for asserting in personam jurisdiction when she was a nonresident defendant.

Only a handful of states still follow the in personam jurisdiction rule that grants custody jurisdiction regardless of the domicile or residence of the child.[57] Whether in personam jurisdiction retains any vitality in even these states is questionable. Of three such states, two have since adopted the UCCJA but not formally abandoned their old in personam decisions, while a third state's highest court has adopted the policies of the Act through case law.[58]

One major criticism that stemmed from use of in personam jurisdiction in the past was that it discouraged parents who thought they might lose their case from willingly subjecting themselves to the jurisdiction of the courts in a second state. In personam jurisdiction, as a result, played a major role in complicating the temporal problems of custody decrees and in causing insecurity for children. Under the Act, the parents' location, so long as it is

---

54. UCCJA § 3.

55. RESTATEMENT (SECOND) OF CONFLICT OF LAWS § 79(c) (1971).

56. Pitrowski v. Pitrowski, 67 App. Div. 2d 743, 412 N.Y.S.2d 316 (1979).

57. *See, e.g.,* Pope v. Pope, 239 Ark. 352, 389 S.W.2d 425 (1965). Sharpe v. Sharpe, 77 Ill. App. 2d 295, 221 N.E.2d 340 (1966); Green v. Green, 351 Mass. 466, 221 N.E.2d 857 (1966).

58. Both Arkansas and Illinois have adopted the act by legislation. The Massachusetts Supreme Judicial Court has adopted the policies of the Act by case law. *See* Murphy v. Murphy, 80 Mass. Adv. Sh. 2517, 404 N.E.2d 69 (1980).

known, is not strictly relevant to the question of exercising jurisdiction.

The authors of the Act offered an example:

> The father removed the child prior to any custody proceedings and a few weeks later petitioned for custody in a new state. The mother, glad to learn the whereabouts of the child from the service of process, rushed to the other state and appeared in the proceedings; but the father obtained custody. Under the UCCJA, the mother's submission to the jurisdiction of a state where the child was merely present did not give subject matter jurisdiction to the court because no enacting state is required to honor the resulting decree.[59]

The result of a court exercising jurisdiction upon a mere submission to proceedings on a party's part is that any resulting decree is not entitled to recognition, enforcement, or any semblance of validity (see Chapter IV). This may seem harsh, but if the Act is to accomplish its goals, a reduction of cases based on in personam jurisdiction will be required. It should not, however, lead to a new round of interstate judicial competition in which states disregard one another's decrees; the prohibition is aimed only at misuse of in personam jurisdiction. As with other provisions of the Act, the cases show that the courts are capable of giving this provision the intended restrictive application; and a second court cannot disregard another's in personam–based decree unless the second court itself would originally have been the appropriate court under the Act's terms.

---

59. Bodenheimer, *supra* note 51.

IV. Full Faith and Credit and Comity

The major stated goal of the Uniform Child Custody Jurisdiction Act is to prevent two courts, or a series of courts, from exercising jurisdiction over any single child custody case at a time. The confusion caused by multiple jurisdiction, and the rapid increase in the number of interstate cases (see Chapters II and III), is primarily traceable to the confusion and leeway that have resulted from a series of U.S. Supreme Court opinions dealing with the effect of the Full Faith and Credit Clause of the U.S. Constitution[1] upon child custody determinations in the state courts. These cases also offered guidance and instruction to the state courts on the questions of jurisdiction and res judicata in child custody cases. The UCCJA attempts to deal with the effects of these cases by redefining the bases for jurisdiction, res judicata, recognition, and enforcement; it pointedly avoids any direct clash with constitutional cases, however, because a state law may not override federal law.

The UCCJA, without saying so explicitly, codifies the doctrine of comity whereby one state's courts grant deference, respect, and, occasionally, recognition, to the decrees of another state's courts. Comity is adopted in the Act both because it avoids any constitutional challenge and offers more flexibility then full faith and credit can; since flexibility, even if reduced, is a hallmark of the UCCJA, the use of comity is virtually required.

---

1. U.S. CONST. art. IV, § 1: Full Faith and Credit shall be given in each State to the public Acts, Records, and judicial Proceedings of every other State. And the Congress may by general Laws prescribe the Manner in which such Acts, Records and Proceedings shall be proved, and the Effect thereof.

A. The Supreme Court Cases—
Full Faith and Credit Prior to the Act

Four major U.S. Supreme Court cases—*May v. Anderson;*[2] *People ex rel. Halvey v. Halvey;*[3] *Kovacs v. Brewer;*[4] *Ford v. Ford*[5] —taken together, have come to represent an overall federal approach to the question of full faith and credit for child custody decrees. This has been in practice a "hands-off" approach. There has been no important Supreme Court case dealing with child custody since *Ford* was decided in 1962; as the Court has repeatedly declined to hear appeals on child custody cases since then.

Both *Halvey* and *Kovacs* stand for the principle that a custody decree rendered in one state is entitled to full faith and credit in a second, but only if jurisdiction was proper and *if* there are no changed circumstances to justify a change of custody. Since the law in all states provides that a custody decree given in that state is modifiable at all times upon a sufficient showing of changed circumstances,[6] the Supreme Court reasoned that a custody decree should be just as modifiable if the issue were presented to a second court. Technically, then, a second state's court would be required to grant full faith and credit to another state's decree if a parent who sought modification in the second state were unable to present evidence of changed circumstances that would satisfy a court in the state. In practice, this did not occur, largely because the Supreme Court itself did not consider its decision a technical one.

> Because the child's welfare is the controlling guide in custody determination, a custody decree is of an essentially transitory nature. The passage of even a relatively short period of time may work great changes, although difficult of ascertainment, in the needs of a developing child. Subtle, almost imperceptible, changes in the fitness and adaptability of custodians to provide for such needs may develop with corresponding rapidity. A court that is called upon to determine to whom and under what circumstances custody of an infant will be granted cannot, if it is to perform its function responsibly, be bound by a prior decree of another court.[7]

---

2. 345 U.S. 528 (1953).

3. 330 U.S. 610 (1947).

4. 356 U.S. 604 (1958).

5. 371 U.S. 187 (1962).

6. H. CLARK, LAW OF DOMESTIC RELATIONS IN THE UNITED STATES § 11.5 (1968).

7. Kovacs v. Brewer, 356 U.S. at 612.

As this language makes clear, in both *Kovacs* and *Halvey* the Supreme Court was more anxious to say what full faith and credit did not, rather than what it did, cover; not wishing to restrict the discretion of the state courts in any meaningful way.

In neither case does the Court discuss the order of events needed to show a sufficient change in circumstances to warrant a change in custody. Normally, changed circumstances are thought to be events or conditions that have occurred since the original custody decree was issued.[8] Under these cases, the change circumstances upon which a modification action in a second state is based need not be subsequent to the original decree. The parent who seeks modification might plead that the first court ignored relevant evidence, or even that the first court made an error of judgment, and possibly find a sympathetic judicial ear.[9]

Another question that lurked in the background in *Halvey* and *Kovacs* was that of jurisdiction. In *Halvey*, both parents appeared before a New York court that was hearing a modification request. Although the facts offered a chance to discuss the problem of a parent acquiescing to jurisdiction, it was not discussed. In *Kovacs*, a modification action was brought in a North Carolina court, the state where the grandmother who had legally been granted custody by another court resided. The mother, not a resident, sought modification and submitted herself to the North Carolina court's jurisdiction. Although jurisdiction in *Halvey* and *Kovacs* could have been justified by and based upon the jurisdictional standards then used by the states in interstate custody cases (see Chapters II and III), the Court still passed up a chance to clarify a confused situation, one it had helped complicate in *May*. Instead, the Court approved the jurisdiction *sub silentio*, although this result may simply be an example of a court not reaching an issue that is not plainly presented by the parties in the case.[10]

Jurisdiction and full faith and credit go hand in hand. *May* is the Supreme Court's expression of the constitutional requirements for proper jurisdiction—the kind that will entitle a decree to full faith and credit—but the case has produced more confusion

---

8. CLARK, *supra* note 6, § 17.7.

9. *See* discussion, subsection C, and in Chapters II, III, and VI.

10. "It is a cardinal principle that this Court will first ascertain whether a construction of the statute is fairly possible by which the constitutional question may be avoided." Ashwander v. TVA, 297 U.S. 288, 346 (1936) (Brandeis, J., concurring).

than clarity. The mother and father had separated. The mother, by agreement, took the couple's children to Ohio until a course of action was decided upon. A month later, she informed the father that she had no intention of returning to Wisconsin. The father filed in Wisconsin for a divorce and for custody of the children. The mother received a summons and copy of the Wisconsin petition, but she did not appear in the case. The Wisconsin court granted the father the divorce and custody of the children, and the father retrieved the children. Five years later, the father agreed that the mother might exercise visitation rights and took the children to Ohio. The mother refused to return them, and the father filed a habeas corpus action in Ohio to have the children returned, relying upon the Wisconsin decree. The wife contested the validity of that decree, but the Ohio court enforced it.

In a limited holding, the Supreme Court reversed the Ohio courts that had upheld the Wisconsin decree. The Ohio courts had said that the Wisconsin decree was entitled to full faith and credit. The Supreme Court held that the Wisconsin court's jurisdiction in the original custody determination was improper; and, without proper jurisdiction, the decree was not necessarily entitled to full faith and credit. To have been valid, the original judgment should have been based on in personam jurisdiction over the mother. The fact that the mother had been personally served in Ohio did not serve to repair the jurisdictional defect.

The Supreme Court split on the reasoning for its decision in *May*, however; the state courts have remained split ever since. Justice Burton's plurality opinion stressed the relationships among states, urging strict adherence to the jurisdictional requirements offered in the opinion. Justice Frankfurter concurred to the extent that the opinion did not grant full faith and credit to the original Wisconsin decree. But Frankfurter urged that the Court decide flatly that child custody decrees are never entitled to full faith and credit in a second state; instead, he felt that the states' custody decrees should be enforced on the basis of comity, if at all. The Frankfurter opinion was based on the argument that the best interests of the child were the ultimate concern in child custody cases. He felt that the state courts were best able to make this determination, and his comity approach would implicitly limit the role of the federal courts in child custody appeals. He did not believe that the federalism principles expressed in the Full Faith and Credit Clause were important enough to prevail over the primary state role and state concern for children, an approach close to that of parens patriae (see Chapters II and III). Since there was no majority for any opinion in *May*, the state courts were not bound by its reasoning, only by its result. Frankfurter's concurrence has had a continuing impact, largely because most states eventually adopted a form of his analysis.

Two dissenting opinions in *May* have also had a continuing impact. Justice Jackson felt that, if the sole basis of the result in the case was in fact jurisdictional defect, the Wisconsin decree must be invalid not only in Ohio but also in the issuing state of Wisconsin. More important, Jackson urged that the Supreme Court, and the state courts in turn, use a balancing test that would make one state—the one primarily concerned with the child's welfare—the sole or initial arbiter on custody questions. This is the beginning of the concept of a child's home state adopted in the UCCJA.[11] The other dissenting justice, Justice Minton, made a technical argument; he felt that the mother should have contested jurisdiction in Wisconsin rather than Ohio.

Each of the separate opinions in *May* has attracted followers, but until passage of the UCCJA began, most states followed the Frankfurter approach. All states, however, were careful to obtain jurisdiction in personam over both parents if at all possible; since *May* was a plurality opinion, even in personam jurisdiction was not felt to be a strict requirement. It must be emphasized that *May* was an unusual interstate case; more often, a parent who is legally entitled to custody obtains the initial decree in the family's state of residence. In *May*, the wife apparently had established separate residence in Ohio. She also showed unusual forbearance; in most interstate custody disputes, either parent follows to the state where a custody action is in progress. There is another notable feature in this case: in the final analysis, the Court decided much as it would have had the subject in dispute been property rather than children (see Chapters II and III).

In *Ford*, the South Carolina Supreme Court had held that a custody agreement negotiated by the parents in Virginia was binding in South Carolina, both on res judicata grounds and on

---

11. UCCJA §§ 2(5), 3(a)(1).

full faith and credit. The negotiated agreement had resulted in the dismissal of an ongoing Virginia court action. The Supreme Court reversed, holding that the agreement was not necessarily binding upon South Carolina, on either res judicata or full faith and credit grounds. The result turned on a question of Virginia state law: Did a dismissal operate in the same way as an adjudication of an issue? *Ford* added a new element to the mixture of child custody law made in the previous three cases. Apparently, the principle of res judicata, which provides that once a question has been decided on its merits it cannot be retried without new facts,[12] only applies if the court, rather than the parents, settles the custody issue. This opened yet another door for reconsidering child custody cases.

In its discussion in *Ford*, the Supreme Court tied together the purposes of res judicata and full faith and credit. A first state's custody decree is res judicata only if custody was granted as part of an adversary process; the factual and legal issues become binding upon a second state's court. If the non-custodial parent seeks modification in a second state, and fails to offer evidence of changed circumstances, the initial decree is entitled to full faith and credit. But if the non-custodial parent offers evidence of changed circumstances, the initial decree is entitled to full faith and credit only to the extent that some of the same issues are presented. This discussion is a logical extension from *Halvey*, reinforcing the need to present subsequent facts in a later modification hearing.

There are two other interesting aspects of *Ford*. First, the opinion implicitly says that the welfare of the child cannot be properly protected when the child's parents are allowed to privately arrange for its custody; the child's rights and welfare cannot be decided by contract. This is a curious implication, since the majority of custody cases are negotiated and settled without court supervision.[13] A second oddity is that the Supreme Court could have dealt again with a jurisdictional question after the out-of-state parent acquiesced to jurisdiction in South Carolina. The case, in fact, did not decide any federal or constitutional law question; it was termed solely an interpretation of Virginia law. As a result,

---

12. BLACK'S LAW DICTIONARY 1470 (4th rev. ed. 1968).
13. CLARK, *supra* note 6, §§ 16.10, 16.13.

the Supreme Court said that South Carolina was free to give res judicata and full faith and credit, or comity, to the Virginia decree, but did not have to.

These four Supreme Court cases set the legal stage for the glut of interstate child custody cases that have arisen in the past ten years. Full faith and credit, if it applied at all, was limited to an original decree made upon proper jurisdiction. When a non-custodial parent left the first state with a child, followed by the custodial parent, who shortly brought an action to enforce the original decree in the second state, the action to enforce justified a second state court's exercise of jurisdiction. This jurisdiction was not only for the limited purpose of enforcement, but also for a modification request by the non-custodial parent.[14] On occasion, both parents would ask for modification simultaneously. The second state in assuming jurisdiction was perfectly correct. Both parents and the child were personally subject to its power and control. And it was a simple matter for a parent to produce some evidence, however tenuous, of changed circumstances.[15]

B. State Cases—Full Faith and Credit Prior to the Act

The state courts have followed the U.S. Supreme Court fairly closely, the majority holding that another state's custody decree is entitled to full faith and credit—but only to the extent that the facts that supported the original decree continue to exist, and only so long as no additional facts have been developed. This closely follows the Supreme Court's advice in *Halvey* and *Kovacs*, emphasizing that custody decrees are made to be modified.[16] A custody decree is a court's final judgment, but not for long. Under this analysis, both original and modified custody decrees were granted full faith and credit. Unfortunately, in most cases the second state's court found that the original facts were stale.

The states deviated from the *Halvey/Kovacs* approach in one significant way. The Supreme Court had noted that the first state's decree was only as good in a second state as it would be in

---

14. Ratner, *Child Custody in a Federal System,* 62 MICH. L. REV. 795, 807 (1964).

15. *See, e.g.,* King v. King, 114 R.I. 329, 333 A.2d 135 (1975); CLARK, *supra* note 6, at 598–601.

16. Note, *Legalized Kidnapping of Children by Their Parents,* 80 DICK. L. REV. 305 (1976).

the first. The logical method for a second state court to follow when faced with a request for modification would have been to determine what would qualify as sufficiently changed circumstances to justify a modification in the first state. This would have given the original decree the exact effect it would have had in the issuing state and would not have been difficult since all state courts are adept at borrowing other states' laws.[17] In practice, however, a second state's court would normally apply *its own* statutory modification standards, resulting in a second state decree modifying and changing custody.[18]

In a typical case, a non-custodial parent who temporarily had legal custody—as on a visit—in a second state would ask that state to modify the original decree. So long as the second state had proper jurisdiction, it was free to modify. Such a modification could be had for all the usual list of changed circumstances (see Chapter V).

A particularly comprehensive case on the subject of modification in a second state was heard by a New Mexico Supreme Court.[19] Although it concerned a request to modify the visitation portions of a custody decree, the court discussed the law governing all interstate custody modifications at length. Following their California divorce in 1970, the father and mother waged a continuing battle of nerves and attrition over the father's visitation rights. The mother, after having obtained court permission to move to New Mexico, tried repeatedly to have the California courts limit the father's visits and to loosen her travel restrictions. She eventually brought an action in New Mexico to modify the California decree, alleging changed circumstances, and the trial court modified it. The state supreme court reversed, finding that the mother's alleged evidence of changed circumstances was frivolous. She claimed, among other things, that because of the father's visits the children missed the opportunity to appear in school plays, that paying for the costs of transporting the children to California for visits was too onerous, and that, since she and the father had become increasingly hostile toward one another, the visits could not be good for the children. In another case, the

---

17. *See generally* LEFLAR, AMERICAN CONFLICTS LAW, ch. 9 (1977).
18. Wilsonoff v. Wilsonoff, 514 P.2d 1264 (Alaska 1973).
19. Orason v. Allgood, 85 N.M. 260, 511 P.2d 746 (1973).

court said, it might be more willing to go along with the trial court because the trial court has considerable discretion in child custody awards.[20] But here, the alleged changed circumstances were only inconveniences; and only one, the school plays argument, concerned the children directly. In essence, the court reaffirmed the proverbial rule that a modification should only be made when it is clearly in a child's best interests. Although the state supreme court did not closely define what changed circumstances it felt would justify modification, it implied a loose standard. Here, however, the alleged circumstances applied at both the time of the original decree and ever after; only the mother's address had changed. There were no subsequent events that materially affected the children. Charitably, the court did not remind the mother that she herself had engineered her complaints. Since modification was not in order, the California decree was granted full faith and credit and effect as res judicata. The laxity of the modification rules in New Mexico is implicit in the fact that the mother's lawyer even believed that the modification case might be won; he guessed right, at least at the trial level. The simple fact that a child custody decree is always modifiable, therefore, creates an almost automatic exception to the full faith and credit requirement. If the mother had presented even a single claim of substance, the appeals court was prepared to affirm the trial result.

The steps in avoiding the full faith and credit requirement where no illegality is involved are simple. First, the second state court recognizes that the original decree is entitled to full faith and credit; normally, the parent entitled to custody under the original decree enters it as proof of his or her claim. Then the non-custodial parent seeking modification pleads changed circumstances. (On occasion the parent granted custody also seeks modification.) The pleading that circumstances have changed effectively makes granting of full faith and credit to the original decree merely a rebuttable presumption, one on which the second state court is free to proceed and make its own custody determination. This process is repeated in hundreds of cases. Since it was so simple, granting full faith and credit to other states' custody decrees became largely a matter of lip service, especially when the

---

20. *See* Murphy v. Murphy, 196 Kan. 118, 410 P.2d 252 (1966).

parent urging modification of the original decree was not guilty of violating it.

May had a strong effect on the state courts. They became extremely reluctant to issue ex parte custody orders. In practice, ex parte divorce and custody trials are not at all rare, but are typically cases in which the spouses negotiate the result. When a state court issues an ex parte decree that is later contested, it is almost certain to be modified by the state where it is contested. In a 1976 New Hampshire case,[21] the mother had obtained an ex parte divorce and custody decree in Arizona, but neither the children nor the father were in Arizona at the time. Furthermore, the father had not consented to Arizona's jurisdiction. The New Hampshire court readily modified the Arizona decree to give him custody; full faith was simply denied when jurisdiction was improper.

A few states took the rather extreme position that, whenever a parent petitioned for modification of another state's custody decree, the original decree was not owed full faith and credit and comity recognition. This stems from a 1930 Kansas case,[22] and the position came to be known as the "Kansas rule." The rule was valid only when the child was physically within the court's jurisdiction; in that event, the court reasoned that it might ignore another state's decree and decide for itself and on its own terms what is in the child's best interests. It is an expansive version of the parens patriae jurisdiction by which many courts heard custody cases. In effect, the court taking the Kansas rule found that the fact that the child was now subject to a second state's jurisdiction—its own—was changed circumstance enough to justify reopening the original decree.

The major difference between the absolute Kansas rule and normal parens patriae jurisdiction was that a court using the later approach was more likely to respect another state's decree on the basis of comity. Prior to the promulgation of the UCCJA, the strict best-interests/parens patriae jurisdictional approach was winning converts in many states. Typically, the parens patriae court gave a preexisting decree "strong consideration," but no more. The Alaska Supreme Court held,[23] shortly before the UCCJA went into effect in that state, that full faith and credit did

---

21. Willett v. Willett, 116 N.H. 829, 367 A.2d 607 (1976).
22. Wear v. Wear, 130 Kan. 205, 285 P. 606 (1930).
23. Layman v. DeHart, 560 P.2d 1206 (Alaska 1977).

not apply to custody decrees whatsoever, and that, under the facts of the case, neither did comity. Therefore, changed circumstances were not required to modify another state's custody decree, so long as the trial court was satisfied that the result was in the child's best interests. The court granted custody to the mother, the Alaska resident.

California has long held to an express best-interests standard; its major case espoused the dominance of the parens patriae/best-interests principle.[24] As noted later, it appears to be an open question whether this rule survives under the UCCJA in California.

A few states have taken the position that, in rejecting full faith and credit and comity treatment for custody decrees, they are merely abandoning the pretense of offering them, but they then erase them, opinion by opinion. Often a state argues that sister-state decrees would be no more likely to be modified than under the usual full faith and credit and comity rules. Whatever the merits of this approach, it saved a court from the tedious job of justifying almost every case as an exception to the full faith and comity consideration. If it felt the first state court was right, the decree was upheld; if not, it was modified.[25]

Without some type of additional safeguards, the results would be like open invitations to parents who had lost custody cases. They could simply abduct their children and flock to those states with the most lenient full faith and credit and comity policies. The clean-hands doctrine, which exists to prevent such a flood of child snatching, has been used by almost all state courts and is now codified in the UCCJA. "Clean hands" is a code name for a maxim holding that a wrongdoer should not be allowed to benefit from his wrong.[26] In an interstate child custody case, it means that a parent who has taken a child to a second state in violation of an existing custody decree should not be allowed to bring a modification action in the second state. Jurisdiction over the parent and the child in the second state exists only because of the wrongdoing; for a court to hear the parent's modification case would be to let the parent benefit from his wrongdoing. The clean-hands doctrine was especially important in custody cases in those states that

---

24. *In re* Walker, 228 Cal. App. 2d 217, 39 Cal. Rptr. 243 (1964).
25. *See, e.g.*, Matter of Burns, 49 Hawaii 20, 407 P.2d 885 (1965).
26. BLACK'S LAW DICTIONARY 317 (4th rev. ed. 1968).

did not grant full faith and credit or comity recognition, and was often the only way the abducting parent could be forced to return the child. The major exception to the docrine was emergency jurisdiction (see discussion, *infra*, and in other chapters).[27]

While the clean-hands doctrine has no direct connection to the question of whether a state should grant an original decree, full faith and credit or not, it effectively confers full faith and credit upon the original decree for the limited purpose of denying jurisdiction to a wrongdoing parent. Another explanation might be that the wrongdoing parent is essentially estopped from denying the validity of the original decree. Courts typically discuss clean hands only in terms of its jurisdictional effect, and occasionally hint that the denial of jurisdiction can be punishment against the wrongdoing parent for misusing the legal system.

Clean hands has not operated smoothly, however. Jurisdiction was typically denied when the wrongdoing parent filed for modification. But the rules change completely when the parent entitled to custody under the original decree brings an action in the second state (*i.e.*, habeas corpus) to enforce the original decree and retrieve the child first. Under these circumstances, many state courts have concluded that the original decree is not necessarily entitled to full faith and credit or even comity (see Chapter VI).[28] A wrongdoer who has abandoned a child usually counters the enforcement petition with a petition for modification. The courts apparently reasoned that the parent who sought enforcement of the original decree had also put the validity of that decree into issue. At any rate, clean hands lost its teeth, and the modification hearing was held. The custody case was tried all over again, and the abducting parent got a second chance despite the fact that he still had dirty hands. The difference in these circumstances is that the second state court had jurisdiction over both parents and the child. With the *May* requirements met, the court felt free to reconsider the case.[29] Typical cases are examined in Chapter VI.

In an unusual habeas corpus/modification case,[30] the father had

---

27. The major emergency jurisdiction case, both before and after the UCCJA, is Ferreira v. Ferreira, 9 Cal. 3d 824, 512 P.2d 304 (1973).

28. Annot., 35 A.L.R.3d 520, §§ 5, 8 (1971).

29. *See, e.g.*, Wicks v. Cox, 146 Tex. 489, 208 S.W.2d 876 (1948).

30. Ferster v. Ferster, 220 Ga. 319, 138 S.E.2d 674 (1964).

been granted permanent custody by a Maryland court. The mother took the children, left Maryland, and moved to Georgia. The father brought a habeas corpus action in Georgia, and the mother countered with a petition for modification. Eventually the Georgia Supreme Court enforced the original Maryland decree, but only after it concluded that the mother had failed to prove changed circumstances to justify a modification. In other words, the father was required to win his case twice.

Clean hands may lose all force when an emergency threatens a child, or if enforcement of a custody decree in a second state's court would violate its public policy. In a compelling example of a court using both emergency and public policy to effectively ignore a parent's dirty hands,[31] the parents were divorced in Colorado, and custody of the couple's two children was granted to the mother. Later the husband moved to Nebraska and, later yet, removed the children to that state, refusing to return them. The mother brought habeas corpus action in Nebraska. The father defended by introducing evidence that the mother had become a prostitute and was, in fact, raising the children in a "bawdy house." The trial court denied the mother's petition.

On appeal, the Nebraska Supreme Court first determined that the Colorado decree was entitled to no more weight than it had when it was first issued, citing *Halvey*. Next the court discussed its policy on comity. Ordinarily, comity will be extended to a sister-state decree by a Nebraska court, but "extraordinary circumstances" (not quite the same as emergency) will justify a court's failure to grant comity recognition. In this case the court felt that the evidence of the mother's profession was so extraordinary that both comity and the clean-hands doctrine were irrelevant. Although the opinion did not explicitly discuss public policy, its emphasis on the immorality of the mother's lifestyle left no doubt that public policy would have been invoked if necessary to keep the children with the father. The court did not investigate Colorado's public policy concerning the mother's habits, but it is safe to assume the same result if it had. (The problems of this case under the UCCJA will be discussed later in this chapter.)

The Nebraska court found a third justification for its exercise of jurisdiction—a modified version of parens patriae. The court

---

31. Copple v. Copple, 186 Neb. 696, 185 N.W.2d 846 (1971).

said that when a child's custody is sought in a habeas corpus action, the child becomes a ward of the state in which the action is
brought, and the child's custody is dealt with under a strict best-
interests standard that pushes full faith and credit and comity considerations to a secondary level. Although the "ward of the state"
rule exists for habeas corpus in all states, it is seldom relied on in
child custody cases. The net impression left by this case is that the
court used—and would use—every and any argument available to
keep the children from the mother's unfortunate influence. The
question of the father's dirty hands was ignored; he was practically applauded for his action.

C. Comity Prior to the UCCJA

The U.S. Supreme Court has never laid down any explicit rules
on how state courts should use principles of comity to recognize
other states' child custody decrees. Although a definitive ruling
from the Supreme Court may have helped avoid the confusion,
repetitive litigation, and profusion of legal theories in this area of
the law, such a decision would not fit the Supreme Court's role.
The Supreme Court and other federal courts have become involved in family law cases in general and child custody cases in
particular only on rare occasions and usually only when a federal
constitutional issue, such as the scope of the Full Faith and Credit
Clause, is raised.[32] Occasionally, however, the various justices'
opinions in *May, Halvey, Kovacs,* and *Ford* have advised state
courts to which the cases were being remanded that they were
free to use a policy of comity to recognize one another's decrees.

Comity, which became strictly a matter of state law, technically
involves one sovereign court's deference or respect for another,
resulting in a foreign decree being recognized and/or enforced[33]
The function of comity is best exemplified in a United States
court, perhaps a county court in Iowa, faced with a decree from
another country, say, Mexico. Comity urges the Iowa court to
recognize the sovereign Mexican court's decree. The states, however, are considered sovereign themselves within the American
legal system so long as they are dealing with areas of law that have
not been preempted by the federal government. So comity be-

---

32. In recent years, however, as family law matters have become constitu-
tionalized, the U.S. Supreme Court has been reviewing matters dealing with
substantive family law issues. *See generally* Note, *Developments in the
Law—the Constitution and the Family,* 96 HARV. L. REV. 1156 (1980).

33. LEFLAR, *supra* note 17, § 84.

tween states in theory operates exactly as it does between courts of separate countries. The notion of sovereignty, and the resulting separateness, seems to have played a major role in the developments in child custody law that the UCCJA means to avoid.

Approximately one-third of the states have used comity as their primary means of avoiding interstate disputes and legal inconsistencies in child custody decrees. But comity has been very elastic, and not all states defined their policies similarly. New York's comity policy for child custody decrees was fairly typical, perhaps because many other states followed it. The New York Court of Appeals,[34] in an opinion written shortly before the UCCJA went into effect there, declared that all its policies that refused a forum in interstate child custody cases were based on comity. In this case a parent who had abducted a child sought modification of another state's decree in a New York court. The court noted that, although clean hands was applicable in most states to abduction, clean hands itself was like a subsection of comity. Full faith and credit, it said, simply did not apply. This was the last installment in a series of New York cases over twenty years that had established the general outlines of comity policy. It is but a short step to the UCCJA.

In most cases, comity was simply another step in the process by which a court decided whether to hear a case involving another state's decree. It was a matter left largely to the discretion of trial judges, who were expected to treat and consider a sister-state's decree with respect and restraint and, if necessary, enforce it. But if a trial judge determined that the facts warranted reappraisal of the previous decree, he was relatively free to reappraise it. The state appellate courts were unlikely to second-guess the trial judge.[35] According to a New York court,[36] in the absence of other evidence, another state's custody decree should be given validity in that state; a showing that adverse circumstances affected the child's health or welfare justified exercise of emergency jurisdiction, however. Despite the apparently absolute language—that only an emergency justified an exception to the general New York comity rule—the trial judges' broad discretion was usually upheld. For example, the New York Court of Appeals[37] upheld the modification of a custody decree issued by a Puerto Rico

34. Martin v. Martin, 45 N.Y.2d 739, 408 N.Y.S.2d 479 (1978).
35. *See, e.g.*, Metz v. Morley, 29 App. Div. 2d 462, 289 N.Y.S.2d 364 (1968).
36. *Id.*
37. Bachman v. Mejias, 1 N.Y.2d 575, 136 N.E.2d 866 (1956).

court. The state's parens patriae and concern for children were cited as justifications for exercising jurisdiction.

A number of states have placed less discretion in a trial judge's hands. The Indiana Court of Appeals[38] held that comity, on the state level, operated similarly to full faith and credit on the federal constitutional level. Only genuinely changed circumstances therefore, justified an Indiana court to set aside another state's custody decrees. And, to the extent that some issues were identical with those in the original case, an Indiana court was bound by the original decision. The result was required even when an Indiana court had obtained jurisdiction over the parties that was normally satisfactory and might justify reopening if the case were brought in some other state.

Minnesota has perhaps brought is comity policy closest to the principles urged by Justice Jackson in *May*. The Minnesota Supreme Court said that in interstate child custody cases:

> Probably, the better rule is that it does not involve constitutional issues at all, but is simply a matter of comity, and that the courts of the state which has the greatest interest in the child ought to be permitted to determine its custody.[39]

Thus, a Minnesota court would use comity to refuse a parent who abducted his child a forum in that state when another state remained the one with the greatest interest in the child. Minnesota courts concluded that their state did not necessarily have the greatest interest in a child who simply entered its borders. This and several similar cases definitely foreshadowed the UCCJA.

An Alabama case anticipating the UCCJA[40] was decided not long before the Act went into effect there. It held that an Alabama court could refuse to hear a request for modification of another state's decree on comity grounds alone, so long as the other state court exercised continuing jurisdiction.

It is not unusual for a court to speak of both full faith and credit and comity in the same opinion. The tendency to refer to both concepts underscores several patterns that recur from case to case:

1. Many interstate child custody cases treat full faith and credit as a step in an analytical process that must be gotten over

---

38. Kniffen v. Courtney, 148 Ind. App. 358, 266 N.E.2d 72 (1971).
39. *In re* Welfare of Longseth, 282 Minn. 28, 162 N.W.2d 365 (1968).
40. Fawkes v. Fawkes, 360 So. 2d 719 (Ala. App. 1978).

before the court may move on to the real issue at hand, *i.e.,* modification.

2. The state courts have been and remain confused on just what difference there is between full faith and credit and comity and as a result talk of both in order to cover all their bases.

3. The difference between full faith and credit and comity may be seen as a legal rather than decisional distinction. Whichever is applied in a given case, the result is virtually the same.

State judges are correct in seeing the difference between full faith and credit and comity as an interesting question of legal theory only. When a decree is entitled to full faith and credit, the U.S. Supreme Court and the Constitution make it a requirement; of course, full faith and credit was easily sidestepped by use of the Supreme Court's analysis in *Halvey* and *May.* Comity, rather than being a requirement, is something a court should offer to another court's actions; of course, it is also easily avoided. The major difference between the two doctrines appears to be that in some states a decree entitled to full faith and credit required changed circumstances to justify a modification, whereas comity itself might justify a reappraisal of another state's decree. Even this difference was of little importance since most states required changed circumstances under comity, and parties in an interstate case pleaded changed circumstances in any event, just to feel sure the case would be heard.[41]

While comity occasionally resulted in the recognition or enforcement of a custody decree in a case where full faith and credit would not—which is the central reason for a state to have a comity policy—comity was elastic in practice. As a result, the states' comity policies often resulted in interstate problems that stemmed from the U.S. Supreme Court's full faith and credit decisions. Comity did, however, require the courts to think twice before jumping into an interstate custody dispute, at least if there was no emergency. In an emergency, comity did not apply at all.

D. Res Judicata Prior to the UCCJA

The doctrine of res judicata has not played a major role in the interstate child custody area. For one thing, in *Ford* the U.S. Supreme Court did not actually give the state courts any valuable

---

41. *See generally* Annot., note 28, *supra.*

advice, since that case turned on a peculiarity of Virginia law. The essential rules of the doctrine have been of little aid in interstate custody cases simply because the normal rules seldom apply. The general rule is that the questions of fact and law decided by a first state's court are binding upon any subsequent court faced with identical issues. In practice, courts that face an identical action, in a tort or contract case, for example, simply refuse jurisdiction.[42] Res judicata seldom comes into a custody action brought in a second state because that action is for modification—by definition a *different* action. If some issues in the modification are identical with those in the first state proceeding, many state courts hold that res judicata principles prevent them from retrying those issues;[43] in areas of law other than child custody, a partial bar on some issues is typically referred to as collateral estoppel.[44]

The Supreme Court itself noted, a year after *Ford*, that the facts in that case were unusual,[45] if not downright strange. Basically, it stands for the principle that, as regards res judicata effect, a first state decree is entitled to no more binding effect in a second state than in the first. Unlike Virginia, most states provided either that a negotiated settlement acted as res judicata or made such settlements effective.[46]

The introduction of res judicata may have contributed to judicial confusion, however. Apparently, some state courts felt that full faith and credit and res judicata were the same thing, at least for child custody purposes. The state courts mixed the Supreme Court's jurisdiction and res judicata principles. If another state's decree had been rendered upon improper or insufficient jurisdiction, a second state court felt free to modify since neither full faith and credit, nor res judicata, applied to the decree. This analysis was unfortunate, although state courts were technically correct. Res judicata applies to the rationale of a case and the state courts should perhaps have considered the reasoning, if applicable, from cases where jurisdiction was faulty.

---

42. EHRENZWEIG & LOUISELL, JURISDICTION IN A NUTSHELL § 29 (3d ed. 1973).

43. *See, e.g.,* Dowden v. Fischer, 338 S.W.2d 534 (Tex. Civ. App. 1960).

44. EHRENZWEIG, *supra* note 42.

45. Durfee v. Duke, 375 U.S. 106 (1963).

46. CLARK, *supra* note 6, § 16.10.

One confused case was brought in the Texas Supreme Court,[47] which enforced an Illinois voluntary child custody agreement entered into by the divorced parents. According to Illinois law res judicata had effect in that state. The Texas court said it was bound under principles of full faith and credit to give recognition and enforcement to the Illinois decree.

Most cases that considered the res judicata aspects of custody (and it should be noted that res judicata is always involved even if it has no ultimate effect) stressed that the decree of a first state is entitled to res judicata effect only to the extent of the factual and legal situation that pertained when the original order was issued.[48] This, of course, meant that changed circumstances negated any res judicata effects, just as changed circumstances negated full faith and credit and comity.

E. Full Faith and Credit and Comity under the UCCJA

The terms "full faith and credit" and "comity" are not mentioned in the text of the UCCJA itself. The Commissioners' Prefatory Note,[49] however, specifically refers to the confusion that reigned in interstate child custody litigation and stresses that the Act is designed to prevent all, or most of, this confusion. It is plain by reading the UCCJA that virtually every section is designed in some way to overcome the legacy of the U.S. Supreme Court child custody decisions. Plainly, to do so requires that the Act deal with both full faith and credit and comity, even if obliquely.

Analysis of full faith and credit and comity in cases brought under the UCCJA is made rather difficult. First, few cases discuss either topic. Second, the Act's comity principles pervade its various sections; as a result, reference to comity itself is seldom necessary to reach a decision that grants what amounted to comity, before UCCJA enactment to another state's decree. The cases indicate that the Act is working, through comity principles, to prevent multiple litigations.

---

47. Rodgers v. Williamson, 489 S.W.2d 558 (Tex. 1973).

48. *See, e.g.*, People *ex rel.* Bukovich v. Bukovich, 39 Ill. 2d 76, 233 N.E.2d 382 (1968).

49. Commissioners' Prefatory Notes to the UCCJA.

One oddity today is that the Act makes no claim to codify a principle of full faith and credit, and in fact eschews any such interpretation.[50] State cases that granted full faith and credit to sister-state decrees are not and cannot be superseded by the UCCJA; those cases are apparently good law until the state courts decide otherwise. The same is true of old comity cases. The most accurate approach to the full faith and credit issue is probably to presume that the Act makes the issue of full faith and credit irrelevant.[51] One state has, at least temporarily, held that the UCCJA requires a state where the Act is in effect to grant full faith and credit to another state's decree.[52] The court here found that result in the provisions of § 13. The case, however, involved a father who had abducted his children and then sought an Ohio forum, and the father's case could have been denied jurisdiction under the clean-hands terms of § 8. The mother's original decree could then have been enforced via § 13 without reaching any jurisdictional question.

An interpretation that holds that the UCCJA requires courts to grant full faith and credit to decrees rendered by courts in other states where the Act is in effect is fraught with troubles. The U.S. Supreme Court has simply and repeatedly said that decrees are not entitled to full faith and credit the minute the circumstances change, but that the states are free to extend comity recognition. First, an interpretation that the Act requires the granting of full faith and credit places a state court in direct opposition to the Supreme Court custody cases. The Act is designed specifically to avoid this confrontation:

> Although the full faith and credit clause may perhaps not require the recognition of out-of-state custody decrees, the states are free to recognize and enforce them. This section (13) declares as a matter of state law, that custody decrees of sister states will be recognized and enforced.[53]

In other words, the framers of the Act intend a policy of comity. Of course, a state court is free to disagree with the Commissioners and determine that the Act actually requires full faith and

---

50. Commissioners' Notes to UCCJA § 14.

51. Crouch, Interstate and International Custody Disputes in the 1980s—Something Can Be Done 11 (unpublished manuscript, 1980).

52. Matter of Potter, 10 Ohio Op. 3d 214, 377 N.E.2d 536 (1978).

53. Commissioners' Notes to UCCJA § 13.

credit, since the Commissioners' Notes are merely advisory. The second problem with the interpretation is that the Supreme Court cases are avoided as intended, and the same loopholes that created the interstate child custody problem may remain intact.

No case has arisen that explicitly challenges the constitutionality of the UCCJA on federal full faith and credit grounds. In one, however, the North Dakota Supreme Court[54] rejected a parent's claim that the UCCJA's notice provisions, contained in §§ 4 and 5, did not meet standards created by the U.S. Supreme Court. The North Dakota court held that the Act's provisions did in fact satisfy federal constitutional notice and due process requirements.

The UCCJA tries to get as close to ensuring full faith and credit as possible without intruding on the U.S. Supreme Court's legal territory. Section 3 on jurisdiction and §§ 4 and 5 on notice and opportunity to be heard (see Chapters II and III for discussion) are designed to meet the requirements of the jurisdiction case, *May*. Sections 12, 13, and 14 of the Act present a scheme that attempts to meet the problems of *Halvey, Kovacs,* and *Ford*. Section 12 establishes that a decree rendered upon proper jurisdiction as defined in § 3 and in accord with the notice provisions—also a key problem in *May*—will be given res judicata effect in that state when the Act is in effect. The Act's res judicata provision, when enacted, becomes the voluntary res judicata law of the state, and *Ford* makes it clear that a state's voluntary rules will be respected. The Commissioners' Note to § 12 refers to the res judicata policy expressed there as a problem that pertains to the validity of decrees only, not to their recognition. This interpretation helps to prevent the confusion that had developed over the interplay between res judicata, full faith and credit, and comity. In the past, of course, the validity of a decree was seldom relevant, since the modification rules developed after *Halvey* ensured that recognition was avoidable.

Section 13, separately, provides for the recognition of any original or modification decree issued by another state under provisions substantially similar to those of the Act. It appears that the term "substantially similar" is meant to allow a court to recognize decrees that emanate from states where the UCCJA is not yet in effect. (In addition, the term "substantially similar" would allow

---

54. Giddings v. Giddings, 228 N.W.2d 915 (N.D. 1975).

for variations in the UCCJA as it is enacted by particular states. This concern seems unnecessary, however, because there have been very few variations from the original text of the Act. Those that exist are minor and cannot be expected to result in a conflict among states.) According to the Commissioners' Note to § 13, a decree that is valid under § 12 is entitled to recognition and enforcement under § 13. It becomes, in effect, res judicata in the second state court, deserving of comity. This two-step approach may seem as tautological as the discussions in pre-UCCJA opinions concerning the interplay of res judicata, comity, and full faith and credit, but the approach seems necessary or at least advisable as a safeguard to establish the requirements for recognition as outlined by the U.S. Supreme Court. There may still be a federal constitutional question—*May* in personam jurisdiction—lurking in the workings of §§ 3, 5, 12, and 13. This possibility is not likely to become a problem, according to the Commissioners' Note to § 13, because of the strong provisions for giving notice and an opportunity to be heard.

Section 14 is the major comity provision of the UCCJA. The Commissioners' Note to the section comments that the policy of refraining from exercising jurisdiction is "respect for the continuing jurisdiction of another state" rather than comity. Section 14 is technically, however, a provision that restricts a court's ability to enter modifications of another state's decrees (see Chapter V) through jurisdictional qualifications rather than vague notions of deference and respect. Consequently, it is not necessary for the section to mention comity as such, although its extension results when the section is properly used. Whether a second state may entertain an action for modification of another state's original child custody decree does not depend upon the rules of *Halvey* or *Brewer*, but upon the § 3 jurisdictional requirements. These two opinions, of course, cannot be overruled by a state law; the UCCJA simply avoids them. Only an emergency affecting the child, supported by competent evidence, justifies a second court's disregard of another court's continuing jurisdiction under § 14. The clean-hands doctrine of § 8 appears to have been freed of any comity or full faith and credit connotations that may have accrued to the doctrine in past court opinions.[55] A fuller discussion of § 14 is contained in Chapter V.

The majority of those few cases that treat full faith and credit and comity within the context of the UCCJA have decided, ex-

---

55. Commissioners' Notes to UCCJA § 8.

plicitly or implicitly, that the Act codifies a policy of comity. The New York Supreme Court[56] discussed the comity effects of the UCCJA at length when a Puerto Rico custody decree was disputed. The New York court held that if the Puerto Rico court had issued the decree under jurisdictional requirements substantially similar to those of the UCCJA, New York would be required to enforce and recognize the Puerto Rico decree. This result, it said, was a policy of comity, not merely of jurisdiction. However, the custody decree had been issued in an ex parte proceeding and Puerto Rico had not enacted the UCCJA. Since Puerto Rico's jurisdictional standards did not fundamentally conform with those of the Act, the New York court held that it could modify the decree consistent with the Act. An interesting possibility under § 13 would be an interpretation that the section makes recognition turn on whether a second state's court considers the original decree a result of substantially similar jurisdiction as that required under the Act. Under such an interpretation, a second state court would be free to question the soundness of jurisdiction of any original decree, whether the state that issued the decree had the UCCJA in effect or not. There are at present no cases with such an interpretation. The Commissioners' Note to § 13 does call for a state that has the UCCJA to automatically recognize the decrees of another state, even if the other state has not enacted the UCCJA, but the text itself seems slightly narrower.[57]

If courts are free to reconsider the jurisdictional basis of the original decree, dire results may be expected. For example, once the New York court determined that the Puerto Rico court's jurisdiction was improperly exercised, the original order was treated as if null, or never in existence. If a decree is based on improper jurisdiction, in New York at least, the question is no longer whether modification is proper but whether the second state court may take jurisdiction and grant what amounts to an original custody decree.

The result is similar to that in some international custody cases. Discussions in opinions concerning decrees issued in countries where the political or cultural traditions vary markedly from those of the United States are often marked by barely concealed disparagement of the foreign country's legal, political, or cultural

---

56. Fernandez v. Rodriquez, 97 Misc. 2d 353, 411 N.Y.S.2d 134 (1978).
57. UCCJA § 13: Commissioners' Notes to UCCJA § 13.

systems. The UCCJA provides in § 23 that child custody decrees of other nations be recognized and enforced so long as the decree was issued after reasonable notice and an opportunity to be heard was granted to all interested parties. This means that an ex parte foreign decree will not be granted comity. Section 23 made the California Supreme Court's decision[58] rather simple and allowed the court to avoid other sticky issues. The father, a resident of Australia came to California to enforce a recent Australia modification decree. The Australia courts originally had granted custody to the mother, but she had violated provisions of the decree, and her violations appear to have led to the modification. The California court enforced the Australia modification decree, despite evidence that it was punitive. It may be significant that the Australian way of life is quite similar to ours, however.

The California Supreme Court,[59] in a case decided just after the UCCJA went into effect in that state, was faced with similar facts. The major exceptions were that the original decree had been issued in Czechoslovakia and that all the significant events had taken place before the UCCJA took effect in California. The California Supreme Court dodged the question of the validity of a Czechoslovakia decree by citing cases that made the welfare of the children paramount; the court then noted that the question of whether their remaining in California was best for the children was left almost entirely to the discretion of the trial court. On remand, the trial court issued a decree keeping the children in California, influenced in large part by expert testimony that they would live better and more well-adjusted lives there than in Czechoslovakia. Both § 23 and the home-state principle of the UCCJA—plus the parental preference rules that California applied in the case—should probably have returned the children to the mother.

When the custody dispute is strictly a matter between states, the UCCJA as an entirety expresses a policy of comity, according to the action discussed at note 34. In that case, the New York Court of Appeals, just prior to the Act's effective date in that state, laid out its concept of how the Act affected comity. It specifically ruled that the policy of forum non conveniens (see Chapter III) that permeates the Act as a way of avoiding interstate dis-

---

58. Miller v. Superior Court, 22 Cal. 3d 923, 587 P.2d 723 (1978).
59. *In re* B.G., 11 Cal. 3d 679, 523 P.2d 244 (1974).

putes reflects a policy of comity as well as of jurisdiction. The court held that prior to the Act comity depended largely upon how a particular state or even a particular judge viewed it, but under the Act it became a uniform policy with distinct rules to be followed. It stresses that even under the UCCJA the ultimate concern is the best interests of the child, which, the court said, are normally served by the regular operation of the Act, the only exception being an emergency of immediate possible physical harm. A mere detriment is not enough to allow a New York court to step in and override another state's continuing jurisdiction.[60] The New York court's interpretation of forum non conveniens as a comity process is something of a departure. In the past, forum non conveniens was treated mainly as a jurisdictional and conflict of laws question.[61]

One marked effect that the UCCJA has been having in judicial opinions is that cases which would have called forth a discussion of full faith and credit or comity in the past simply do not mention the topic.[62] Several recent ones have used the forum non conveniens policies and provisions in the UCCJA to return a case to the court that originally exercised jurisdiction. Apparently, the Act is doing its job—providing comity—in these cases even though comity is not brought up.

One recent Montana Supreme Court case[63] contains a lengthy discussion in which comity principles are applied but the word is not mentioned. A father, a California resident, sought a return of his child who was living legally with an aunt and uncle in Montana, pleading a California modification decree. But the Montana court found that the father had failed to properly notify the aunt and uncle, as interested parties to the California modification action, according to the provisions of the UCCJA. As a result, the California court's exercise of jurisdiction and issuance of a modification decree were held improper, with the validity, recognition, and enforcement of the decree disallowed. (This may also be an example of one state with the Act examining the jurisdiction of another court in a state that also uses it.) However,

---

60. Martin v. Martin, 45 N.Y.2d at 742.

61. *See, e.g.,* Fahrenbuch v. Colorado, 109 Colo. 70, 453 P.2d 601 (1969).

62. *In re* Marriage of Verbin, 595 P.2d 905 (Wash. 1979); Pierce v. Pierce 287 N.W.2d 879 (Iowa 1980); Beebe v. Chavez, 602 P.2d 1279 (Kan. 1979); Winkelman v. Moses, 279 N.W.2d 897 (S.D. 1979).

63. Wenz v. Schwartze, 598 P.2d 1086 (Mont. 1979).

Montana was for this case, the child's home state as defined in the UCCJA. On that basis, the Montana court granted permanent custody to the aunt and uncle, taking pains to assure that the California decree would have been recognized had the notice been properly made; it would have reached that result even though the evidence did not support a conclusion that the California decree was in the child's best interests.

Emergencies pose the most interesting full faith and credit and comity questions according to the Commissioners' Note to § 3:

> Paragraph (3) of subsection (a) retains and reaffirms parens patriae jurisdiction, usually exercised by a juvenile court, which a state must assume when a child is in a situation requiring immediate protection. This jurisdiction exists when a child has been abandoned and in emergency cases of child neglect. Presence of the child in the state is the only prerequisite. This extraordinary jurisdiction is reserved for extraordinary circumstances. When there is child neglect without emergency or abandonment, jurisdiction cannot be based upon this paragraph.[64]

The emergency exception is plainly meant to override any comity or recognition provisions of the Act. But emergency jurisdiction is meant to be applied very narrowly. The rules applied in *Ferreira v. Ferreira*[65] (also discussed in Chapters II and VI) seem to have influenced other states. The Commissioners' Note itself cites *Application of Lang*,[66] in which the importance of danger, almost always physical, as an element required for emergency jurisdiction under New York's pre-UCCJA comity rules was stressed. Although the Commissioners' Note refers to parens patriae jurisdiction as the basis for the § 3 emergency exception, Professor Clark has noted[67] that the standard explanation that parens patriae powers derive from the government's right and duty to protect those under its jurisdiction is too facile an explanation. That power, at least as used in the UCCJA and in most state child neglect laws, is child-centered not government-centered; it reflects a state public policy of protecting important legally recognized rights of children. Although these rights are left undefined, they can be seen as including health, safety, and perhaps freedom as

---

64. Commissioners' Notes to UCCJA § 3.
65. Ferreira v. Ferreira, 9 Cal. 3d 824, 512 P.2d 304 (1973).
66. 99 App. Div. 2d 401, 193 N.Y.S.2d 763 (1959).
67. CLARK, *supra* note 6, § 17.1.

well.[68] Whether they have a federal constitutional dimension, as scholars suggest they do, is uncertain. But the rights need not be constitutionally based in order to override comity, since comity is not itself constitutionally based.

Consider again the fact pattern of the prostitute mother, as previously discussed. The emergency exception of the Act is meant to apply only to immediate dangers, and the court cases interpreting the exception have so far generally agreed. But what would a court under the UCCJA do in a case like this where there is prostitution—plainly grounds for modification in the original decree-issuing state—but no evidence that the harm to the children is either immediate or physical? The threat to the children must be active, and under the UCCJA the fact that children are living in a bawdy house appears to be of insufficient immediacy to justify a father's claim for emergency jurisdiction in Nebraska to modify a Colorado decree. Section 14 tells the Nebraska court to return the father to Colorado to press his modification claims under Colorado's changed-circumstances rules. It is hard to imagine that any court would willingly return a child to a prostitute mother; if instead the court wants to prevent returning the child, it will be required to give a tortured interpretation of immediacy that may loosen the Act considerably. Furthermore, the Act does not have an explicit public policy exception that would provide the needed leeway in such an exceptional case.

Another exceptional case is one in which a child himself pleads for or desires a change of custody. The UCCJA is meant to apply generally; as such, it may not apply appropriately in cases where a mature minor requests a change of custody in a second state court. Many states grant heavy consideration to the wishes of a mature minor.[69] Still another exceptional case is one in which a child runs away from the parent legally entitled to custody. A father presented evidence to a Florida Court of Appeals[70] that his children had run away from their mother as proof that the Florida

---

68. Kleinfeld, *The Balance of Power among Infants, Their Parents and the State,* 4 FAM. L.Q. 319 (1970); Inker and Perretta, *A Child's Right to Counsel in Custody Cases,* 5 FAM. L.Q. 108 (1971); Wisconsin v. Yoder, 406 U.S. 205 (1972) (Douglas, J., dissenting).

69. Siegel and Hurley, *The Role of the Child's Preference in Custody Proceedings,* 11 FAM. L.Q. 1 (1977).

70. Moser v. Davis, 364 So. 2d 521 (Fla. App. 1978).

courts should exercise jurisdiction to modify a North Carolina decree. The court assumed jurisdiction.

The Act's provisions for the filing, enforcement, and certification of original state decrees in other states, in §§ 15, 16, and 17, also carry comity ramifications. The Georgia Supreme Court[71] held that, under Georgia's version of the UCCJA, a decree that was properly "domesticated" pursuant to §§ 15, 16, and 17 was entitled to full faith and credit. It became, effectively, a Georgia decree. The holding was softened somewhat three months later.[72] The same court said that the earlier case merely demonstrated that properly domesticated decrees were enforceable in Georgia. This appears to be a retreat to comity.

---

71. Roehl v. O'Keefe, 243 Ga. 696, 256 S.E.2d 375 (1979).
72. Sandifer v. Lynch, 244 Ga. 369, 260 S.E.2d 78 (1979).

V. Modification

Throughout the UCCJA, emphasis is not on what law a court should apply in making a custody determination, but on which court is best able to make it. Nowhere is this emphasis stronger than in § 14, concerning modification. The actual law by which a custody decree may be modified probably remains the local law of the state court that considers the request. In most states, a modification decree is issued only on a showing of changed circumstances.[1] It must be noted, however, that changed circumstances themselves may have different shades of meaning in different states. A few states take a strict and limited view of changed circumstances, allowing modification only if a child's home life and upbringing appear to pose a definite hazard; even if the hazard is shown, the court must be convinced that an alternative disposition will be better for the child. Other states take a broader view. Cases in which a parent was denied custody because of personal lifestyle, sexual habits, or friendships disapproved by a court continue to appear.[2] The question of which state's law is to apply to a modification proceeding, then, may be credited for the petitioner's chances to succeed. Whether disparities in state modification standards encouraged child snatchings in the same manner that other jurisdictional bases did is uncertain; it may safely be assumed that at least a few parents were moved to act by the variations. Section 14, then, may be seen both as a means of limiting

---

1. H. CLARK, LAW OF DOMESTIC RELATIONS IN THE UNITED STATES § 17.7 (1968).

2. *See, e.g.,* Feldman v. Feldman, 45 App. Div. 2d 320, 358 N.Y.S.2d 507 (1974) (choice of lesser evil as between two parents' lifestyles); King v. King, 114 R.I. 329, 333 A.2d 135 (1975) (mere change in child's age qualifies as changed circumstances).

the various states' abilities to modify another's decrees and as a limit on which state law should apply.

The provisions of § 14 appear simple. Subsection (a) provides that a second state court shall not modify an existing decree from another state unless the first state no longer has jurisdiction and the second does. The first state's continuing jurisdiction, or lack of it, is to be judged on whether it still has jurisdiction according to the initial standards set forth in § 3 (see Chapters II and III). Subsection (b) requires a second state court that obtains jurisdiction under subsection (a) to give "due consideration" to the transcript and other documents from the initial custody proceeding.

The Commissioners' Note to § 14 seems somewhat at odds with the plain meaning of the section itself, advising that:

> [A]ll petitions for modification are to be addressed to the prior state if that state has sufficient contact with the case to satisfy section 3. The fact that the court had previously considered the case may be one factor favoring its continued jurisdiction. If, however, all the persons involved have moved away or the contact with the state has otherwise become slight, modification jurisdiction would shift elsewhere.[3]

Although the child's home state is the primary standard for determining initial custody jurisdiction (see Chapter III), the Commissioners' Note implies (but does not say) that significant-contacts jurisdiction, a secondary basis for initial jurisdiction under § 3, should be the primary modification basis for the first state to continue jurisdiction. Professor Bodenheimer argues that the intent of § 14(a) is to grant exclusive continuing jurisdiction to the initial custody court until either all parties have moved elsewhere or the initial court declines to exercise its continuing jurisdiction;[4] her interpretation of § 14 is more in keeping with the spirit of the UCCJA, since it would more surely prevent forum shopping. Section 14, however, appears to be intentionally more open than other sections, perhaps in an attempt to prevent parties from becoming bound to a court that may in the future have little or no relevant connection to the case. At any rate, no court at this time has squarely held that a first state's continuing jurisdiction lasts indefinitely. Cases that have recognized another state's continuing ju-

---

3. UCCJA § 3.

4. Bodenheimer, Curbing Child Snatching on Three Fronts, State, National, and International, and the Uniform Child Custody Jurisdiction Act 8 (May 29, 1980) (unpublished manuscript).

risdiction have generally involved fact patterns where either a parent who has improperly taken a child to the second state was refused a hearing,[5] or the second state court determines, even if implicitly, that the first state court's jurisdiction continues to meet § 3 standards.[6]

Another intriguing question suggested by § 14 but not yet posed to the courts is contained in the Commissioners' Note:

> The prior court has jurisdiction to modify under this section even though its original assumption of jurisdiction did not meet the standards of this Act, as long as it would have jurisdiction *now*, that is, at the time of the petition for modification.[7]

The Note implies that the original decree may be modified in the original state despite a jurisdictional flaw in the issuance of the first decree, which would give it a degree of validity. It seems more likely that, since § 13 allows a *second* state to modify or ignore a jurisdictionally flawed initial decree (see Chapters III and IV), a modification petition in the court that issued that decree may be treated as an original proceeding rather than a modification, as it may be in a second state. A flawed decree is entitled to no recognition, no comity, and no res judicata effect. If the Commissioners' Note grants any of these effects of validity to some extent, it will be at odds with § 13.

The major question under § 13—which court should hear a modification request—appears to have become a judgment call in many cases. The only clear case occurs when all interested parties have left the state of initial jurisdiction. The rule developing in such a case is that the state where the parent entitled to custody and the child live is the one that should exercise jurisdiction,[8] regardless of where the other parent or other interested parties live. Of course, after six months under these facts, the child's home state would become the one to which a custodial parent and child moved.

Where one parent remains in the state of initial jurisdiction, the courts have reached differing conclusions. In one case[9] proceedings were brought in both California and Oregon. The California

---

5. *See, e.g.,* Woodhouse v. District Court, 196 Colo. 558, 587 P.2d 1199 (1978).

6. *See, e.g.,* Fry v. Ball, 190 Colo. 28, 544 P.2d 402 (1975).

7. UCCJA § 14.

8. Neal v. Superior Court, 84 Cal. App. 3d 847, 148 Cal. Rptr. 841 (1978).

9. Carson v. Carson, 29 Or. App. 861, 565 P.2d 763 (1977).

courts, as required by § 14, determined that they had continuing jurisdiction over the matter. The Oregon Court of Appeals also determined that the Oregon courts had jurisdiction on the home-state jurisdictional basis, again ostensibly after consideration as required by § 14. A conflict was avoided, however, because the Oregon courts, apparently convinced that California was a better forum, deferred to that state. Professor Bodenheimer criticized this case[10] because a finding that a court of initial jurisdiction and a second state court have concurrent modification jurisdiction makes custody determinations less stable, which cannot be denied. The Act, however, does not clearly provide for jurisdiction in only one state at a time for modification purposes. The needed stability might be provided by resort to a significant-connections test for modification rather than a home-state rule. Since home state has been made the primary basis for initial jurisdiction under § 3, it has naturally become the focus of many courts in determining whether they have modification jurisdiction.[11] If a parent and child move to a new state, it becomes the child's home state at least in a technical sense; if at the same time the non-custodial parent remains in the original state, that parent's presence, plus the presence of many relevant court and other records, seems plainly to satisfy the significant-connections test, particularly if the parent with custody and the child have been in the second state only a short time. It is doubtful that this possibility of dual or concurrent jurisdiction was intended by the authors of the Act, but the text of § 14 appears to allow it. The enthusiasm of some courts for the home-state rule appears to have hastened the likelihood of concurrent jurisdiction cases.

As Professor Bodenheimer suggests, an arrangement more in keeping with the spirit of the UCCJA would be to require the party or parties seeking modification to petition the court of original jurisdiction.[12] In other words, the initial state's jurisdiction would be presumed until the initial state court itself declined to exercise it. Once jurisdiction has been declined, § 14 (a) allows the second state to hear the case. This approach, however, ties the parties to the initial state even after all parties have left, a situation the section appears to wish to prevent.

---

10. Bodenheimer, *supra* note 4, at 24.
11. *See, e.g.,* Howard v. Gish, 373 A.2d 1280 (Md. App. 1977).
12. Bodenheimer, *supra* note 4, at 23–24.

There is confusion inherent in the section and the Commissioners' Notes, as evidenced by cases that have construed both the section and the Notes. Unless a uniform approach to the question of modification jurisdiction is reached, § 14 may create a major loophole. Although it would be difficult to manipulate, parents could manage to enter or leave states according to those states' standards for changed circumstances and stability could suffer.

Another potential § 14 question concerns which state's law to apply in a modification action, once a court has properly assumed jurisdiction of the modification proceeding. The former standard set by the U.S. Supreme Court in *New York ex rel. Halvey v. Halvey*[13] held that since custody decrees were modifiable in the state where they were issued, they were modifiable in a second state as well. Full faith and credit was given a custody decree only to the extent that there had been no changed circumstances (see Chapter IV). Scholars argued that *Halvey* meant a second state court must or should use the internal modification/changed circumstances law of the state that had initially issued the decree. Thus, a decree issued in New York could be modified in New Mexico, but only by New York's standards. As noted in Chapter IV, second states' courts seldom followed this line of reasoning, and instead applied their own internal modification law.

It is an open question if the UCCJA, stressing stability in decrees as it does, intends to bind the parties to the modification law of the state that issues the initial decree. Professor Bodenheimer believes it does.[14] The Act, however, requires only that a second court give strong consideration to the transcript and record from proceedings in the first state;[15] a second court may be required to look into the original records. But there is nothing in the text or in the Commissioners' Note to § 14 that suggests a second court is bound to apply the law of the state used for the initial determination.

A requirement that the first state's internal law is applicable no matter which state later acquires jurisdiction would go a long way toward providing stability and predictability. If the applicable law changes along with jurisdiction, parents are offered an opportunity, however small, to shop for a forum with modification stan-

---

13. 330 U.S. 610 (1947).
14. Bodenheimer, *supra* note 4, at 27.
15. UCCJA § 14(b).

dards more to their liking. No such requirement exists under the strict text of the Act; it could be created only by amending the Act or through case law.

VI. Remedies

The UCCJA itself does not specifically provide for remedies of any sort (see Chapter II). The parent entitled to custody of a child, but unlawfully deprived of it by the non-custodial parent, must still seek relief by a number of traditional, well-established methods, including criminal sanctions, contempt of court, tort liability, and the writ of habeas corpus.

Although the UCCJA does not substantively effect these remedies, it appears to have an indirect bearing. For example, the fact that a court in a second state refuses to entertain a modification action when the first state retains continuing jurisdiction should strengthen the custodial parent's right to relief in a habeas corpus action. If the second state cannot exercise jurisdiction to modify a previous decree, it follows logically that it will enforce the previous decree in a habeas corpus action and return the child. Similarly, an abduction that results in a second state's refusal to exercise jurisdiction may be persuasive evidence that the abducting parent is in contempt of the first state's court.

This chapter is concerned primarily with the historical development and current status of remedies available to a custodial parent following abduction of a child by a non-custodial parent. The UCCJA, both because it is recent and indirect, does not play a major role in most cases cited. Its effect in the area of remedies must remain conjectural.

A. Criminal

State legislatures—most of them only recently—have responded to the problems of child snatching by non-custodial parents by passing statutes that make simple kidnapping or interference with custodial rights, or both, a crime. (Appendix B contains each state statute dealing with kidnapping and interference.) The new laws are aimed directly at preventing the abduction of children by their parents; in the past, kidnapping statutes have concentrated almost exclusively on kidnappings by third parties. Since most of the active legislation is recent, few cases have arisen that have required interpretation of anti-abduction statutes.

Child snatching closely resembles traditional kidnapping. It involves the intentional deprivation of the custodian's recognized legal rights to a child. The federal kidnapping statute, the Lindbergh Act,[1] specifically exempts parents from liability under its provisions, as it has for over forty years. This exclusion was apparently based on a vague notion that parents, even acting wrongly, did what they thought best for the child.[2] The Lindbergh Act, in effect, codifies that notion. Another factor that remained strong until the passage of the Federal Parental Kidnapping Prevention Act of 1980 (see pp. 121–124), was that federal agencies were less than eager to become involved in what they saw as domestic disputes, and did not wish to stretch their limited manpower.

Certain states have kidnapping laws that also exclude parents from liability. In some states, simple kidnapping statutes aimed at child snatching have been passed and exist alongside the old laws. Where they do not specifically include parental abductions, courts have often been willing to hold that the parents' immunity from prosecution was implied.

In one of the first cases to consider the issue, parental immunity was granted by the Pennsylvania Supreme Court.[3] The court interpreted the kidnapping statute's purpose and said it was

> enacted to protect parental and other lawful custody of children against the greed and malice of the kidnapper, not to punish their natural guardian for asserting his claim to the possesion and control of them.[4]

This statement reflects two themes that run through decisions that exempt parents from criminal liability for child snatching. These abductions are not generally viewed as violations of any personal right belonging to the child; abduction is viewed as an infringe-

---

1. 18 U.S.C. § 1201 (1971). The Lindbergh Act was originally passed in 1932.
2. 75 CONG. REC. 13,296 (1932).
3. Burns v. Commonwealth, 129 Pa. 138, 18 A. 756 (1889).
4. *Id.* at 757.

ment of property rights in the child, rights that belong to the custodial parent.[5]

The courts often explained or condoned an abduction because it was considered a natural result of a parent's desire to be with his child.[6] Charges are dismissed in such cases because there is believed to be a lack of unlawful intent, a rationale particularly true if parental kidnapping charges are based on an abduction that occurred before a final decree or order granting custody has been entered. The Georgia Supreme Court[7] examined a charge of kidnapping brought by a mother against a father. Since there was no outstanding custody decree, the court defined the arrest warrant as a nullity because there was no evidence or allegation that the father had in fact ever parted with his parental right of custody, a pattern that has continued to the present day. Until a valid decree vesting custody of a child is entered for the benefit of only one parent, or primarily for one, both parents are presumed to be equally entitled to custody. Therefore, the parent who has abducted the child when there is no decree awarding custody cannot be guilty of the crime of kidnapping.[8]

The Iowa Supreme Court[9] extended the principle of parental immunity further holding that neither the father, nor someone acting on his behalf, could be found guilty of kidnapping without a previously entered custody decree. Immunity of agents has also lasted until the present; the agent is presumed to act in the same capacity as the parent himself. So a parent could hire someone to perform the actual abduction.[10]

A parent or a person assisting a parent in an abduction has been found guilty of the crime of kidnapping when he abducted a child after a valid custody decree was entered, however. In a 1960 case[11] the New Hampshire Supreme Court reasoned:

---

5. *See, e.g.,* Wilborn v. Superior Court, 51 Cal. 2d 828, 337 P.2d 65 (1959); State v. Brandenburg, 232 Mo. 531, 134 S.W.2d 529 (1911).

6. State v. Elliot, 171 La. 306, 131 So. 28 (1930); State v. Switzer, 80 Ohio Abs. 12, 157 N.E.2d 466 (1956); People v. Nelson, 322 Mich. 262, 33 N.W.2d 786 (1948).

7. Hunt v. Hunt, 94 Ga. 257, 21 S.E. 515 (1894).

8. Hard v. Spain, 45 App. D.C. 1 (1916); State v. Beslin, 19 Idaho 185, 112 P. 1053 (1911); Biggs v. State, 13 Wyo. 94, 77 P. 901 (1904); State v. Huhn, 346 Mo. 695, 142 S.W.2d 1064 (1940).

9. State v. Dewey, 155 Iowa 469, 136 N.W. 533 (1912).

10. State v. Angel, 42 Kan. 216, 21 P. 1075 (1889).

11. State v. Farrow, 41 N.H. 53 (1960).

The custody of the child having been, by a decree of this court, assigned to the mother, that custody must be regarded for all purposes, as lawful, even as against the father; and he has no lawful authority to take the child from her. If he does so against her will, for the purpose of carrying it (the child) out of the state, it comes within the statute.[12]

The Tennessee Supreme Court[13] overturned a father's conviction for kidnapping. The father claimed he had been unaware of an ex parte divorce granted to the mother before the abduction took place. This result might have been based on a lack of proper jurisdiction to award custody during an ex parte divorce, or perhaps on the principle that the mother was estopped from, or not allowed to deny, the basic shaky foundation of the custody order, but it was not. The court instead reasoned that the father lacked unlawful intent, since he had no way of suspecting that he was violating the law by abducting the child. The right of custody remained with the mother, however.

Modern child snatching legislation has been used by some states to deal with the problem of parental abductions. In a 1979 case, a mother was convicted under an Arizona child snatching statute,[14] when she knowingly violated a custody order. The court, citing *Lee v. People*,[15] sentenced her to a year in jail and ten years' probation.[16] A father was convicted of child abduction when he fled with his children to Kansas following a grant of custody to the mother.[17] The defendant wrote a letter to his brother that offers interesting insight into the emotional and mental processes an abducting parent may go through.

I'm sorry I wasn't able to contact you sooner, but I have been establishing a new identity. The kids and I have new birth certificates, and I tried a new line of work since I can't use any references or education background. Debbie just started kindergarten, and as far as anyone is concerned, she is five, and for me, she is willing to pretend.
***If anybody thinks that I could give that tramp [his former wife] $50 a week with what she made, and see my children one day a month, he

---

12. *Id.* at 58.
13. Hicks v. State, 158 Tenn. 204, 12 S.W.2d 385 (1928).
14. ARIZ. REV. STAT. § 13–1302.
15. Lee v. People, 53 Colo. 507, 127 P. 1023 (1912).
16. State v. Kracker, 129 Ariz. 294, 599 P.2d 250 (1979).
17. People v. Hyatt, 18 Ca. App. 3d 621, 96 Cal. Rptr. 156 (1971).

is nuts! What I have done may make me a fugitive, but to see how happy the kids are, it's worth it and more.

***I have to be very cautious. If you wish to ever contact me, put an ad in the personal column of the *N. Y. Times*—begin Attention Mr. Miller. I will probably see it, as I usually get the paper in the morning.[18]

Of course, if an abducting parent is this determined and succeeds both in establishing a new identity and interring a former one, no law can be particularly effective. Fortunately, few parents are willing to go to such lengths.

In Oregon, the kidnapping statute[19] allows for the conviction not only of the abducting parent, but of any other person who assists a non-custodial parent in an abduction.[20] In Ohio,[21] it was determined that a mother of minor children was guilty of the offense of child stealing. Under an Ohio statute,[22] she could be convicted for taking her own children from her former husband when the father had been awarded custody under a valid decree.

The criminal legislation dealing with parental abductions falls into two major categories. Many earlier statutes made no distinction between kidnapping by a parent in an ongoing custody dispute and kidnapping by a third party who planned on getting a ransom. Parents, however, tended to obtain immunity as a result of common law decisions in cases where no formal custody order had been issued. The only clear way a parent could be charged with kidnapping under an abduction or kidnapping statue was when the kidnapping took place after a valid custody order was issued. Parents were quick to notice the loophole; since they could not be punished absent a final custody order, abductions were often coterminous with custody proceedings. The UCCJA may limit this loophole (see Chapter II).

The states have reacted to the problem of child snatching by aiming specific statutory language at parents and relatives who take children away from the proper custodian, including an abduction from the person who has temporary custody pending a fi-

---

18. *Id.* at 622, 96 Cal. Rptr. at 158.
19. OR. REV. STAT. § 163.225 (1).
20. State v. Edmiston, 43 Or. App. 13, 602 P.2d 282 (1979).
21. State v. Crafton, 15 Ohio App. 2d 160, 239 N.E.2d 571 (1968).
22. OHIO REV. CODE ANN. § 2901.33 (Baldwin).

nal decree. Some statutes differentiate between concealing a child within the state of residence, which is normally made a misdemeanor, and absconding with the child across the border into a second state, which is typically made a felony. Traditionally, the crime of child stealing or simple kidnapping was classified as a misdemeanor, which often meant that the guilty party could avoid prosecution simply by stepping across the state line, because a misdemeanor is normally not an extraditable offense. Other states today continue to make no distinction between abductions within the state and abductions where the child is removed from the state (see Appendix B), and they appear arbitrarily to denominate the offense as either a felony or misdemeanor. Whatever it is called, the penalty for the crime is seldom as severe when a parent rather than a third party is guilty; in no case examined did a recent conviction provide for a penalty more severe than a year in jail.

In many states, a person, parent or not, may be found guilty of the offense of custodial interference when he removes a child from the person who has lawfully been granted custody.[23] New York's Penal Law[24] allows for the conviction for the crime of custodial interference of anyone who "willfully entices" a child to leave the lawful guardian of his own accord. A further question posed by this language is whether or not a parent who simply abducts, but takes pains not to entice, is guilty. The Minnesota Supreme Court[25] affirmed the 1966 conviction of a father, who had been fined $500 and sentenced to one year in prison, for interference with custody. The father argued in defense that his abduction was a natural result of his ex-wife's refusal to grant him visitation rights given in the original custody decree. The court looked at the explicit wording of the statute,[26] especially "to prevent another from obtaining or retaining his custody pursuant to a court order," and chose to eliminate the concept of visitation from the meaning of the word "custody." The statute was amended in 1967. The quoted phrase was omitted and replaced by "to deny another's rights under an existing court order," which was designed to include visitation within the statute's protections.

---

23. State v. Dirks, 36 Or. App. 33, 581 P.2d 85 (1978).
24. N.Y. PENAL LAW § 135.45 (McKinney).
25. Olsen v. State, 287 Minn. 583, 177 N.W.2d 424 (1970).
26. MINN. STAT. ANN § 609.26 (West).

The court's present interpretations clearly imply that a denial or frustration of visitation rights could lead to a criminal charge.

The same court, in a 1978 case,[27] found another portion of the statute,[28] which covered a parent's failure to return a child to its proper custodian, unconstitutional. Because the statute included the words "whoever intentionally detains his own child under the age of 18 years outside the state of Minnesota," the court found the section invalid, because it authorized the exercise of extraterritorial criminal jurisdiction in violation of both the federal and state constitutions. The Minnesota Legislature revised the statute to have it conform to the court's decree by omitting any reference to carrying the child out of state.[29]

A Wisconsin statute makes it a crime for anyone to take an illegitimate child from the custody of either its mother or father. A father who acknowledged a child as his, but had not taken any legal steps to establish paternity, was convicted of abducting his illegitimate child from its mother.[30] On appeal, the father argued that the statute was unconstitutional because it denied equal protection; the statute[31] presumed that an illegitimate child should automatically be placed in lawful custody of the mother. However, in this case the child had lived with the father for seven months, then with the mother for six months immediately preceding the abduction. Nevertheless, the court found the statute constitutional; the state, it said, has a substantial interest in protecting an illegitimate child whose paternity has not been formally adjudicated or established. Therefore, the father could make no custody claims until his paternal rights were lawfully established. His one-year prison sentence was affirmed. The rationale might be applied in other, more typical cases. An action for divorce or separation almost always brings the custody of minor children, if any, into question. It might be more consistent for the states to conclude, whenever a family is breaking apart, that the issue of custody rights is open, and that neither parent has the right to the exclusive custody of a child until a final decree is issued. Such an analysis would also promote the purposes of the UCCJA. It could

---

27. State v. McCormick, 273 N.W.2d 624 (Minn. 1978).
28. MINN. STAT. ANN § 609.26 (West).
29. *Id.*
30. State v. Hill, 91 Wis. 2, 283 N.W.2d 451 (1979).
31. WIS. STAT. ANN. § 946.71 (4) (West).

avoid unfortunate cases, as the one in which Kansas attempted to prosecute a father for interfering with the custody rights of the mother when he took their child to Iraq.[32] At the time the child was abducted, the parents were in the process of getting a divorce, and no custody order had been entered. As a result, the Kansas Supreme Court held that both parents at that time had an equal right to the custody of the child, and that in the absence of a court order granting custody there was no reason to convict for custodial interference. As a result, the child was permanently removed from its "home" state. Although Kansas had not enacted the UCCJA at that time, its courts had applied the Act's principles in a number of cases.

Once a valid custody order has been decreed, a kidnapping conviction is possible following an abduction, no matter how long the child has been away from the lawful custodian, and no matter how much the circumstances of father, mother, and child have changed. This is the import of a case[33] in which a father was convicted of interfering with custody of his child under a Pennsylvania statute.[34] The father had taken the child to Florida and was able to remain hidden for sixteen months. After being found, he defended himself by arguing that the emotional welfare of the child would be threatened if the child were returned to the mother. The court found the father's defense lacked merit, at least as it related to the offense of custodial interference, and affirmed his conviction.

An example of the effect of classifying abduction as a felony or misdemeanor is found in a case where custody of minor children was awarded to the paternal grandparents.[35] The defendant-mother had removed the children from Arkansas to Puerto Rico without permission of the court that had originally granted custody. Under Arkansas law,[36] the mother was convicted and sentenced to six months' imprisonment, a result affirmed by the Arkansas Supreme Court. Under the present Arkansas statute prohibiting interference with custody,[37] the mother could have

---

32. State v. Al-Turck, 220 Kan. 557, 552 P.2d 1375 (1976).
33. Commonwealth v. Chubb, 3 Pa. D. & C. 3d 676 (1977).
34. 18 PA. CONS. STAT. ANN. § 2904 (Purdon).
35. Estes v. State, 246 Ark. 1145, 442 S.W.2d 221 (1969).
36. ARK. STAT. ANN. § 41-1121 (repealed 1964).
37. ARK. STAT. ANN. § 41-2411.

avoided a felony conviction if she had not taken the children out of the state. Her flight to Puerto Rico would have resulted in a conviction under either version of the statute.

In a more extreme case,[38] a father was found not guilty of kidnapping despite the fact that he had taken the child at gunpoint. He was able to avoid prosecution under a recently enacted law[39] in Maine simply because he had not taken the child out of the state. Most states make it illegal both to remove a child from the state without permission of the guardian and to conceal a child within the state without the permission of the guardian (see Appendix B).

A New York case[40] does not appear to fit the patterns discussed so far. A mother and father were divorced in Nevada in a unilateral divorce action brought by the mother. The father was granted the right to visitation with the child. The mother later moved to Israel, taking the child with her, and the father brought a civil suit in New York against the mother for deprivation of his visitation rights. The father also sued the mother's parents for helping to deprive him of his visitation rights. The father pleaded the original custody decree in both suits. The court held that since the mother had lawful custody of the child, no action for damages was allowable, but that a contempt order could be a proper remedy. Possible transfer of custody to the father, if appropriate in certain cases, would be equivalent to punishment for kidnapping.

Recently, the Illinois Appellate Court determined that a father who was granted joint custody with a mother could be convicted of child abduction if he took the child without the mother's permission. The court said that the purpose of the state kidnapping statute was to deter child snatching and that criminal sanctions should be used because civil remedies were insufficient. The court allowed restitution to the mother for the costs of traveling and long-distance telephone calls incurred while attempting to regain custody.[41] This type of approach, especially in a joint custody case, is remarkably like the reasoning of the court in the illegitimate child case, *supra*. Unlike the results in the New York and

---

38. State v. Banner, 355 A.2d 48 (Me. 1978).
39. ME. REV. STAT. tit. 17A, § 302.
40. McGrady v. Rosenbaum, 62 Misc. 2d 182, 308 N.Y.S.2d 181 (1970).
41. State v. Harrison, 6 FAM. L. REP. 2521 (Ill. App. 1980).

Kansas cases (see notes 40 and 32, *supra*), an equally shared right to custody is seen as a limitation rather than a grant of rights. Kidnapping statutes have another salutary effect when they make the crime a felony; the abducting party becomes subject to extradition from a second state to the first, which has jurisdiction. The effectiveness of these statutes depends on the willingness of states' attorneys and prosecutors to enforce them. Still, the new statutes that make kidnapping and custodial interference a criminal act work in harmony with the UCCJA in this regard. Proper use of extradition procedures in criminal actions can act as another way to prevent custody from being relitigated in a second state.

A criminal action brought against a parent who has abducted his child, while it may be a deterrent, is not of itself a remedy for the parent who has wrongfully been denied a lawful right to custody. If applied strictly, criminal sanctions apply only to the question of wrongdoing; they do not ensure that custody is returned to the proper parent. In practice, however, the child is typically returned to the parent who was originally entitled to custody. A non-custodial parent, incarcerated, is not in a position to press custody claims; even if the penalty were less severe, the fact of abduction alone is normally enough to place custody again with the lawful custodian and is persuasive evidence that the abducting parent should not be granted custody later.

B. Tort Liability

Actions brought to establish civil liability under a tort claim have been rare; for this reason alone tort has not historically deterred child snatching. Some states have given tort liability for child snatching fresh life in recent years; decisions in those states may serve as an example for others.

In the late nineteenth and early twentieth centuries, a tort action was most often brought by fathers to recover the value of the services, and therefore custody, of a child. At that time, a child was often valued more for the work he could perform or the money he could earn than for himself. A father who during divorce had negotiated an agreement that granted him custody was allowed to recover the expenses involved in recovering a child after its abduction. The North Carolina Supreme Court also allowed him to collect punitive damages from the mother.[42] In Ohio, a

---

42. Howell v. Howell, 162 N.C. 283, 78 S.E. 222 (1913).

grandfather who had custody of his son's children by agreement was allowed to recover the value of the loss of the children's services and the value of their possession.[43] The same result obtains when the father has obtained custody through a court decree. A Massachusetts father recovered damages for reasonable expenses incurred while pursuing his child, who had been abducted by an agent of the mother.[44] In a New York case, both a grandfather and a father were granted damages for injuries to their feelings (*i.e.*, mental cruelty) when the mother of the minor children abducted the children.[45] As minor children began to be considered other than the exclusive personal property and private labor force of their fathers, this civil remedy was used less often. An action for a child's services is virtually unthinkable today, but the tort action has survived in different forms. A Louisiana court awarded damages to a father on two grounds.[46] First, it ruled that the mother, as the non-custodial parent, owed the father a legal duty not to deprive him of lawful custody. That duty, as defined in Louisiana simple kidnapping statute, had been violated, which alone justified an award of damages, the court said. The father also recovered damages for mental anguish. The use of the kidnapping statute as a standard for tort liability closely resembles the general tort law doctrine of negligence per se, which holds that proof of violation of a statute is also proof of a tort.[47]

A mother and child brought suit in California against the child's father and grandfather for abducting the child and hiding it from its mother.[48] There was no custody decree in effect, but the father and grandfather were both found guilty of violating the California kidnapping statute,[49] which forbids the abduction of a child from a parent, largely because the court read the statute broadly. It explicitly held that a parent, even if entitled to custody in his own right, cannot deprive the other parent of the benefit of the child's company. As a result, the mother was entitled to damages, as was

---

43. Clark v. Bayer, 32 Ohio St. 299 (1877).

44. Rice v. Nickerson, 91 Mass. 478 (1864).

45. Pickle *et al.* v. Page, 252 N.Y. 474, 169 N.E. 650 (1930).

46. Spencer v. Terebelo, 373 So. 2d 200 (La. 1979).

47. *See* RESTATEMENT (SECOND) OF TORTS § 874A.

48. Rosefeld v. Rosefeld, 221 Cal. App. 2d 431, 34 Cal. Rptr. 479 (1963).

49. CAL. CIV. CODE § 49 (West).

the child because he had been denied the care and affection of his mother.

Tort damages are also possible when a parent simply fails to play fair in a custody dispute. A father and mother had been divorced in Illinois, with custody granted to the father. The following year, the mother convinced the original Illinois court that it should modify its order and grant custody to her. The father then sent the children to their paternal grandparents' home in California and later initiated a California proceeding to have custody given to the grandparents.[50] The California court instead granted a petition brought by the mother to force the grandfather to produce the children and hand them over to her. The grandfather appealed, claiming that an emergency situation existed which justified not only the court's exercise of jurisdiction but also a modification that would grant custody to him. The court found the grandfather's claim "patently thin to non-existent."[51] The court then awarded the mother her costs plus the sum of $1,500, assessed against the grandfather as a penalty for bringing the frivolous action. It may be significant that California at the time was operating under the UCCJA. Frivolous actions are seldom condoned, but this case offers the hope that emergency jurisdiction under the Act will be strictly construed and policed for abuse; a failure to allege an emergency dire enough to meet the standards of the UCCJA may be sufficient evidence that a party has abused legal process.

The Missouri Court of Appeals[52] found an actionable tort when anyone knowingly entices or decoys a minor from his home with the intent to deprive the parents (or parent) or lawful custodian of the child's services. Although children's services have not played a large role, a tort may be brought between parents when one is entitled to sole custody and the one who is not entices the minor away. In this case, the mother was able to avoid paying damages only because the father could not establish that he was entitled to sole custody.

---

50. *In re* Marriage of Schwander, 79 Cal. App. 3d 1013, 145 Cal. Rptr. 325 (1978).

51. *Id.* at 329.

52. Kipper v. Vokolek, 546 S.W.2d 521 (Mo. App. 1977).

The New York Court of Appeals recently held that a father could be found liable for damages resulting from the abduction of his child when he has contractually agreed—as in a separation agreement—to surrender custody to the mother. The court said that because of the agreement, the mother had a superior (although not necessarily absolute) right to custody and was entitled to bring an action for actual damages, apparently based on the contract, up to what it had cost her. In addition, she received damages for emotional harm and mental cruelty plus punitive damages.[53]

The California Court of Appeals[54] affirmed a jury's finding of damages. The mother and father had been divorced with custody of the children granted to the mother. Later, the father, with the help of his mother, abducted the children. Both the father and grandmother were liable for damages, the grandmother solely on the basis of her aiding, abetting, and assisting the father in his plans to deprive the mother of custody. Actual damages were $50,000 and punitive $40,000.

In another variation to cases where a relative or agent has helped a parent to unlawfully abduct a child, a federal district court in New York decided that a child and the mother can recover for the traditional tort of false imprisonment when the child has been abducted and detained without the permission of the custodial parent.[55] But because the father had fled with the child to Yugoslavia, the court said the mother could recover against the, relatives who had helped in the abduction, on a claim of mental distress. The relatives remained in the United States, and it appeared that the father would never return the child.

Tort liability as a remedy for child snatching is, like criminal sanctions, one step removed from the ultimate goal of the parent who seeks the return of the unlawfully detained child. Alone, it does not promise the child's return. But tort action, if available, grants the custodial parent a means of recovering the costs of retrieving the child. Virtually every case grants actual damages up to all the costs of recovery. A custodial parent who has suffered

---

53. Laranjo v. Laranjo, 6 FAM. L. REP. 2522 (Fam. Ct. N.Y. 1980).
54. Gibson v. Gibson, 15 Cal. App. 3d 943, 93 Cal. Rptr. 617 (1971).
55. *In re* Kajtazi, 4 FAM. L. REP. 2703 (E.D.N.Y. 1978).

genuine emotional or mental anguish may be awarded special damages. If the illegal detention of the child is flagrant, or if the action clearly violates a relevant state law, a court may award punitive damages as a means of deterring such behavior, both by the abducting parent and potential abducting parents. One major advantage of tort over a criminal remedy is that it will come as close as possible to making the plaintiff, the custodial parent, emotionally and financially whole. It is too early to tell if the UCCJA will play any role in the area of tort remedies. The California case (see note 50, *supra*) only hints at the possibility that a violation of the UCCJA may be a violation of a legal duty owed to the custodial parent as well as contempt against the state that issued the initial custody order.

C. Civil Contempt

Contempt of court, broadly speaking, is "any act which is calculated to embarrass, hinder, or obstruct [the] court in administration of justice, or which is calculated to lessen its authority or its dignity."[56] The distinctions between civil and criminal contempt are hazy at best; generally, contempt is criminal when the injury is directly against the court or the administration of justice. The purpose of a civil contempt proceeding, however, is to provide a remedy for an injured suitor by compelling compliance with a court order.[57] A person found in contempt can be fined, subjected to forfeiture of a previously posted bond, and even imprisoned for a continued refusal to comply with a court order.[58]

When a court has made a custody determination, and issued a decree granting custody and visitation rights, any violation of the decree by either parent is technically an act in contempt of court. It is clear that a parent who has abducted his child in defiance of a valid custody decree may be held in contempt. Child snatching is the most serious act in contempt of a custody decree. The West Virginia Supreme Court used its contempt power against a grandfather who had abducted a child, although the grandfather was not a party to the original custody proceedings.[59] This shows the broad application of the courts' contempt powers; the person held

---

56. BLACK'S LAW DICTIONARY 390 (rev. 4th ed. 1968).
57. MCCLINTOCK, PRINCIPLES OF EQUITY (1948).
58. 17 AM. JUR., *Contempt* § 4, pt. 7.
59. Hendershot v. Handlan, 248 S.E.2d 273 (W. Va. 1978).

in contempt need only know that his action is frustrating proper legal process. It was sufficient to show that the grandfather had knowledge of the existing decree that granted custody to his former daughter-in-law.

Contempt citations are widely used as a remedy for child snatching. A New York lower court granted a mother custody of two minor children following a dissolution of marriage. One child disappeared, and the mother accused the father of masterminding a kidnapping, pointing to the father's lack of interest and concern over locating the child as support for her charge. The court found the father was in contempt for failure to comply with the custody decree, and he was put in jail. The New York Court of Appeals reversed this result because it found the evidence insufficient to prove that the father actually knew where the child was.[60] When the complaining parent has adequate proof, however, a finding of contempt is likely to hold up on appeal. A mother was held in contempt of court for removing her children from Florida to New York in violation of a custody order issued by a Pennsylvania court at the time of the divorce.[61]

Generally, a contempt citation is only as broad as the jurisdiction of the court that issues it. When a parent removes a child from the state where the issuing court is located, there is no assurance that the citation will be enforced. In practice, however, the courts often cooperate under the principles of comity (see Chapter IV). Just as courts typically recognize the validity of another state's custody decree, they also recognize that violation of another state's custody decree is an act in contempt of court. Since the second state's court is not the one that issued the original decree it may be reluctant to issue a contempt citation on its own authority; however, it will often also be reluctant to grant the parent who has acted in contempt a legal forum.

A New York mother was granted custody of two minor children by a New York trial court and given permission to move with the children to Connecticut, and the father was given visitation rights.[62] The mother moved the children to Illinois, where she brought an action to modify the original custody order. The father brought his own action in New York, seeking a modification of the original custody order and to have the mother held in con-

60. Pereira v. Pereira, 35 N.Y.2d 301, 361 N.Y.S.2d 148 (1974).
61. Spriggs v. Carson, 470 Pa. 290, 368 A.2d 635 (1977).
62. Entwistle v. Entwistle, 61 App. Div. 2d 380, 402 N.Y.S.2d 213 (1978).

tempt. The New York court found that the mother had willfully interfered with the father's visitation rights. The court found the action of taking the children, and thereby preventing the children from seeing their father, an act "so inconsistent with the best interests of the children as to, per se, raise a strong probability that the mother is unfit to act as a custodial parent."[63] The appeals court sent the case back to a trial court, however, to see if the mother should be held in contempt and to decide if custody should be granted to the father because of the denial of visitation rights. More evidence was needed. Although the appeals court granted neither of the father's requests, it is clear that the mother would be held to account for actions if she returned to the state.

Courts may be flexible when using the contempt power. The Tennessee Supreme Court held a father in contempt for violating a court's restraining order enjoining him from removing the children from the state.[64] The father had brought an action to modify the original custody decree and stressed that he worried for the safety and welfare of his children if custody reverted to the mother. The court said that when the welfare of the minor child is in doubt, the father is not required to purge himself of the contempt charge (by obeying the original order) before the modification question is heard. The father had essentially asserted that the court was faced with an emergency and should exercise emergency jurisdiction, a result that would accord with the emergency jurisdiction provisions of the UCCJA (see Chapter II). At the time, the UCCJA had not been enacted in Tennessee. Now that it is in force there, the decision should remain authoritative.[65]

In most cases where children have been removed from the state where an original custody decree was issued, the issuing state can do nothing. A mother who had fled to Florida in violation of a California custody and visitation decree was found in contempt of court.[66] But as the court noted, "Jurisdiction is gone for all practical purposes when the children are living in another state, for no effective order can be made modifying the custody provisions of

---

63. *Id.* at 385.

64. Segelike v. Segelike, 584 S.W.2d 211 (Tenn. 1979).

65. For an analogous case, *see* Perry v. Superior Court, 7 Cal. App. 3d 236, 86 Cal. Rptr. 607 (1970).

66. Rosin v. Superior Court, 181 Cal. App. 2d 486, 5 Cal. Rptr. 421 (1960).

the [original] decree."[67] In a similar case, the Pennsylvania Supreme Court assessed a fine of $100 a week against a father who had abducted his child in an attempt to compel delivery of the child to the court.[68] The penalty was of doubtful value, however, because the father was out of state and his whereabouts unknown. The case recognized that an 1894 decision, *Sage v. Sage,*[69] was still correct in many ways. There the Pennsylvania Supreme Court had held that it could not compel a Pennsylvania resident who had previously removed her child from New Jersey to return to that state and submit herself to civil contempt proceedings. The second state's court simply lacked the power. The use of fines that accrue so long as the violation continues is of little use to a parent who primarily wants his or her child returned, but there is little else a court can do.

A typical pattern of a parent abducting a child and leaving the state that issued the original custody decree is shown in a New York action.[70] The mother fled with her child, who had been visiting her legally pursuant to a valid custody and visitation decree that had vested primary custody with the father. The court held the mother in contempt during an action by the father, but in the process recognized that its contempt citation was of little force: "Even in the absence of the defendant, and the possibility that the orders of this court cannot be immediately effectuated, the motion is granted."[71] The mother could purge her contempt citation by returning the child to the state and bringing the child before the court; a return to the state but a continued failure to comply with court orders could result in imprisonment.

Courts have, in the past, often been willing to disregard or modify the custody orders of another state by granting more favorable custody arrangements to a parent who has abducted a child. This occurred even when the second jurisdiction was aware that the parent who now brought a modification action had explicity violated the existing custody provisions ordered by the first jurisdiction. A mother was legally vested with custody of her minor daughter by a decree of the U.S. District Court for the Virgin

67. *Id.* at 491.
68. Commonwealth *ex rel.* v. McKinney, 476 Pa. 1, 381 A.2d 453 (1977).
69. 160 Pa. 389, 28 A. 863 (1894).
70. Greenberg v. Greenberg, 81 Misc. 2d 180, 365 N.Y.S.2d 400 (1975).
71. *Id.* at 404.

Islands.[72] Under its law, that federal district court has jurisdiction to award custody when it has also heard a divorce case.[73] The normal pattern is for state courts to have exclusive jurisdiction over both divorce and child custody disputes. In this case, the father, now a resident of New York, attempted to modify the custody decree when the child was visiting with him. The U.S. Court of Appeals, in a rare excursion into family law, applied New York law and held that when a child is in New York, that state's court (and therefore a federal court in diversity cases) has jurisdiction to entertain the father's application for a modification. The court traced the history of the Full Faith and Credit Clause of the U.S. Constitution (see Chapter IV) and held that the New York court was not required to recognize the continuing validity of the Virgin Islands decree; as a result, a contempt citation issued by the Virgin Islands court was set aside. The appeals court ruled that the latter court had erred by failing to take into account the fact that New York could have valid jurisdiction, and that principles of comity also dictated that the Virgin Islands court defer to New York. This case is an extreme example of an ineffective contempt citation. The Supreme Court of Vermont held that a contempt order it had issued when a mother had abducted a child who was visiting in California remained effective, despite the fact that a California court subsequently entered a modification decree in the mother's favor.[74] The court reasoned that the contempt citation must stand because it was issued prior to the modification by the California court. Curiously, the Vermont court then found that it must grant full faith and credit to the later California decree and did not discuss the question of why the California court had not offered the same type of full faith and credit reciprocation, in kind, when the mother had abducted the child originally.

Neither of these cases should reach the same decision today under the UCCJA, unless an emergency is pleaded and proved. The second state's court is abjured to decline jurisdiction under both the clean-hands and forum non conveniens provisions. The possibility that the California court was not aware of the Vermont custody decree, its terms, or both, is limited under the UCCJA by the requirement that courts cooperate by disseminating informa-

---

72. Bergen v. Bergen, 439 F.2d 1008 (3d Cir. 1971).
73. V.I. CODE ANN, tit. 16, § 109.
74. Brooks v. Brooks, 131 Vt. 86, 300 A.2d 531 (1973).

tion on custody cases among themselves; in addition, the father could have registered his original custody decree with California officials (see Chapter II). Under the UCCJA, then, the second state court must defer to the original jurisdiction; the abducting parent cannot totally escape the consequences of contemptible conduct.

Even before the UCCJA was adopted by a vast majority of states, some courts recognized that allowing parents to abduct children and escape the powers of the original trial court prevented the proper operation of the custody law process. The Pennsylvania Supreme Court attempted to apply the full faith and credit clause to contempt citations rather than to custody decrees themselves.[75] The father was awarded visitation rights; each summer the children stayed with him in Ohio. During one of these visits, the father refused to return the children and initiated a custody modification action in Ohio. The Pennsylvania trial court held that the father was in civil contempt for his willful failure to return the children; it imposed an unconditional compensatory fine, including an option of imprisonment. In an unusual provision, the court said that the fine could be paid either to the state or directly to the aggrieved party, the mother. The Pennsylvania Supreme Court held that the Ohio courts should not act on the modification claim:

> [W]here there is no proof of changed circumstances, comity alone should prevent an Ohio court from interfering with or changing the Amended Custody Order of the Butler County [Pa.] Court. Even more important the Full-Faith and Credit clause . . . would seem to require every court in Ohio to give full faith and credit to the Pennsylvania Court's Custody Order and, in the absence of substantial and important change circumstances, an Ohio Court should not be permitted to ignore or modify the Pennsylvania Court's custody order.[76]

By going to the Ohio Court for a custody decree, the father was unable to purge himself of the contempt found by the Pennsylvania court.

Effective use of the civil contempt power is predicated on the hope that the court, either in the first or second state, will consider a parent's action before making a determination or modifica-

---

75. Brocker v. Brocker, 429 Pa. 513, 241 A.2d 336 (1968).
76. *Id.* at 341.

tion of an existing custody decree.[77] Under the UCCJA, courts in a second state can be expected to pay closer attention to both the custody decrees and contempt findings of other jurisdictions. In a California case,[78] the mother and father were residents of Australia. Custody of the children had been granted to the mother, but she could not leave Australia without obtaining the agreement of both the father and the court. She violated the decree by taking the children to California. The father secured a modification of the original custody decree in an Australia court, primarily because of the mother's unlawful acts. The California court, in this case, asked by the father to return the children to him, side-stepped the issue of whether or not the Australia court's modification decree was punitive. It was enough that the Australia court had originally exercised jurisdiction over the custody dispute that was essentially in accord with the jurisdictional requirements of the UCCJA. The court upheld a contempt citation against the mother and ordered her to deliver custody of the children to the father. She was also required to pay attorney fees, costs, and other expenses incurred by the father.

The reasoning, if not the result, could be a model for other states that have enacted the UCCJA, when they are faced with both domestic and international cases. The original custody decree was unusual, and the California court felt it was beyond its ken to decide if the modification decree was punitive: all the evidence was in Australia. It definitely reverses the historical pattern of multi-state contempt cases where abducting parents traditionally had the upper hand. Technically, however, pre-UCCJA contempt cases are still good law in most states simply because they have not been reinterpreted in light of the UCCJA.

D. Habeas Corpus

The writ of habeas corpus is widely recognized as the primary remedy for persons who claim before a court that they are legally entitled to the custody of a minor child.[79] Most nonlawyers are familiar with the writ of habeas corpus, which developed primarily as a criminal remedy by which a convicted prisoner pleads to a

---

77. *See, e.g.,* Bankston v. Bankston, 355 So. 2d 58 (Ct. App. La. 1978).

78. Miller v. Superior Court, 22 Cal. 3d 923, 51 Cal. Rptr. 6, 587 P.2d 723 (1978).

79. H. CLARK, LAW OF DOMESTIC RELATIONS IN THE UNITED STATES § 17.13 (1968).

court that his incarceration is not legal and claims a right to be free. In either a criminal or child custody case, the person seeking a writ of habeas corpus must convince a court that there is at least a likelihood that that person will prevail. If, for example, a parent claims a legal right to custody but cannot prove the existence of a valid court order granting custody, a court may decline to hear the case at all. If instead the parent seeking custody proves a legal right, a court will issue the writ of habeas corpus, which means literally that the person wrongfully holding the child must bring the "body" (the child) before the court and under its jurisdiction.[80]

The use of the writ of habeas corpus in interstate custody disputes is notable more for the ways it does not follow the traditional decision-making pattern of habeas corpus cases rather than for the way it is consistent with them. The petitioner in a child custody habeas corpus proceeding usually faces one of two situations. First, the parent or guardian has previously been granted custody pursuant to a valid court order and is attempting to obtain actual physical custody of the child, a pattern close to the traditional one for habeas corpus cases: the petitioner is merely seeking to enforce legal rights that have already been granted and are currently in force.

The second pattern occurs when the parent is seeking to obtain a modification of a previous custody order that granted custody to someone else, and is most often seen in interstate child custody and child snatching cases. Often a petitioning non-custodial parent argues, essentially, that the court that issued the original decree was wrong, and that the child's best interests require a change of custody. If the court agrees, a modified custody order could be issued, and the petitioning parent could then bring a habeas corpus action on the new order. Occasionally a non-custodial parent seeking modification of an existing order relies on a writ of habeas corpus; the writ is used as a means of getting the custodial parent into court.

Habeas corpus has been a proper remedy both for parents who are legally entitled to custody and those who are not. The remedy as applied to child custody cases is much broader and more flexible than in a criminal case. Before the UCCJA became widely accepted, habeas corpus was used in most jurisdictions, much as it

---

80. *See* BLACK'S LAW DICTIONARY 837 (rev. 4th ed. 1968).

has been described. The inquiry often extended far beyond the mere legal issues; the case was not limited to deciding who had a legally enforceable right to custody.[81] Under parens patriae, most courts looked into the broader question of what would ultimately be in the child's best interests. Those best interests could, and usually did, include a petition for modification of an original custody decree; the non-custodial parent was allowed to present evidence to show the need for a change. Parens patriae derives from the idea that the state is the ultimate protector of its citizens, particularly children.[82]

A child custody habeas corpus action is far different from that of the original proceeding. The issue of custody is usually part of the divorce action itself. Habeas corpus, however, resembles an action *in rem*—an action about a piece of property—in which the property is the child;[83] and, as property must be within the court's jurisdiction, so must the child. In most states, prior to the UCCJA, this requirement meant that a child must be physically within a state before a court could entertain an action for a writ of habeas corpus.[84] Without the child before it the court cannot, in the terms of habeas corpus, hand the "body" over. The petitioner must follow the child to wherever he resides and file a petition for the writ in the state's courts.

Interstate custody disputes form the majority of cases in which habeas corpus relief is sought. The effect of the UCCJA is not entirely clear. Most authorities agree that the Act is designed to prevent the practice of seeking different orders in different state courts (see Chapter II). According to the standard, a second state's courts should hear a habeas corpus action based on another state court's decree only to the extent necessary to determine who is lawfully entitled to custody, the traditional habeas corpus pattern. Where the UCCJA has not been enacted, however, this result may not be uniform. Even under the UCCJA, a few courts have interpreted the Act to allow consideration of the broader question of permanent custody by way of an action for modification of an original custody decree. A modification may also be ef-

---

81. Annot., 4 A.L.R.3d 1277.

82. CLARK, *supra* note 79, § 17.1.

83. 36 C.J.S. § 124; *see* State v. Glasier, 272 Minn. 62, 137 N.W.2d 549 (1965).

84. Beebe v. Chavez, 226 Kan. 591, 602 P.2d 1279 (1979).

fected inadvertently if the second state court, to which a child has been abducted, denies the request of a petitioning parent who is validly entitled to custody according to the terms of an original decree by refusing to enforce it. Such a result also implicitly recognizes the validity or legitimacy of the kidnapping which actually brought the case before the second state court.

Cases where a non-custodial parent has brought a petition for a writ of habeas corpus have increased in recent years. Often the person legally entitled to custody moves with the child to another state. The non-custodial parent follows them to the new state and files a petition for habeas corpus; in reality, however, the petition is used as a means of getting the second state's court to consider a possible modification. The non-custodial parent usually claims that the child has not been been receiving proper care from the other parent. If the UCCJA is strictly applied, a second state court should decline to exercise jurisdiction under these circumstances;[85] only a genuine emergency would justify a departure from this standard of judicial restraint (see Chapter II). But, as noted, even in states where the UCCJA has been enacted, the writ of habeas corpus may, under some circumstances, justify a modification.

Prior to the UCCJA, courts entertaining modification requests as part of a habeas corpus proceeding simply claimed that they were attempting to clarify what would be in the best interests of the child.[86] The courts typically claim that if in hearing a habeas corpus claim they are allowed to rehear the entire custody issue, they are in the best position not only to determine the right to custody, but also to protect the child's interests and welfare. In their eagerness to modify prior custody decrees on this basis, courts have unintentionally encouraged interstate child abduction.[87]

A major goal of the Uniform Act is to restrict the availability of modification of custody decrees in a second, or even third, state. Professor Bodenheimer stressed the need to encourage enforcement of existing custody decrees:

---

85. UCCJA § 3.

86. Wicks v. Cox, 146 Tex. 489, 208 S.W.2d 876 (1948).

87. *See* Bodenheimer, *Progress under the Uniform Child Custody Jurisdiction Act and Remaining Problems: Punitive Decrees, Joint Custody, and Excessive Modification,* 65 CALIF. L. REV. 978 (1977).

The Uniform Act requires courts of a state that adopts it to recognize and enforce the custody decree of another state if that state had jurisdiction to render the decree. Jurisdiction of the rendering state exists and must be honored if it was assumed under statutory standards substantially in accordance with those of the Act, or if the facts of the case would justify that state's jurisdiction under the Act.[88]

The UCCJA, however, does not specifically cover use of the writ of habeas corpus in child custody disputes. It applies, on its face, only to jurisdiction; but jurisdiction as used in the Act must be interpreted to apply to the habeas corpus remedy, and all other remedies, if the Act is to have its intended effect, or any effect whatsoever. Habeas corpus jurisdiction has been denied in a number of cases precisely because the UCCJA was in effect in the state hearing the petition. These cases, and the Act itself, evince an intent and interpretation that the scope of the writ of habeas corpus be narrowed from a broad, flexible, and unpredictable remedy to a strict enforcement mechanism. The writ, under this view, should rarely if ever be available for the purpose of modifying custody decrees. The scope of the relief available in habeas corpus, at least in these cases, has been theoretically restricted to a determination of the initial issue—the legality of the contested restraint of the minor child in question.

A Colorado Supreme Court decision concerned an interstate custody claim.[89] A father detained his eldest son at the end of an authorized visitation period. The mother brought a habeas corpus action in one county in Colorado while the father brought an action for modification in another county where the court of original jurisdiction was located. Although a second state's courts were not involved, and the father actually brought his modification action in the proper court for UCCJA purposes, the supreme court held that the court which heard the habeas corpus petition, but not the arguments for modification, was correct in not considering modification. The court said that in the absence of an emergency situation or of significant connection between the state and the person seeking modification, habeas corpus is useful only as a remedy to enforce a prior custody decree: once a court determines where legal custody lies, it is obligated to defer to a previous decree, and then enforce that decree by demanding that the

---

88. *Id.* at 983.
89. Wood v. District Court, 181 Colo. 95, 508 P.2d 124 (1973).

child be turned over to the lawful custodian. Modification, if considered at all, can only be considered after the child is returned. The case stresses that a modification action should only take place when the existing decree, or status quo, is in effect. This is quite close to the doctrine of clean hands (see Chapter II).

A petitioner cannot use the writ of habeas corpus unless he can establish a prima facie, or plainly obvious, right to custody.[90] This requirement has been read broadly by some courts in the past, however. Once this right has been established, the petitioning parent becomes a legitimate party to the proceeding.

Until recently, the combination of the best-interests-of-the-child standard and the doctrine of parens patriae have combined to produce a confusing legacy. In a habeas corpus action by a father to obtain custody from a maternal great-aunt of his minor children, the father established that he was a party to the original decree. (It should be noted that natural parents have an advantage over third parties in custody disputes generally.) Nonetheless, the court held that, "A proceeding in habeas corpus involving the custody of a minor child is of an equitable nature," and awarded custody to the aunt. It used its judicial discretion to determine what the child's best interests were, and decided they were served propitiously by the aunt.[91] The determination that habeas corpus in child custody disputes is an equitable rather than legal remedy is very important; it means that a court may apply much greater discretion. And, as seen in many habeas corpus cases, discretion given becomes discretion used.

Jurisdiction in habeas corpus proceedings in custody disputes was particularly indefinite prior to widespread adoption of the UCCJA. Some courts have held that jurisdiction once established by a given court becomes continuous. Other courts have allowed for the possibility of concurrent, or shared, jurisdiction between the state that heard the original case and issued the original decree and the second state which is now the minor child's domicile or residence. Still others require only that the child be physically present in the state to exercise jurisdiction.[92] It was usually true that, whatever the basis for jurisdiction, a state's courts would exercise it.

---

90. Roberts v. Staples, 79 N.M. 298, 442 P.2d 788 (1968).
91. Daugherty v. Nelson, 241 Mo. App. 121, 234 S.W.2d 353 (1950).
92. Johnson v. Johnson, 405 Ariz. 233, 462 P.2d 182 (1969).

Physical presence of the child is perhaps the most widespread of these bases. States with this standard tended to follow the reasoning of Justice Benjamin Cardozo in his opinion from a New York Court of Appeals case:

> The jurisdiction of a state to regulate the custody of infants found within its territory does not depend upon the domicile of the parents. It has its origin in the protection that is due to the incompetent or helpless. . . . [F]or this, the residence of the child suffices though the domicile be elsewhere.[93]

The courts have further extended this parens patriae argument over the years. Often they say that since the child is in the state and within the court's jurisdiction, that court is the best equipped and informed to inquire into the environment affecting the child's welfare. The Florida Supreme Court assumed jurisdiction after a lower state court had refused to exercise jurisdiction on a habeas corpus petition proceeding brought by a mother after a father had absconded to Florida with a child in violation of and following a California trial court decree that had granted permanent custody to the mother. The court said:

> . . . [T]he law is and has been from time immemorial that each state is not only empowered, but is charged with the duty to regulate the custody of infants within its borders. This is true even though the parents may be residents of another state.[94]

In *Wicks v. Cox,* the court summed up the question of the exercise of concurrent jurisdiction:

> Ordinarily the courts of the domiciliary state are in a better position to pass intelligently on the matter of the child's welfare, and good order frequently requires that they do so to the exclusion of courts of other states in which the child is temporarily resident. But where the latter are in a more or less equally good position to determine the child's best interest, and their doing so appears to involve no particular prejudice to good order or social welfare, they have no jurisdiction.[95]

An Iowa Supreme Court case[96] involved a mother who abducted her minor children to that state from Missouri, where a court had granted permanent custody to the father. When the fa-

---

93. Finlay v. Finlay, 240 N.Y. 429, 148 N.E. 624 (1925).
94. DiGeorgio v. DiGeorgio, 153 Fla. 24, 13 So. 2d 596 (1943).
95. 208 S.W.2d at 878.
96. Helton v. Crawley, 241 Iowa 296, 41 N.W.2d 60 (1950).

ther, acting in reliance on the Missouri custody decree, brought a petition for a writ of habeas corpus in Iowa, that state's court granted itself jurisdiction over the children and awarded custody to the mother. The Iowa Supreme Court affirmed, relying on the paramount importance, in its opinion, of the best-interests-of-the-child doctrine. Jurisdiction over the child, and over the case, was based on the child's presence.

Certain courts recognized, even before the UCCJA, that the jurisdiction over a custody dispute should remain with the court that made the original custody award. The Kentucky Supreme Court affirmed a trial court's order in a habeas corpus case.[97] The trial court had ordered that a child be returned to the father on the basis of the original decree that granted custody to him. The court required that the mother hand the child over, but noted she had the right to challenge in an action for modification if it were brought in a proper forum, such as the court that originally made a custody determination. A Missouri Supreme Court case[98] recognized that once custody has been initially determined, the original court retains jurisdiction over all subsequent custody questions.

Unless there is an emergency, or there exist significant connections with a second state's courts that justify jurisdiction, the UCCJA seems to prohibit a second state's court from assuming jurisdiction over a child custody issue solely on the basis of the child's physical presence in the state, especially in a habeas corpus proceeding. The Kansas Supreme Court in note 84, *supra*, held that Kansas lacked jurisdiction to hear a habeas corpus proceeding in which Arizona had continuous jurisdiction over custody matters under and by virtue of a previous determination. Although emergency jurisdiction under the UCCJA was pleaded, the court found the facts insufficient for it to assume jurisdiction under the emergency jurisdiction provisions of the Act. The Kansas legislature, when adopting the UCCJA, specifically chose to deal with the jurisdictional dispute in its supreme court case; the court's result and the legislative intent are identical.

The Arizona Court of Appeals also declined jurisdiction when

---

97. Wright v. Wright, 305 Ky. 680, 205 S.W.2d 49 (1949).
98. *In re* Wakefield, 365 Mo. 415, 283 S.W.2d 467 (1955).

it attempted to settle a case that featured repeated abductions.[99] The paternal grandmother, who lived in Alabama, had been granted permanent custody in a valid Alabama court order. There followed a series of abductions: the mother, who now lived in Arizona, would snatch the child in Alabama and return to Arizona; the grandmother would then travel to Arizona, snatch the child, and return to Alabama. Finally a petition for a writ of habeas corpus was brought by the grandmother in an Arizona court while the child was in that state with the mother. The grandmother relied upon the original Alabama decree. The Arizona court returned the child to the grandmother, noting that it would not and could not go further into the case to consider the remaining custody issues, absent an emergency or threat to the child's welfare. Modification could be considered only in the original court in Alabama.

A California Supreme Court case illustrates that, although the writ of habeas corpus is now primarily only an enforcement mechanism, the courts must retain a degree of flexibility in child custody matters. Under the UCCJA, emergency jurisdiction, which remains largely undefined (see Chapter II) provides this flexibility. The father, a resident of California, was able to temporarily defeat a habeas corpus petition brought by the mother, an Alabama resident. The original decree granting custody to the mother was issued in Idaho. The court reasoned that it must consider the best interest of the children above all else. And while the policy of restraint in the UCCJA provides for the child's best interests in the majority of cases, it cannot be exclusive. The father asserted that the minor children would be placed in peril if they were returned to and continued to live with the mother in Alabama. The mother countered by arguing that the doctrine of forum non conveniens (see Chapter II), long recognized in California as a means of avoiding conflicting child custody adjudications, should apply to the case. The California Supreme Court held that the trial court had erred by declining to hear the father's emergency arguments:

> Charges of beating or other serious misconduct affecting the health or safety of a child compel an inquiry by the court. The requirement of

---

99. Stuard v. Bean, 27 Ariz. App. 350, 554 P.2d 1293 (1976).

allegation and proof that the child's health or safety will be "jeopardized" includes a showing of substantial emotional harm or other forms of injury *in addition to* physical mistreatment; it does, however, suggest that such showing encompass competent proof of some substantial harm to the child. A mere allegation that an award of custody to the resident (the father) would further the "best interest" or "welfare" of the child, an allegation tendered in all these cases, is not sufficient grounds for denying enforcement to the foreign decree. (Emphasis added.)[100]

Since the father's case had been denied, and not a shred of evidence had been presented on whether his allegations had substance, the trial court was directed to stay enforcement of the wife's existing decree until he was heard. The court, preferring caution to strict legalism when a child's safety *might* be at stake, created a procedural right. A parent claiming endangerment to a child has the right to have his claim presented and evidence heard before a court will decline modification jurisdiction. If the petitioning parent has shown the substantial harms that the California Supreme Court enumerated, the trial court will be justified in exercising emergency jurisdiction. If, however, the father failed to make his case, the mother's petition for a writ of habeas corpus would be granted. The result, although preceding the adoption of the UCCJA in California, appears to be consistent with the Act, which would find jurisdiction where:

the child is physically present in this state and (i) the child has been abandoned or (ii) it is necessary in an emergency to protect the child because he has been subjected to or threatened with mistreatment or abuse or is otherwise neglected.[101]

The court based its jurisdiction on an oft-cited California case, *In re Walker*,[102] which had said that in making a determination whether to modify an existing custody decree as part of a habeas corpus proceeding, "the court's primary, paramount and controlling consideration [is] . . . the welfare of the child." The California Supreme Court limited *Walker*, however, by holding that exercise of jurisdiction to modify is the exception rather than the

---

100. Ferreira v. Ferreira, 9 Cal. 3d 824, 836, 109 Cal. Rptr. 80, 88, 512 P.2d 304, 312 (1973).
101. UCCJA § 3(a)(3).
102. 228 Cal. App. 2d 217, 39 Cal. Rptr. 243 (1964).

rule. Apparently in anticipation of the UCCJA, the court held that declining jurisdiction, and thereby declining to issue a custody order that conflicts with that of another state, is normally the course that is in a child's best interest.

In a Florida case,[103] a mother who had been granted custody through an existing decree brought a petition for a writ of habeas corpus in Florida after her child was abducted by the father and taken from its home in New York to Florida. The father claimed emergency, and the Florida court refused to grant the writ until the question of the mother's fitness to have custody was settled. But once the mother was able to establish that she was a fit parent, the Florida court held that it was without jurisdiction to modify the original decree under the UCCJA and simply enforced the New York custody decree. Claims of emergency are likely to become standard for a parent who seeks modification in this type of case, at least until the state courts in states that have passed the UCCJA reach a uniform approach.

Colorado has been inconsistent in its interpretations of how the Act affects jurisdiction to hear a modification request during a habeas corpus proceeding. In 1974, the Colorado Supreme Court allowed a modification[104] when a mother refused to return her minor child to its legal custodian. The mother was a Colorado resident, whereas the legal custodian, a third party, lived in Montana. The custodian brought a habeas corpus petition in Colorado in an attempt to regain custody. The father also lived in Colorado, and this fact appears to have affected the court's decision. It held that a modification proceeding could be consolidated with a habeas corpus proceeding, and that a court in Colorado is competent to hear the matter if:

> it is in the best interests of the child that a court of this state assume jurisdiction because the child and his parents, or the child and at least one contestant, have a significant connection with the state, and there is available in this state substantial evidence concerning the child's present or future care, protection, training and personal relationships.[105]

Quoting the UCCJA as adopted by Colorado,[106] the court found

---

103. Trujillo v. Trujillo, 378 So. 2d 812 (Fla. 1979).
104. Nelson v. District Court, 186 Colo. 381, 527 P.2d 811 (1974).
105. *Id.* at 813.
106. 36 Colo. App. 96; 1973 Colo. Sess. Laws ch. 163, 46-6-3 (1) (c).

that the parents' domicile in Colorado, along with the child's interest in being with its parents, combined to make enough of a connection to confer jurisdiction on a Colorado court.

In 1975, the Colorado Court of Appeals[107] refused to exercise jurisdiction to hear the modification request of a father who lived in Colorado and had temporary custody of his child as part of the visitation order of an existing custody decree. The court could find no emergency situation or such significant connections as would allow it to assume jurisdiction. Therefore, under the UCCJA, Kansas, the mother's home and the state where the original custody decree was issued, retained jurisdiction to hear any custody dispute. The Colorado court ordered the child to be returned to its mother.

The case is consistent with Colorado's most recent pronouncement on the subject, *Woodhouse v. District Court.*[108] The parents had been divorced in England, and the decree granted custody of the couple's son and daughter to the mother. The father later moved to the United States and subsequently abducted his son, taking him to Colorado. When the mother petitioned for a writ of habeas corpus in Colorado, the father moved for a modification of the original custody order. The court granted the mother's petition, citing England's continuing connections with the parties and the absence of any emergency under which it could assume jurisdiction. The court did not apparently rely on the UCCJA provision that calls for recognition of decrees from other countries (see Chapter II).[109] Instead, it simply held that England had continuing jurisdiction over the custody issue and noted that the clean-hands doctrine was sufficient reason to decline jurisdiction. The courts in most states that have adopted the Act agree with the *Woodhouse* interpretation in cases where an emergency is not claimed and will not assume jurisdiction to hear a modification request as part of a habeas corpus proceeding.[110]

A father who was granted custody of a minor child in a Texas decree temporarily placed the child with his mother and father in Arizona while he tried to get himself settled. When the grandparents refused to return the child, the father brought a habeas cor-

---

107. *In re* Custody of Thomas, 36 Colo. App. 96, 537 P.2d 1095 (1975).
108. 196 Colo. 558, 587 P.2d 1199 (1978).
109. UCCJA § 23.
110. *See, e.g.,* Reid v. Adams, 241 Ga. 521, 246 S.E.2d 655 (1978).

pus petition in Arizona.[111] At about the same time, the Arizona Court of Appeals affirmed a grant of temporary custody to the grandparents in a separate action and dismissed the habeas corpus petition. The Arizona Supreme Court reversed the decision, holding that unless there is an emergency, that state has no right or power under the UCCJA to hear the modification request of the grandparents. This case follows the *Woodhouse* analysis.

In a 1978 case, the Iowa Supreme Court[112] followed the *Ferreira* (note 100, *supra*) line of thought. The court, granting the habeas corpus petition and refusing to exercise jurisdiction over the modification issue, delayed enforcement. Modification would have to be heard in the state that had continuing jurisdiction. Until the question had been decided, the Iowa court would delay enforcement of the habeas corpus writ. As a result, the lawful custodian was required to wait for a remedy.

E. International Disputes

The UCCJA is designed to apply to custody disputes and incidents of child snatching that involve United States and foreign courts. As long as the jurisdictional requirements and the provisions for notice and appearances used by the foreign court are substantially similar to those required in an American court under the UCCJA, the Act will recognize the validity of the foreign decree (see Chapter II). Most international disputes anticipated by the UCCJA are expected to be cases in which a parent brings a child to the United States from another country.

A federal district court[113] has granted parents who are residents of the United States a specific remedy when a minor child has been abducted by the other parent from the United States to another country. The court held that the State Department's regulations relating to the issuance and revocation of passports[114] provided that, in the event of such an abduction, the child could lose his "documentation," and thus be forced to return to the United States. The mother had been granted custody of the child; the father took the child to France. Later, the mother brought an action to compel the Secretary of State to revoke the child's passport and to deny issuance of a new one. The father argued that

---

111. McNeal v. Mahoney, 117 Ariz. 543, 574 P.2d (1978).
112. Barcus v. Barcus, 278 N.W.2d 646 (Iowa 1978).
113. Morgan v. Vance, 4 Fam. L. Rep. 2252 (N.D. Cal. 1978).
114. 22 C.F.R. § 51.27 (d) (1978).

the regulations were enacted only to deter the issuance of a passport in the first instance, and only when custody was in dispute. Since the child was already abroad, the father claimed, the regulations should not apply. He also maintained that the regulations in question were meant for criminal rather than civil cases. The court disagreed. The present regulation dealing with this matter reads:

e. *Objection by parent or guardian in cases involving the custody of the minor.* When there is a controversy concerning the custody of a minor, the passport issuing office will issue a passport to the minor unless it receives a court order giving custody of the minor to the objecting parent, legal guardian, or person in loco parentis.[115]

F. Parental Kidnapping Prevention Act of 1980

On December 28, 1980, President Carter signed H.R. 8406, the Pneumococcal Vaccine Bill, into law. Sections 6 through 10 of that legislation constitute the Parental Kidnapping Prevention Act of 1980, which grew out of S. 105, a bill introduced by Senator Malcolm Wallop (R-Wyo.) in January 1979.

In Section 7, Congress recognized that custody and visitation disputes are an ever-increasing problem in the United States and that judicial decisions concerning these disputes have been marked by inconsistent and conflicting results among the various jurisdictions. To discourage parental kidnapping, Congress has mandated a national system to locate parents and children who have traveled from one jurisdiction to another while involved in such disputes. National standards to determine and resolve jurisdictional disputes, as well as to determine what effect the court decrees of one jurisdiction shall have on another, have also been established.

The stated purposes of this Act are to:

1. promote cooperation between state courts to ensure that the state that can best decide the case in the best interests of the child maintains jurisdiction;

2. promote cooperation between states in providing information and assistance to each state involved in a custody dispute;

3. promote enforcement of custody decrees of sister states;

---

115. 22 C.F.R. § 51.27 (e) (1979). For a discussion of international child abduction, *see* Bodenheimer, *The Hague Draft Convention in International Child Abduction,* 14 FAM. L.Q. 99 (1980).

4. promote and secure a stable home environment and a strong family relationship by discouraging continuing interstate controversies over child custody;

5. avoid jurisdictional disputes between state courts in matters that have resulted in the past in shifting children from state to state;

6. deter interstate abductions and unilateral removals of children undertaken to obtain custody awards.

Section 8 contains the full faith and credit provisions, which state that the appropriate authorities of every state shall enforce and not modify any child custody determination entered by a court of another state exercising jurisdiction consistent with the provisions of the law, which are derived from the Uniform Child Custody Jurisdiction Act. The immediate goal of this provision is to require those jurisdictions that have not enacted the UCCJA to enforce and not modify custody determinations (including custody and visitation rights) made by sister states that follow the Act. This section is intended to close the doors of these nonenacting jurisdictions (Massachusetts, New Mexico, Mississippi, South Carolina, West Virginia, Texas, the District of Columbia, Puerto Rico, and the Virgin Islands)[116] to forum-shopping child snatchers. If indeed the parent who abducts a child seeks the protection of a court in one of these states, it will be under a federal obligation to recognize and enforce the decree of the "home state" that took jurisdiction under UCCJA standards.

The child custody determination, to receive full faith and credit, must comply with certain provisions of Section 1738A of 28 U.S. Code. These include meeting one of the following conditions:

a. the court entering the decree is the "home state" of the child; *or*

b. no other state has jurisdiction based on paragraph a, and it would be in the child's best interests for this court to assume jurisdiction because the child has significant connections with the state, and the state can show sufficient evidence concerning the child's future welfare; *or*

c. the child is physically present in the state and has been abondoned, or an emergency situation exists because the

---

116. *But see,* Murphy v. Murphy, 80 Mass. Adv. Sh. 2517, 404 N.E.2d 69 (1980), in which Massachusetts judicially adopted a scheme of rules similar to the UCCJA. Texas has adopted certain provisions. While this book was in press, the governor of New Mexico signed S.B. 83 (UCCJA) and the governor of West Virginia signed H.B. 785 (UCCJA). *See* 7 Fam. L. Rep. 2393 (1981).

child's welfare is threatened; *or*

    d. no other state appears to have jurisdiction under paragraphs a, b, c, or e, or another state has refused to exercise jurisdiction because it believes jurisdiction rests with the state whose jurisdiction is in issue; *or*

    e. the court has continuing jurisdiction because it has previously made a custody determination, maintains jurisdiction for any of the reasons above, and continues to be the home of the child or any of the contestants.

For a child custody determination to be made, notice and an opportunity to be heard have to be presented to the interested parties. This determination can only be modified by the court of another state if the modifying state has, and the original state no longer has, jurisdiction or has refused to exercise it. The second court must not exercise jurisdiction where a proceeding is pending in another state whose court has properly exercised jurisdiction. To encourage the purposes of Section 1738A, the state courts are permitted to award attorneys' fees, travel and other incidental expenses incurred in connection with such custody disputes when a child has been wrongfully abducted from his home state.

Section 9 of H.R. 8406 authorizes the Secretary of Health and Human Services to enter into agreements with states to use the Federal Parent Locator Service to find any absent parent or child when his location is needed to make or enforce a child custody determination, or to enforce any state or federal law with respect to the unlawful taking or restraint of a child. The new law does not impose a mandatory duty upon the states to transmit requests to the Federal Parent Locator Service. Rather, any state that is able and willing to may agree to receive requests to locate children and to send such requests directly to the Federal Parent Locator Service for processing.

The Federal Parent Locator Service is to respond to requests made by: any representative of any state that has an agreement with the FPLS when that representative has the authority under state law to enforce a child custody determination; any court having jurisdiction to make or enforce such a child custody determination, or any agent of such court; any agent or attorney of the United States, or of a state, who has the duty or authority to investigate, enforce, or bring prosecutions for the wrongful taking or restraint of a child. Parents cannot apply directly to the Federal Parent Locator Service for assistance, nor can their legal representatives. However, a parent or his or her attorney can, for example, petition the court to request the FPLS to locate the absconding parent and missing child. A parent can request the local prosecutor to make such a request provided that person has the authority to enforce whatever laws exist in the state relative to the taking or restraint of a child.

Section 10 clarifies congressional intent that the Fugitive Felon Act, 18 U.S. Code § 1073, shall apply in state felony parental kidnapping cases. The original bill, S. 105, which also applied in state felony parental kidnapping cases, proposed a federal misdemeanor offense, punishable by a heavy fine and possible jail term, for interstate child abduction. House-Senate conferees rejected this approach in favor of revitalizing the Fugitive Felon Act in serious state felony child-stealing cases.

Congress deemed it necessary to state its position with respect to federal involvement in state felony child-stealing cases because of the Justice Department's policy not to intervene except in rare instances. Congress stated its belief that the federal government should assist states in the prosecution of their child-stealing laws by issuing federal warrants, which in turn will involve the FBI in the investigation, location, apprehension, and return of the fugitive parent sought by state authorities for alleged violation of the underlying state felony custodial interference/kidnapping statute. Once the fugitive parent returns to the prosecuting state, the federal charges would be dropped and prosecution would proceed under state law. At present about 60 percent of the states make custodial interference a felony.

Practically speaking, the Department of Justice is required by this law to revise the U.S. Attorney's Manual to reflect the new policy. Congress specifically rejected the previous standards for federal involvement that led to rare FBI assistance—threat of serious, imminent *physical* injury to the child or a pattern of harmful conduct by the abductor-parent. Federal court jurisdiction is not expressly foreclosed by the new law. And, while the history of the legislation seems to reflect a congressional intent to keep child custody litigation in the state courts, there is movement in the direction of granting jurisdiction to the federal courts in these cases.[117]

---

117. On January 5, 1981, Congressman Fish (R-N.Y.) introduced a bill, H.R. 223, to grant jurisdiction to the district courts to enforce any custody order of a state court against a parent who, in contravention of the order, takes a child to another state. The bill was referred to the House Judiciary Committee. On January 28, 1981, Congressman Sawyer (R-Mich.) introduced a bill, H.R. 1440, to make child snatching a federal crime. The bill was referred to the House Judiciary Committee.

Appendix A

Table of Jurisdictions under the
Uniform Child Custody Jurisdiction Act

Jurisdiction	Laws	Effective Date	Statutory Citation*
Alabama	1980, No. 92	3-20-80	To be codified
Alaska	1977, c. 61	7-1-77	AS 25.30.010 to 25.30.910
Arizona	1978, c. 16	4-21-78†	A.R.S. §§ 8-401 to 8-424
Arkansas	1979, No. 91 § 26	3-6-79	A.S.A. 34-2701 to 34-2706
California	1973, c. 693	1-1-74	West's Ann.Civ.Code §§ 5150 to 5174
Colorado	1973, c. 163	7-1-73	C.R.S. '73, 14-13-101 to14-13-126
Connecticut	1978, P.A. 78-113	10-1-78	C.G.S.A. §§ 46b-90 to 46B-114

*The form of statutory citation utilized in this table is that employed in 9 ULA 8 (Supp. 1980).
†Date of approval.

125

Table of Jurisdictions—*continued*

Jurisdiction	Laws	Effective Date	Statutory Citation
Delaware	60 Del.Laws, c.368	4-19-76	13 Del.C. §§ 1901 to 1925.
District of Columbia[1]			
Florida	1977, c. 77– 433	10-1-77	West's F.S.A. §§ 61.1302 to 61.1348
Georgia	1978, p. 258	1-1-79	Code, §§ 74-501 to 74.525
Hawaii	1973, c. 88		HRS §§ 583-1 to 583-26
Idaho	1977, c. 214	7-1-77	I.C. §§ 5-1001 to 5-1025
Illinois	1979, P.A. 81-541	9-11-79	S.H.A. ch. 40, §§ 2101 to 2126
Indiana	1977, H. 1040	8-1-77	IC 31-1-11.6-1 to 31-1-11.6-24
Iowa	1977, c. 139	7-1-77	I.C.A. §§ 598A.1 to 598A.25

1. No action by legislature.

Jurisdiction	Laws	Effective Date	Statutory Citation
Kansas	1978, c. 231	1-1-79	K.S.A. 38-1301 to 38-1326
Kentucky	1980, ch. 69	7-15-80	K.R.S. 403.400 to 403.630
Maine	1979, c. 481	9-14-79	19 M.R.S.A. §§ 801 to 825
Maryland	1975, c. 265	7-1-75	Code 1967, art. 16, §§ 184 to 207
Massachusetts[2]			
Michigan	1975, P.A. 297	12-14-75	M.C.L.A. §§ 600.651 to 600.673
Minnesota	1977, c. 8	4-1-77	M.S.A. §§ 518A.01 to 518A.25
Mississippi[3]			
Missouri	1978, H.B. No. 914	8-13-78	V.A.M.S. §§ 452.440 to 452.550
Montana	1977, c. 537	7-1-77	R.C.M. 1977, §§ 61-401 to 61-425
Nebraska	1979, L.B. 19	8-24-79	N.R.S. §§ 43-1201 to 43-1225
Nevada	1979, c. 85	3-23-79	To be codified

2. *See Murphy v. Murphy*, 404 N.E.2d 69 (Mass. 1980), wherein the Supreme Judicial Court adopted a scheme of rules similar to the UCCJA.

3. No action by legislature.

Table of Jurisdictions—*continued*

Jurisdiction	Laws	Effective Date	Statutory Citation
New Hampshire	1979, ch. 345	9-1-79	N.H.R.S.A. §§ 458A:1 to 458A:25
New Jersey	1979, c. 124	7-3-79	N.J.S.A. 2A:34-28 to 2A:34-52
New Mexico[4]	1981, c. 119	7-1-81	
New York	1977, c. 493	9-1-78	McKinney's Domestic Relations Law, §§ 75-a to 75-z
North Carolina	1979, c. 110	7-1-79	G.S. §§ 50A-1 to 50A-25
North Dakota	1969, c. 154	7-1-69	NDCC 14-14-01 to 14-14-26
Ohio	1977, SB 135	10-25-77	R.C. §§ 3109.21 to 3109.37
Oklahoma[5]			
Oregon	1973, c. 375	10-5-73	ORS 109.700 to 109.930
Pennsylvania	1977, No. 20	7-1-77	11 P.S. §§ 2301 to 2325
Puerto Rico[6]			
Rhode Island	1978, c. 185	7-1-78	Gen. Laws 1956, §§ 15-14-1 to 15-14-26
South Carolina[7]			

4. As of the publication date of this book, no statutory citation was available.
5. H.B.1741 enacting UCCJA has been passed, pending in the Senate. (See 6 FAM. L. REV. 2582 (1980).)
6. Pending in legislature.
7. Pending in legislature.

Jurisdiction	Laws	Effective Date	Statutory Citation
South Dakota	1978, c. 1980		SDCL 26-5-5 to 26-5-52
Tennessee	1979, ch. 383	5-25-79	T.C.A. tit.36 ch. 13
Texas[8]			
Utah	1980, H.B. 50	7-1-80	U.C.A. 78-45C-1 to 78-45C-26
Vermont	1980, Act 136	4-22-80	15 V.S.A. 19
Virginia	1979, c. 229	1-1-80	Code 1950, §§ 20-125 to 20-146
Virgin Islands[9]			
Washington	1979, c. 98	6-7-79	RCWA 26.27.010 to 26.27.910
West Virginia[10]	1981, H.B. 785		W. Va. C. ch. 48-10-1 to 48-10-26
Wisconsin	1975, c. 283	5-28-76	W.S.A. 822.01 to 822.25
Wyoming	1973, c. 240	3-7-73	W.S.1977, §§ 20-5-101 to 20-5-125

8. Passed in a localized version.
9. No action by legislature.
10. The law was enacted as this book went to press.

Uniform Child Custody Jurisdiction Act

1968 Act

Be it enacted . . .

§ 1. [Purposes of Act; Construction of Provisions]

(a) The general purposes of this Act are to:

(1) avoid jurisdictional competition and conflict with courts of other states in matters of child custody which have in the past resulted in the shifting of children from state to state with harmful effects on their well-being;

(2) promote cooperation with the courts of other states to the end that a custody decree is rendered in that state which can best decide the case in the interest of the child;

(3) assure that litigation concerning the custody of a child take place ordinarily in the state with which the child and his family have the closest connection and where significant evidence concerning his care, protection, training, and personal relationships is most readily available, and that courts of this state decline the exercise of jurisdiction when the child and his family have a closer connection with another state;

(4) discourage continuing controversies over child custody in the interest of greater stability of home environment and of secure family relationships for the child;

(5) deter abductions and other unilateral removals of children undertaken to obtain custody awards;

(6) avoid re-litigation of custody decisions of other states in in this state insofar as feasible;

(7) facilitate the enforcement of custody decrees of other states;

(8) promote and expand the exchange of information and other forms of mutual assistance between the courts of this state and those of other states concerned with the same child; and

(9) make uniform the law of those states which enact it.

(b) This Act shall be construed to promote the general purposes stated in this section.

Commissioners' Note

Because this uniform law breaks new ground not previously covered by legislation, its purposes are stated in some detail. Each section must be read and applied with these purposes in mind.

§ 2. [Definitions]

As used in this Act:

(1) "contestant" means a person, including a parent, who claims a right to custody or visitation rights with respect to a child;

(2) "custody determination" means a court decision and court orders and instructions providing for the custody of a child, in-

cluding visitation rights; it does not include a decision relating to child support or any other monetary obligation of any person;

(3) "custody proceeding" includes proceedings in which a custody determination is one of several issues, such as an action for divorce or separation, and includes child neglect and dependency proceedings;

(4) "decree" or "custody decree" means a custody determination contained in a judicial decree or order made in a custody proceeding, and includes an initial decree and a modification decree;

(5) "home state" means the state in which the child immediately preceding the time involved lived with his parents, a parent, or a person acting as parent, for at least 6 consecutive months, and in the case of a child less than 6 months old the state in which the child lived from birth with any of the persons mentioned. Periods of temporary absence of any of the named persons are counted as part of the 6-month or other period;

(6) "initial decree" means the first custody decree concerning a particular child;

(7) "modification decree" means a custody decree which modifies or replaces a prior decree, whether made by the court which rendered the prior decree or by another court;

(8) "physical custody" means actual possession and control of a child;

(9) "person acting as parent" means a person, other than a parent, who has physical custody of a child and who has either been awarded custody by a court or claims a right to custody; and

(10) "state" means any state, territory, or possession of the United States, the Commonwealth of Puerto Rico, and the District of Columbia.

Commissioners' Note

Subsection (3) indicates that "custody proceeding" is to be understood in a broad sense. The term covers habeas corpus actions, guardianship petitions, and other proceedings available under general state law to determine custody. See Clark, Domestic Relations 576–582 (1968).

Other definitions are explained, if necessary, in the comments to the sections which use the terms defined.

§ 3. [Jurisdiction]

(a) A court of this State which is competent to decide child custody matters has jurisdiction to make a child custody determination by initial or modification decree if:

(1) this State (i) is the home state of the child at the time of commencement of the proceeding, or (ii) had been the child's home state within 6 months before commencement of the proceeding and the child is absent from this State because of his removal or retention by a person claiming his custody or for other reasons, and a parent or person acting as parent continues to live in this State; or

(2) it is in the best interest of the child that a court of this State assume jurisdiction because (i) the child and his parents, or the child and at least one contestant, have a significant connection with this State, and (ii) there is available in this State substantial evidence concerning the child's present or future care, protection, training, and personal relationships; or

(3) the child is physically present in this State and (i) the child has been abandoned or (ii) it is necessary in an emergency to protect the child because he has been subjected to or threatened with mistreatment or abuse or is otherwise neglected [or dependent]; or

(4) (i) it appears that no other state would have jurisdiction under prerequisites substantially in accordance with paragraphs (1), (2), or (3), or another state has declined to exercise jurisdiction on the ground that this State is the more appropriate forum to determine the custody of the child, and (ii) it is in the best interest of the child that this court assume jurisdiction.

(b) Except under paragraphs (3) and (4) of subsection (a), physical presence in this State of the child, or of the child and one of the contestants, is not alone sufficient to confer jurisdiction on a court of this State to make a child custody determination.

(c) Physical presence of the child, while desirable, is not a prerequisite for jurisdiction to determine his custody.

Commissioners' Note
Paragraphs (1) and (2) of subsection (a) establish the two major bases for jurisdiction. In the first place, a court in the child's home state has jurisdiction, and secondly, if there is no home state or the child and his family have equal or stronger ties with another state, a court in that state has jurisdiction. If this alternative test produces concurrent jurisdiction in more than one state, the mechanisms provided in sections 6 and 7 are used to assure that only one state makes the custody decision.

"Home state" is defined in section 2(5). A 6-month period has been selected in order to have a definite and certain test which is at the same time based on a reasonable assumption of fact. See Ratner, Child Custody in a Federal System, 62 Mich.L.Rev. 795, 818 (1964) who explains:

"Most American children are integrated into an American community after living there six months; consequently this period of residence would seem to provide a reasonable criterion for identifying the established home."

Subparagraph (ii) of paragraph (1) extends the home state rule for an additional six-month period in order to permit suit in the home state after the child's departure. The main objective is to protect a parent who has been left by his spouse taking the child along. The provision makes clear that the stay-at-home parent, if he acts promptly, may start proceedings in his own state if he desires, without the necessity of attempting to base jurisdiction on paragraph (2). This changes the law in those states which required presence of the child as a condition for jurisdiction and consequently forced the person left behind to follow the departed person to another state, perhaps to several states in succession. See also subsection (c).

Paragraph (2) comes into play either when the home state test cannot be met or as an alternative to that test. The first situation arises, for example, when a family has moved frequently and there is no state where the child has lived for 6 months prior to suit, or if the child has recently been removed from his home state and the person who was left behind has also moved away. See paragraph (1), last clause. A typical example of alternative jurisdiction is the case in which the stay-at-home parent chooses to follow the departed spouse to state 2 (where the child has lived for several months with the other parent) and starts proceedings there. Whether the departed parent also has access to a court in state 2, depends on the strength of the family ties in that state and on the applicability of clean hands provision of section 8. If state 2, for example, was the state of the matrimonial home where the entire family lived for two years before moving to the "home state" for 6 months, and the wife returned to state 2 with the child with the consent of the husband, state 2 might well have jurisdiction upon petition of the wife. The same may be true if the wife returned to her parents in her former home state where the child had spent several months every year before. Compare Willmore v. Willmore, 273 Minn. 537, 143 N.W.2d 630 (1966), cert. denied 385 U.S. 898 (1966). While jurisdiction may exist in two states in these instances, it will not be *exercised* in both states. See sections 6 and 7.

Paragraph (2) of subsection (a) is supplemented by subsection (b) which is designed to discourage unilateral removal of children to other states and to guard generally against too liberal an interpretation of paragraph (2). Short-term presence in the state is not enough even though there may be an intent to stay longer, perhaps an intent to establish a technical "domicile" for divorce or other purposes.

Paragraph (2) perhaps more than any other provision of the Act requires that it be interpreted in the spirit of the legislative purposes expressed in section 1. The paragraph was phrased in general terms in order to be flexible enough to cover many fact situations too diverse to lend themselves to exact description. But its purposes is to limit jurisdiction rather then to proliferate it. The first clause of the paragraph is important: jurisdiction exists jurisdictional requirement. Subsequent sections are designed to assure the appearance of the child before the court.

This section governs jurisdiction to make an initial decree as well as a modification decree, only if it is in the *child's* interest, not merely the interest or convenience of the feuding parties, to determine custody in a particular state. The interest of the child is served when the forum has optimum access to relevant evidence about the child and family. There must be maximum rather than minimum contact with the state. The submission of the parties to a forum, perhaps for purposes of divorce, is not sufficient without additional factors establishing closer ties with the state. Divorce jurisdiction does not necessarily include custody jurisdiction. See Clark, Domestic Relations 578 (1968).

Paragraph (3) of subsection (a) retains and reaffirms *parens patriae* jurisdiction, usually exercised by a juvenile court, which a state must assume when a child is in a situation requiring immediate protection. This jurisdiction exists when a child has been abandoned and in emergency cases of child neglect. Presence of the child in the state is the only prerequisite. This extraordinary jurisdiction is reserved for extraordinary circumstances. See Application of Lang, 9 App. Div. 2d 401, 193 N.Y.S.2d 763 (1959). When there is child neglect without emergency or abandonment, jurisdiction cannot be based on this paragraph.

Paragraph (4) of subsection (a) provides a final basis for jurisdiction which is subsidiary in nature. It is to be resorted to only if no other state could, or would, assume jurisdiction under the other criteria of this section.

Subsection (c) makes it clear that presence of the child is not a prerequisite for jurisdiction. Both terms are defined in section 2. Jurisdiction to modify an initial or modification decree of another state is subject to additional restrictions contained in sections 8(b) an 14(a).

§ 4. [Notice and Opportunity to Be Heard]

Before making a decree under this Act, reasonable notice and opportunity to be heard shall be given to the contestants, any parent whose parental rights have not been previously terminated, and any person who has physical custody of the child. If any of these persons is outside this State, notice and opportunity to be heard shall be given pursuant to section 5.

Commissioners' Note

This section lists the persons who must be notified and given an opportunity to be heard to satisfy due process requirements. As to persons in the forum state, the general law of the state applies; others are notified in accordance with section 5. Strict compliance with sections 4 and 5 is essential for the validity of a custody decree within the state and its recognition and enforcement in other states under sections 12, 13, and 15. See Restatement of the Law Second, Conflict of Laws, Proposed Official Draft sec. 69 (1967); and compare Armstrong v. Manzo, 380 U.S. 545, 85 S.Ct. 1187, 14 L.Ed.2d 62 (1965).

§ 5. [Notice to Persons Outside This State; Submission to Jurisdiction]

(a) Notice required for the exercise of jurisdiction over a person outside this State shall be given in a manner reasonably calculated to give actual notice, and may be:

(1) by personal delivery outside this State in the manner prescribed for service of process within this State;

(2) in the manner prescribed by the law of the place in which the service is made for service of process in that place in an action in any of its courts of general jurisdiction;

(3) by any form of mail addressed to the person to be served and requesting a receipt; or

(4) as directed by the court [including publication, if other means of notification are ineffective].

(b) Notice under this section shall be served, mailed, or delivered, [or last published] at least [10, 20] days before any hearing in this State.

(c) Proof of service outside this State may be made by affidavit of the individual who made the service, or in the manner prescribed by the law of this State, the order pursuant to which the service is made, or the law of the place in which the service is made. If service is made by mail, proof may be a receipt signed by the addressee or other evidence of delivery to the addressee.

(d) Notice is not required if a person submits to the jurisdiction of the court.

Commissioners' Note

Section 2.01 of the Uniform Interstate and International Procedure Act has been followed to a large extent. See 9B U.L.A. 315 (1966). If at all possible, actual notice should be received by the affected persons; but efforts to impart notice in a manner reasonably calculated to give actual notice are sufficient when a person who may perhaps conceal his whereabouts, cannot be reached. See Mullane v. Central Hanover Bank and Trust Co., 339 U.S. 306, 70 S.Ct. 652, 94 L.Ed. 865 (1950) and Shroeder v. City of New York, 371 U.S. 208, 83 S.Ct. 279, 9 L.Ed.2d 255 (1962). Notice by publication in lieu of other means of notification is not included because of its doubtful constitutionality. See Mullane v. Central Hanover Bank and Trust Co., *supra*; and see Hazard, A General Theory of State-Court Jurisdiction, 1965 Supreme Court Rev. 241, 277, 286–87. Paragraph (4) of subsection (a) lists notice by publication in brackets for the benefit of those states which desire to use published notices *in addition* to the modes of notification provided in this section when these modes prove ineffective to impart actual notice.

The provisions of this section, and paragraphs (2) and (4) of subsection (a) in particular, are subject to the caveat that notice and opportunity to be heard must always meet due process requirements as they exist at the time of the proceeding.

§ 6. [Simultaneous Proceedings in Other States]

(a) A court of this State shall not exercise its jurisdiction under this Act if at the time of filing the petition a proceeding concerning the custody of the child was pending in a court of another state exercising jurisdiction substantially in comformity with this Act, unless the proceeding is stayed by the court of the other state because this State is a more appropriate forum or for other reasons.

(b) Before hearing the petition in a custody proceeding the court shall examine the pleadings and other information supplied by the parties under section 9 and shall consult the child custody registry established under section 16 concerning the pendency of proceedings with respect to the child in other states. If the court has reason to believe that proceedings may be pending in another state it shall direct an inquiry to the state court administrator or other appropriate official of the other state.

(c) If the court is informed during the course of the proceeding that a proceeding concerning the custody of the child was pending in another state before the court assumed jurisdiction it shall stay the proceeding and communicate with the court in which the other proceeding is pending to the end that the issue may be litigated in the more appropriate forum and that information be exchanged in accordance with sections 19 through 22. If a court of this State has made a custody decree before being informed of a pending proceeding in a court of another state it shall immediately inform that court of the fact. If the court is informed that a proceeding was commenced in another state after it assumed jurisdiction it shall likewise inform the other court to the end that the issues may be litigated in the more appropriate forum.

Commissioners' Note
Because of the havoc wreaked by simultaneous and competitive jurisdiction which has been described in the Prefatory Note, this section seeks

to avoid jurisdictional conflict with all feasible means, including novel methods. Courts are expected to take an active part under this section in seeking out information about custody proceedings concerning the same child pending in other states. In a proper case jurisdiction is yielded to the other state either under this section or under section 7. Both sections must be read together.

When the courts of more than one state have jurisdiction under sections 3 or 14, priority in time determines which court will proceed with the action, but the application of the inconvenient forum principle of section 7 may result in the handling of the case by the other court.

While jurisdiction need not be yielded under subsection (a) if the other court would not have jurisdiction under the criteria of this Act, the policy against simultaneous custody proceedings is so strong that it might in a particular situation be appropriate to leave the case to the other court even under such circumstances. See subsection (3) and section 7.

Once a custody decree has been rendered in one state, jurisdiction is determined by sections 8 and 14.

§ 7. [Inconvenient Forum]

(a) A court which has jurisdiction under this Act to make an initial or modification decree may decline to exercise its jurisdiction any time before making a decree if it finds that it is an inconvenient forum to make a custody determination under the circumstances of the case and that a court of another state is a more appropriate forum.

(b) A finding of inconvenient forum may be made upon the court's own motion or upon motion of a party or a guardian ad litem or other representative of the child.

(c) In determining if it is an inconvenient forum, the court shall consider if it is in the interest of the child that another state assume jurisdiction. For this purpose it may take into account the following factors, among others:

(1) if another state is or recently was the child's home state;

(2) if another state has a closer connection with the child and his family or with the child and one or more of the contestants;

(3) if substantial evidence concerning the child's present or future care, protection, training, and personal relationships is more readily available in another state;

(4) if the parties have agreed on another forum which is no less appropriate; and

(5) if the exercise of jurisdiction by a court of this state would contravene any of the purposes stated in section 1.

(d) Before determining whether to decline or retain jurisdiction the court may communicate with a court of another state and exchange information pertinent to the assumption of jurisdiction by either court with a view to assuring that jurisdiction will be exercised by the more appropriate court and that a forum will be available to the parties.

(e) If the court finds that it is an inconvenient forum and that a court of another state is a more appropriate forum, it may dismiss the proceedings, or it may stay the proceedings upon condition that a custody proceeding be promptly commenced in another named state or upon any other conditions which may be just and proper, including the condition that a moving party stipulate his consent and submission to the jurisdiction of the other forum.

(f) The court may decline to exercise its jurisdiction under this Act if a custody determination is incidental to an action for divorce or another proceeding while retaining jurisdiction over the divorce or other proceeding.

(g) If it appears to the court that it is clearly an inappropriate forum it may require the party who commenced the proceedings to pay, in addition to the costs of the proceedings in this State, necessary travel and other expenses, including attorneys' fees, incurred by other parties or their witnesses. Payment is to be made to the clerk of the court for remittance to the proper party.

(h) Upon dismissal or stay of proceedings under this section the court shall inform the court found to be the more appropriate forum of this fact or, if the court which would have jurisdiction in the other state is not certainly known, shall transmit the information to the court administrator or other appropriate official for forwarding to the appropriate court.

(i) Any communication received from another state informing this State of a finding of inconvenient forum because a court of this State is the more appropriate forum shall be filed in the custody registry of the appropriate court. Upon assuming jurisdiction the court of this State shall inform the original court of this fact.

Commissioners' Note
The purpose of this provision is to encourage judicial restraint in exercising jurisdiction whenever another state appears to be in a better position to determine custody of a child. It serves as a second check on jurisdiction once the test of sections 3 or 14 has been met.

The section is a particular application of the inconvenient forum principle, recognized in most states by judicial law, adapted to the special needs of child custody cases. The terminology used follows section 84 of the Restatement of the Law Second, Conflict of Laws, Proposed Official Draft (1967). Judicial restrictions or exceptions to the inconvenient forum rule made in some states do not apply to this statutory scheme which is limited to child custody cases.

Like section 6, this section stresses interstate judicial communication and cooperation. When there is doubt as to which is the more appropriate forum, the question may be resolved by consultation and cooperation among the courts involved.

Paragraphs (1) through (5) of subsection (c) specify some, but not all, considerations which enter into a court determination of inconvenient forum. Factors customarily listed for purposes of the general principle of the inconvenient forum (such as convenience of the parties and hardship to the defendant) are also pertinent, but may under the circumstances be of secondary importance because the child who is not a party is the central figure in the proceedings.

Part of subsection (e) is derived from Wis.Stat.Ann., sec. 262.19(1).

Subsection (f) makes it clear that a court may divide a case, that is, dismiss part of it and retain the rest. See section 1.05 of the Uniform Interstate and International Procedure Act. When the custody issue comes up in a divorce proceeding, courts may have frequent occasion to decline jurisdiction as to that issue (assuming that custody jurisdiction exists under sections 3 or 14).

Subsection (g) is an adaptation of Wis.Stat.Ann., sec. 262.20. Its purpose is to serve as a deterrent against "frivolous jurisdiction claims," as G. W. Foster states in the Revision Notes to the Wisconsin provision. It applies when the forum chosen is seriously inappropriate considering the jurisdictional requirements of the Act.

§ 8. [Jurisdiction Declined by Reason of Conduct]

(a) If the petitioner for an initial decree has wrongfully taken the child from another state or has engaged in similar reprehensible conduct the court may decline to exercise jurisdiction if this is just and proper under the circumstances.

(b) Unless required in the interest of the child, the court shall not exercise its jurisdiction to modify a custody decree of another state if the petitioner, without consent of the person entitled to custody, has improperly removed the child from the physical custody of the person entitled to custody or has improperly retained the child after a visit or other temporary relinquishment of physical custody. If the petitioner has violated any other provision of a custody decree of another state the court may decline to exercise its jurisdiction if this is just and proper under the circumstances.

(c) In appropriate cases a court dismissing a petition under this section may charge the petitioner with necessary travel and other expenses, including attorneys' fees, incurred by other parties or their witnesses.

Commissioners' Note

This section incorporates the "clean hands doctrine," so named by Ehrenzweig, Interstate Recognition of Custody Decrees, 51 Mich. L.Rev. 345 (1953). Under this doctrine courts refuse to assume jurisdiction to reexamine an out-of-state custody decree when the petitioner has abducted the child or has engaged in some other objectionable scheme to gain or retain physical custody of the child in violation of the decree. See Fain, Custody of Children, The California Family Lawyer I, 539, 548 (1961); Ex Parte Mullins, 26 Wash.2d 419, 174 P.2d 790 (1946); Crocker v. Crocker, 122 Colo. 49, 219 P.2d 311 (1950); and Leathers v. Leathers, 162 Cal.App.2d 768, 328 P.2d 853 (1958). But when adherence to this rule would lead to punishment of the parent at the expense of the well-being of the child, it is often not applied. See Smith v. Smith, 135 Cal.App.2d 100, 286 P.2d 1909 (1955) and In re Guardianship of Rodgers, 100 Ariz. 269, 413 P.2d 744 (1966).

Subsection (a) extends the clean hands principle to cases in which a custody decree has not yet been rendered in any state. For example, if upon a de facto separation the wife returned to her own home with the children without objection by her husband and lived there for two years without hearing from him, and the husband without warning forcibly removes the children one night and brings them to another state, a court in that state although it has jurisdiction after 6 months may decline to hear the husband's custody petition. "Wrongfully" taking under this subsection does not mean that a "right" has been violated—both husband and wife as a rule have a right to custody until a court determination is made —but that one party's conduct is so objectionable that a court in the exercise of its inherent equity powers cannot in good conscience permit that party access to its jurisdiction.

Subsection (b) does not come into operation unless the court has power under section 14 to modify the custody decree of another state. It is a codification of the clean hands rule, except that it differentiates between (1) a taking or retention of the child and (2) other violations of custody decrees. In the case of illegal removal or retention refusal of jurisdiction is mandatory unless the harm done to the child by a denial of jurisdiction outweighs the parental misconduct. Compare Smith v. Smith and In Re Guardianship of Rodgers, *supra;* and see In Re Walter, 228 Cal. App.2d 217, 39 Cal.Rptrs. 243 (1964) where the court assumed jurisdiction after both parents had been guilty of misconduct. The qualifying word "improperly" is added to exclude cases in which a child is withheld because of illness or other emergency or in which there are other special justifying circumstances.

The most common violation of the second category is the removal of the child from the state by the parent who has the right to custody, thereby frustrating the exercise of visitation rights of the other parent. The second sentence of subsection (b) makes refusal of jurisdiction entirely discretionary in this situation because it depends on the circumstances whether non-compliance with the court order is serious enough to warrant the drastic sanction of denial of jurisdiction.

Subsection (c) adds a financial deterrent to child stealing and similar reprehensible conduct.

§ 9. [Information under Oath to Be Submitted to the Court]

(a) Every party in a custody proceeding in his first pleading or in an affidavit attached to that pleading shall give information under oath as to the child's present address, the places where the child has lived within the last 5 years, and the names and present addresses of the persons with whom the child has lived during that period. In this pleading or affidavit every party shall further declare under oath whether:

(1) he has participated (as a party, witness, or in any other capacity) in any other litigation concerning the custody of the same child in this or any other state;

(2) he has information of any custody proceeding concerning the child pending in a court of this or any other state; and

(3) he knows of any person not a party to the proceedings who has physical custody of the child or claims to have custody or visitation rights with respect to the child.

(b) If the declaration as to any of the above items is in the affirmative the declarant shall give additional information under oath as required by the court. The court may examine the parties under oath as to details of the information furnished and as to other matters pertinent to the court's jurisdiction and the disposition of the case.

(c) Each party has a continuing duty to inform the court of any custody proceeding concerning the child in this or any other state of which he obtained information during this proceeding.

Commissioners' Note

It is important for the court to receive the information listed and other pertinent facts as early as possible for purposes of determining its jurisdiction, the joinder of additional parties, and the identification of courts in other states which are to be contacted under various provisions of the Act. Information as to custody litigation and other pertinent facts occurring in other countries may also be elicited under this section in combination with section 23.

§ 10. [Additional Parties]

If the court learns from information furnished by the parties pursuant to section 9 or from other sources that a person not a party to the custody proceeding has physical custody of the child or claims to have custody or visitation rights with respect to the child, it shall order that person to be joined as a party and to be duly notified of the pendency of the proceeding and of his joinder as a party. If the person joined as a party is outside this State he shall be served with process or otherwise notified in accordance with section 5.

Commissioners' Note
The purpose of this section is to prevent re-litigations of the custody issue when these would be for the benefit of third claimants rather than the child. If the immediate controversy, for example, is between the parents, but relatives inside or outside the state also claim custody or have physical custody which may lead to a future claim to the child, they must be brought into the proceedings. The courts are given an active role here as under other sections of the Act to seek out the necessary information from formal or informal sources.

§ 11. [Appearance of Parties and the Child]

[(a) The court may order any party to the proceeding who is in this State to appear personally before the court. If that party has physical custody of the child the court may order that he appear personally with the child.]

(b) If a party to the proceeding whose presence is desired by the court is outside this State with or without the child the court may order that the notice given under section 5 include a statement directing that party to appear personally with or without the child and declaring that failure to appear may result in a decision adverse to that party.

(c) If a party to the proceeding who is outside this State is directed to appear under subsection (b) or desires to appear personally before the court with or with the child, the court may require another party to pay to the clerk of the court travel and other necessary expenses of the party so appearing and of the child if this is just and proper under the circumstances.

Commissioners' Note

Since a custody proceeding is concerned with the past and future care of
the child by one of the parties, it is of vital importance in most cases that
the judge has an opportunity to see and hear the contestants and the
child. Subsection (a) authorizes the court to order the appearance of
these persons if they are in the state. It is placed in brackets because
states which have such a provision—not only in their juvenile court laws
—may wish to omit it. Subsection (b) relates to the appearance of persons who are outside the state and provides one method of bringing
these before the court; sections 19(b) and 20(b) provide another. Subsection (c) helps to finance travel to the court which may be close to one
of the parties and distant from another; it may be used to equalize the
expense if this is appropriate under the circumstances.

§ 12. [Binding Force and Res Judicata Effect of Custody Decree]

A custody decree rendered by a court of this State which had
jurisdiction under section 3 binds all parties who have been
served in this State or notified in accordance with section 5 or who
have submitted to the jurisdiction of the court, and who have
been given an opportunity to be heard. As to these parties the
custody decree is conclusive as to all issues of law and fact decided
and as to the custody determination made unless and until the determination is modified pursuant to law, including the provisions
of this Act.

Commissioners' Note

This section deals with the intra-state validity of custody decrees which
provides the basis for their interstate recognition and enforcement. The
two prerequisites are (1) jurisdiction under section 3 of this Act and (2)
strict compliance with due process mandates of notice and opportunity
to be heard. There is no requirement for technical personal jurisdiction,
on the traditional theory that custody determinations, as distinguished
from support actions (see section 2(2) *supra*), are proceedings in rem or
proceedings affecting status. See Restatement of the Law Second, Conflict of Laws, Proposed Official Draft, sections 69 and 79 (1967); and
James, Civil Procedure 613 (1965). For a different theory reaching the
same result, see Hazard, A General Theory of State-Court Jurisdiction,
1965 Supreme Court Review 241. The section is not at variance with
May v. Anderson, 345 U.S. 528, 73 S.Ct. 840, 97 L.Ed. 1221 (1953),
which relates to interstate recognition rather than in state validity of custody decrees. See Ehrenzweig and Louisell, Jurisdiction in a Nutshell 76
(2d ed. 1968); and compare Resse, Full Faith and Credit to Foreign Equity Decrees, 42 Iowa L.Rev. 183, 195 (1957). On May v. Anderson, *supra*, see comment to section 13.

Since a custody decree is normally subject to modification in the interest of the child, it does not have absolute finality, but as long as it has not been modified, it is as binding as a final judgment. Compare Restatement of the Law Second, Conflict of Laws, Proposed Official Draft, section 109 (1967).

§ 13. [Recognition of Out-of-State Custody Decrees]

The courts of this State shall recognize and enforce an initial or modification decree of a court of another state which had assumed jurisdiction under statutory provisions substantially in accordance with this Act or which was made under factual circumstances meeting the jurisdictional standards of the Act, so long as this decree has not been modified in accordance with jurisdictional standards substantially similar to those of this Act.

Commissioners' Note

This section and sections 14 and 15 are the key provisions which guarantee a great measure of security and stability of environment to the "interstate child" by discouraging relitigations in other states. See Section 1, and see Ratner, Child Custody in a Federal System, 62 Mich.L.Rev. 795, 828 (1964).

Although the full faith and credit clause may perhaps not require the recognition of out-of-state custody decrees, the states are free to recognize and enforce them. See Restatement of the Law Second, Conflict of Laws, Proposed Official Draft, section 109 (1967), and see the Prefatory Note, *supra*. This section declares as a matter of state law, that custody decrees of sister states will be recognized and enforced. Recognition and enforcement is mandatory if the state in which the prior decree was rendered 1) has adopted this Act, 2) has statutory jurisdictional requirements substantially like this Act, or 3) would have had jurisdiction under the facts of the case if this Act had been the law in the state. Compare Comment, Ford v. Ford: Full Faith and Credit to Child Custody Decrees? 73 Yale L.J. 134, 148 (1963).

"Jurisdiction" or "jurisdictional standards" under this section refers to the requirements of section 3 in the case of initial decrees and to the requirements of sections 3 and 14 in the case of modification decrees. The section leaves open the possibility of discretionary recognition of custody decrees of other states beyond the enumerated situations of mandatory acceptance. For the recognition of custody decrees of other nations, see section 23.

Recognition is accorded to a decree which is valid and binding under section 12. This means, for example, that a court in the state where the father resides will recognize and enforce a custody decree rendered in the home state where the child lives with the mother if the father was duly notified and given enough time to appear in the proceedings. Personal jurisdiction over the father is not required. See comment to section 12. This is in accord with a common interpretation of the inconclusive decision in May v. Anderson, 345 U.S. 528, 73 S.Ct. 840, 97 L.Ed. 1221 (1953). See Restatement of the Law Second, Conflict of Laws, Proposed Official Draft, section 79 and comment thereto, p. 298 (1967). Under this interpretation a state is permitted to recognize a custody decree of another state regardless of lack of personal jurisdiction, as long as due process requirements of notice and opportunity to be heard have been met. See Justice Frankfurter's concurring opinion in May v. Anderson; and compare Clark, Domestic Relations 323–26 (1968), Goodrich, Conflict of Laws 274 (4th ed. by Scoles, 1964); Stumberg, Principles of Conflict of Laws 325 (3rd ed. 1963): and Comment, The Puzzle of Jurisdiction in Child Custody Actions, 38 U.Colo.L.Rev. 541 (1966). The Act emphasizes the need for the personal appearance of the contestants rather than any technical requirement for personal jurisdiction.

The mandate of this section could cause problems if the prior decree is a punitive or disciplinary measure. See Ehrenzweig, Interstate Recognition of Custody Decrees, 51 Mich.L.Rev. 345, 370 (1953). If, for example, a court grants custody to the mother and after 5 years' of continuous life with the mother the child is awarded to the father by the same court for the sole reason that the mother who had moved to another state upon remarriage had not lived up to the visitation requirements of the decree, courts in other states may be reluctant to recognize the changed decree. See Berlin v. Berlin, 21 N.Y.2d 371, 235 N.E.2d 109 (1967); and Stout v. Pate, 120 Cal.App.2d 699, 261 P.2d 788 (1953); Compare Moniz v. Moniz, 142 Cal.App.2d 527, 298 P.2d 710 (1956). Disciplinary decrees of this type can be avoided under this Act by enforcing the visitation provisions of the decree directly in another state. See Section 15. If the original plan for visitation does not fit the new conditions, a petition for modification of the visiting arrangements would be filed in a court which has jurisdiction, that is, in many cases the original court. See section 14.

§ 14. [Modification of Custody Decree of Another State]

(a) If a court of another state has made a custody decree, a court of this State shall not modify that decree unless (1) it appears to the court of this State that the court which rendered the decree does not now have jurisdiction under jurisdictional prerequisites substantially in accordance with this Act or has declined to assume jurisdiction to modify the decree and (2) the court of this State has jurisdiction.

(b) If a court of this State is authorized under subsection (a) and section 8 to modify a custody decree of another state it shall give due consideration to the transcript of the record and other documents of all previous proceedings submitted to it in accordance with section 22.

Commissioners' Note

Courts which render a custody decree normally retain continuing jurisdiction to modify the decree under local law. Courts in other states have in the past often assumed jurisdiction to modify the out-of-state decree themselves without regard to the preexisting jurisdiction of the other state. See People ex rel. Halvey v. Halvey, 330 U.S. 610, 67 S.Ct. 903, 91 L.Ed. 1133 (1947). In order to achieve greater stability of custody arrangements and avoid forum shopping, subsection (a) declares that other states will defer to the continuing jurisdiction of the court of another state as long as that state has jurisdiction under the standards of this Act. In other words, all petitions for modification are to be addressed to the prior state if that state has sufficient contact with the case to satisfy section 3. The fact that the court had previously considered the case may be one factor favoring its continued jurisdiction. If, however, all the persons involved have moved away, or the contact with the state has otherwise become slight, modification jurisdiction would shift elsewhere. Compare, Ratner, Child Custody in a Federal System, 62 Mich.L.Rev. 795, 821-2 (1964).

For example, if custody was awarded to the father in state 1 where he continued to live with the children for two years and thereafter his wife kept the children in state 2 for 6½ months (3½ months beyond her visitation privileges) with or without permission of the husband, state 1 has preferred jurisdiction to modify the decree despite the fact that state 2 has in the meantime become the "home state" of the child. If, however, the father also moved away from state 1, that state loses modification jurisdiction interstate, whether or not its jurisdiction continues under local law. See Clark, Domestic Relations 322–23 (1968). Also, if the father in the same case continued to live in state 1, but let his wife keep the children for several years without asserting his custody rights and without visits of the children in state 1, modification jurisdiction of state 1 would cease. Compare Brengle v. Hurst, 408 S. W. 2d 418 (Ky.1966). The situation would be different if the children had been abducted and their whereabouts could not be discovered by the legal custodian for several years. The abductor would be denied access to the court of another state under section 8(b) and state 1 would have modification jurisdiction in any event under section 3(a) (4). Compare Crocker v. Crocker, 122 Colo. 49, 219 P.2d 311 (1950).

The prior court has jurisdiction to modify under this section even though its original assumption of jurisdiction did not meet the standards of this Act, as long as it would have jurisdiction *now*, that is, at the time of the petition for modification.

If the state of the prior decree declines to assume jurisdiction to modify the decree, another state with jurisdiction under section 3 can proceed with the case. That is not so if the prior court dismissed the petition on its merits.

Respect for the continuing jurisdiction of another state under this section will serve the purposes of this Act only if the prior court will assume a corresponding obligation to make no changes in the existing custody arrangement which are not required for the good of the child. If the court overturns its own decree in order to discipline a mother or father, with whom the child had lived for years, for failure to comply with an order of the court, the objective of greater stability of custody decrees is not achieved. See Comment to section 13 last paragraph, and cases there cited. See also Sharpe v. Sharpe, 77 Ill. App. 295, 222 N.E.2d 340 (1966). Under section 15 of this Act an order of a court contained in a custody decree can be directly enforced in another state.

Under subsection (b) transcripts of prior proceedings if received under section 22 are to be considered by the modifying court. The purpose is to give the judge the opportunity to be as fully informed as possible before making a custody decision. "One court will seldom have so much of the story that another's inquiry is unimportant" says Paulsen, Appointment of a Guardian in the Conflict of Laws, 45 Iowa L.Rev. 212, 226 (1960). See also Ehrenzweig, The Interstate Child and Uniform Legislation: A Plea for Extra-Litigious Proceedings, 64 Mich.L.Rev. 1, 6–7 (1965); and Ratner, Legislative Resolution of the Interstate Custody Problem: A Reply to Professor Currie and a Proposed Uniform Act, 38 S.Cal.L.Rev. 183, 202 (1965). How much consideration is "due" this transcript, whether or under what conditions it is received in evidence, are matters of local, internal law which are not affected by this interstate act.

§ 15. [Filing and Enforcement of Custody Decree of Another State]

(a) A certified copy of a custody decree of another state may be filed in the office of the clerk of any [District Court, Family Court] of this State. The clerk shall treat the decree in the same manner as a custody decree of the [District Court, Family Court] of this State. A custody decree so filed has the same effect and shall be enforced in like manner as a custody decree rendered by a court of this State.

(b) A person violating a custody decree of another state which makes it necessary to enforce the decree in this State may be required to pay necessary travel and other expenses, including attorneys' fees, incurred by the party entitled to the custody or his witnesses.

Commissioners' Note
Out-of-state custody decrees which are required to be recognized are enforced by other states. See section 13. Subsection (a) provides a simplified and speed method of enforcement. It is derived from section 2 of the Uniform Enforcement of Foreign Judgments Act of 1964, 9A U.L. A. 486 (1965). A certified copy of the decree is filed in the appropriate court, and the decree thereupon becomes in effect a decree of the state of filing and is enforceable by any method of enforcement available under the law of that state.

The authority to enforce an out-of-state decree does not include the power to modify it. If modification is desired, the petition must be directed to the court which has jurisdiction to modify under section 14. This does not mean that the state of enforcement may not in an emergency stay enforcement if there is danger of serious mistreatment of the child. See Ratner, Child Custody in a Federal System, 62 Mich.L.Rev. 795, 832–33 (1964).

The right to custody for periods of visitation and other provisions of a custody decree are enforceable in other states in the same manner as the primary right to custody. If visitation privileges provided in the decree have become impractical upon moving to another state, the remedy against automatic enforcement in another state is a petition in the proper court to modify visitation arrangements to fit the new conditions.

Subsection (b) makes it clear that the financial burden of enforcement of a custody decree may be shifted to the wrongdoer. Compare 2 Armstrong, California Family Law 328 (1966 Suppl.), and Crocker v. Crocker, 195 F.2d 236 (1952).

§ 16. [Registry of Out-of-State Custody Decrees and Proceedings]

The clerk of each [District Court, Family Court] shall maintain a registry in which he shall enter the following:

(1) certified copies of custody decrees of other states received for filing;

(2) communications as to the pendency of custody proceedings in other states;

(3) communications concerning a finding of inconvenient forum by a court of another state; and

(4) other communications or documents concerning custody proceedings in another state which may affect the jurisdiction of a court of this State or the disposition to be made by it in a custody proceeding.

Commissioners' Note

The purpose of this section is to gather all information concerning out-of-state custody cases which reaches a court in one designated place. The term "registry" is derived from section 35 of the Uniform Reciprocal Enforcement of Support Act of 1958, 9C U.L.A. 61 (1967 Suppl.). Another term may be used if desired without affecting the uniformity of the Act. The information in the registry is usually incomplete since it contains only those documents which have been specifically requested or which have otherwise found their way to the state. It is therefore necessary in most cases for the court to seek additional information elsewhere.

§ 17. [Certified Copies of Custody Decree]

The Clerk of the [District Court, Family Court] of this State, at the request of the court of another state or at the request of any person who is affected by or has a legitimate interest in a custody decree, shall certify and forward a copy of the decree to that court or person.

§ 18. [Taking Testimony in Another State]

In addition to other procedural devices available to a party, any party to the proceeding or a guardian ad litem or other representative of the child may adduce testimony of witnesses, including parties and the child, by deposition or otherwise, in another state. The court on its own motion may direct that the testimony of a person be taken in another state and may prescribe the manner in which and the terms upon which the testimony shall be taken.

Commissioners' Note

Sections 18 to 22 are derived from sections 3.01 and 3.02 of the Uniform Interstate and International Procedure Act, 9B U.L.A. 305, 321, 326 (1966); from ideas underlying the Uniform Reciprocal Enforcement of Support Act; and from Ehrenzweig, The Interstate Child and Uniform Legislation: A Plea for Extralitigious Proceedings, 64 Mich.L.Rev. 1 (1965). They are designed to fill the partial vacuum which inevitably exists in cases involving an "interstate child" since part of the essential information about the child and his relationship to other persons is always in another state. Even though jurisdiction is assumed under sections 3 and 7 in the state where much (or most) of the pertinent facts are readily available, some important evidence will unavoidably be elsewhere.

Section 18 is derived from portions of section 3.01 of the Uniform Interstate and International Procedure Act, 9B U.L.A. 305, 321. The first sentence relates to depositions, written interrogatories and other discovery devices which may be used by parties or representatives of the child. The procedural rules of the state where the device is used are applicable under this sentence. The second sentence empowers the court itself to initiate the gathering of out-of-state evidence which is often not supplied by the parties in order to give the court a complete picture of the child's situation, especially as it relates to a custody claimant who lives in another state.

§ 19. [Hearings and Studies in Another State; Orders to Appear]

(a) A court of this State may request the appropriate court of another state to hold a hearing to adduce evidence, to order a party to produce or give evidence under other procedures of that state, or to have social studies made with respect to the custody of a child involved in proceedings pending in the court of this State; and to forward to the court of this State certified copies of the transcript of the record of the hearing, the evidence otherwise adduced, or any social studies prepared in compliance with the request. The cost of the services may be assessed against the parties or, if necessary, ordered paid by the [County, State].

(b) A court of this State may request the appropriate court of another state to order a party to custody proceedings pending in the court of this State to appear in the proceedings, and if that party has physical custody of the child, to appear with the child. The request may state that travel and other necessary expenses of the party and of the child whose appearance is desired will be assessed against another party or will otherwise be paid.

Commissioners' Note
Section 19 relates to assistance sought by a court of the forum state from a court of another state. See comment to section 18. Subsection (a) covers any kind of evidentiary procedure available under the law of the assisting state which may aid the court in the requesting state, including custody investigations (social studies) if authorized by the law of the other state. Under what conditions reports of social studies and other evidence collected under this subsection are admissible in the requesting state, is a matter of internal state law not covered in this interstate statute. Subsection (b) serves to bring parties and the child before the requesting court, backed up by the assisting court's contempt powers. See section 11.

§ 20. [Assistance to Courts of
   Other States]

(a) Upon request of the court of another state the courts of this State which are competent to hear custody matters may order a person in this State to appear at a hearing to adduce evidence or to produce or give evidence under other procedures available in this State [or may order social studies to be made for use in a custody proceeding in another state]. A certified copy of the transcript of the record of the hearing or the evidence otherwise adduced [and any social studies prepared] shall be forwarded by the clerk of the court to the requesting court.

(b) A person within this State may voluntarily give his testimony or statement in this State for use in a custody proceeding outside this State.

(c) Upon request of the court of another state a competent court of this State may order a person in this State to appear alone or with the child in a custody proceeding in another state. The court may condition compliance with the request upon assurance by the other state that state travel and other necessary expenses will be advanced or reimbursed.

Commissioners' Note
Section 20 is the counterpart of section 19. It empowers local courts to give help to out-of-state courts in custody cases. See comments to sections 18 and 19. The references to social studies have been placed in brackets so that states without authorization to make social studies outside of juvenile court proceedings may omit them if they wish. Subsection (b) reaffirms the existing freedom of persons within the United States to give evidence for use in proceedings elsewhere. It is derived from section 3.02 (b) of the Interstate and International Procedure Act, 9B U.L.A. 327 (1966).

§ 21. [Preservation of Documents for
   Use in Other States]

In any custody proceeding in this State the court shall preserve the pleadings, orders and decrees, any record that has been made of its hearings, social studies, and other pertinent documents until the child reaches [18, 21] years of age. Upon appropriate request of the court of another state the court shall forward to the other court certified copies of any or all of such documents.

Commissioner's Note
See comments to sections 18 and 19. Documents are to be preserved until the child is old enough that further custody disputes are unlikely. A lower figure than the ones suggested in the brackets may be inserted.

§ 22. [Request for Court Records of Another State]

If a custody decree has been rendered in another state concerning a child involved in a custody proceeding pending in a court of this State, the court of this State upon taking jurisdiction of the case shall request of the court of the other state a certified copy of the transcript of any court record and other documents mentioned in section 21.

Commissioners' Note
This is the counterpart of section 21. See comments to sections 18, 19 and 14(b).

§ 23. [International Application]

The general policies of this Act extend to the international area. The provisions of this Act relating to the recognition and enforcement of custody decrees of other states apply to custody decrees and decrees involving legal institutions similar in nature to custody institutions rendered by appropriate authorities of other nations if reasonable notice and opportunity to be heard were given to all affected persons.

Commissioners' Notes
Not all the provisions of the Act lend themselves to direct application in international custody disputes; but the basic policies of avoiding jurisdictional conflict and multiple litigation are as strong if not stronger when children are moved back and forth from one country to another by feuding relatives. Compare Application of Lang, 9 App.Div.2d 401, 193 N.Y.S.2d 763 (1959) and Swindle v. Bradley, 240 Ark. 903, 403 S.W.2d 63 (1966).

The first sentence makes the general policies of the Act applicable to international cases. This means that the substance of section 1 and the principles underlying provisions like sections 6, 7, 8, and 14 (a), are to be followed when some of the persons involved are in a foreign country or a foreign custody proceeding is pending.

The second sentence declares that custody decrees rendered in other nations by appropriate authorities (which may be judicial or administrative tribunals) are recognized and enforced in this country. The only prerequisite is that reasonable notice and opportunity to be heard was given to the persons affected. It is also to be understood that the foreign tribunal had jurisdictional under its own law rather than under section 3 of this Act. Compare Restatement of the Law Second, Conflict of Laws, Proposed Official Draft, sections 10, 92, 98, and 109(2) (1967). Compare also Goodrich, Conflict of Laws 390–93 (4th ed., Scoles, 1964).

§ 24. [Priority]

Upon the request of a party to a custody proceeding which raises a question of existence or exercise of jurisdiction under this Act the case shall be given calendar priority and handled expeditiously.]

Commissioners' Note
Judicial time spent in determining which court has or should exercise jurisdiction often prolongs the period of uncertainty and turmoil in a child's life more than is necessary. The need for speedy adjudication exists, of course, with respect to all aspects of child custody litigation. The priority requirement is limited to jurisdictional questions because an all encompassing priority would be beyond the scope of this Act. Since some states may have or wish to adopt a statutory provision or court rule of wider scope, this section is placed in brackets and may be omitted.

§ 25. [Severability]

If any provision of this Act or the application thereof to any person or circumstance is held invalid, its invalidity does not affect other provisions or applications of the Act which can be given effect without the invalid provision or application, and to this end the provisions of this Act are severable.

§ 26. [Short Title]

This Act may be cited as the Uniform Child Custody Jurisdiction Act.

§ 27. [Repeal]

The following acts and parts of acts are repealed:
(1)
(2)
(3)

§ 28. [Time of Taking Effect]

This Act shall take effect . . .

Appendix B

Table of Criminal Statutes

Statute	Effective Date	Provisions
ALA. CODE tit. 13A, § 6-45	1977	Custodial interference is a *misdemeanor*, but if the actor is trying to regain lawful custody, there is no offense committed.
ALASKA STAT. § 11.41.320	1978	Custodial interference in first degree is a *felony* when child is removed from state.
ALASKA STAT. § 11.41.330	1978	Custodial interference in second degree is a *misdemeanor* if the child is not removed from the state.
ARIZ. REV. STAT. § 13-1302	1978	Custodial interference is a *felony* unless the child is returned unharmed prior to actor's arrest, in which case it is a *misdemeanor*.

155

Table of Criminal Statutes— *continued*

Statute	Effective Date	Provisions
ARK. STAT. ANN. § 41-2411	1975	Interference with custody is a *felony* if the child is taken out of the state; otherwise it is a *misdemeanor*.
CAL. PENAL CODE § 278 (West)	1977	Child abduction by a person having no right to custody is a *felony*.
CAL. PENAL CODE § 278.5 (West)	1977	Any violation of a custody decree is a *misdemeanor*.
COLO. REV. STAT. § 18-3-304	1963	Violation of custody is a *felony* unless the child was in danger at time of abduction.
CONN. GEN. STAT. ANN. § 53a-97 (West)	1971	Custodial interference in first degree is a *felony* if child is endangered or removed from the state.
CONN. GEN. STAT. ANN. § 53a-98 (West)	1971	Custodial interference in second degree is a *misdemeanor* when child remains in state.
DEL. CODE tit. 11, § 785	1953	Interference with custody is a *misdemeanor*.
D.C. CODE ENCYCL. § 22-2101 (West)	1965	The applicable kidnapping statute specifically exempts parents.
FLA. STAT. ANN. § 787.03 (West)	1977	Interference with custody is a *misdemeanor*. It is a defense that the actor reasonably believed that the child was in danger.
FLA. STAT. ANN. § 787.04 (West)	1974	Taking of child out of state in violation of a court order or during a pending custody proceeding is a *felony*.

Statute	Effective Date	Provisions
GA. CODE ANN. § 26-1312	1978	Interference with custody is a *felony* if the child is removed from the state, otherwise it is a *misdemeanor*.
1979 Hawaii Sess. Laws Act 106	1979	Puts all abductions under the heading "extortion" with violation a *felony*.
IDAHO CODE § 18-4501; § 18-4503	1972	Kidnapping in the second degree is a *felony*.
ILL. ANN. STAT. ch 38, § 10-5 (Smith-Hurd)	1978	A person commits the act of child-abduction if he violates a court order granting custody. It is a defense if he returns child to Illinois court within 72 hours. Violation is a *felony*.
IND. CODE ANN. § 35-1-55-2 (Burns)	1905	Child stealing is a *felony*.
IOWA CODE ANN. § 710.6	1978	Violating a custody order by concealing a child out of the state is a *felony*, concealing the child in the state or violating visitation rights is a *misdemeanor*.
KAN. STAT. § 21-3422	1970	Interference with parental custody is a *misdemeanor*.
KAN. STAT. § 21-3422a	1978	Aggravated interference with parental custody is a *felony* and includes removing the child from state, hiring someone to abduct person or being convicted of § 21-3422 for a second time.
KY. REV. STAT. § 509.070	1974	Custodial interference by a parent is a *misdemeanor*.

Table of Criminal Statutes— *continued*

Statute	Effective Date	Provisions
LA. REV. STAT. ANN. § 14.45 (West)	1966	Simple kidnapping is a *felony*.
ME. REV. STAT. tit. 17-A, § 303	1979	Criminal restraint by a parent is a *misdemeanor*.
MD. ANN. CODE art. 27, § 2A	1978	Child abduction is a *misdemeanor* by a parent or one assisting parent; it is a defense that child is in danger and abducting party submits to jurisdiction of a court within 96 hours to modify custody.
MASS. GEN. LAWS ANN. ch. 265, § 26A (West)	1979	Kidnapping by a relative in violation of a custody order is a *misdemeanor* unless the child is put in danger, in which case it is a *felony*.
MICH. STAT. ANN. § 28.582	1948	Concealment from a proper guardian or parent is a *felony*.
MINN. STAT. ANN. § 609.26 (West)	1979	Violation of a custody order is a *misdemeanor*. The court may assess costs incurred by lawful custodian in obtaining child.
MISS. CODE ANN. § 97-3-51	1942	Kidnapping is a *felony*.
MO. ANN. STAT. § 565.150	1979	Interference with custody is a *misdemeanor* unless the child is removed from state in which case it is a *felony*.
MONT. REV. CODES ANN. § 45-5-304	1979	Custodial interference is a *felony* unless the child is returned prior to arraignment in which case it is not an offense; if actor left state and returns the child prior to arrest it is not an offense.

Statute	Effective Date	Provisions
NEB. REV. STAT. § 28-316	1979	Violation of the natural custody rights of the legal custodian is a *misdemeanor*, but violation of the court's custody decree is a *felony*.
NEV. REV. STAT. § 200.359	1975	Violation of a court's custody decree is a *misdemeanor*.
N.H. REV. STAT. ANN. § 633	1973	Kidnapping includes avoidance of apprehension by a law enforcement official, but parents would seem to be exempted. Violation is a *felony*.
N.J. STAT. ANN. § 2C:13-4 (West)	1979	Interference with custody by a parent is a *misdemeanor* unless the child was in danger or the child was 14 years old and went of his own volition. A third party abducting a child is guilty of a *felony* if his action causes serious alarm for the child's safety.
N.M. STAT. ANN. § 30-4-4	1977	Custodial interference by removal of a child from the state is a *felony*.
N.Y. [PENAL] § 135.45	1965	Custodial interference in second degree is a *misdemeanor* when parent takes child from custodian.
N.Y. [PENAL] § 135.50	1965	Custodial interference in first degree is a *felony* when the child is placed in danger.

Table of Criminal Statutes– *continued*

Statute	Effective Date	Provisions
N.C. GEN. STAT. § 14-320.1	1969	It is a *felony* to transport a child out of state in violation of a custody order.
N.D. CENT. CODE § 14-14-22.1 (Supp. 1979)	1979	It is a *felony* to transport a child out of state in violation of a custody order.
OHIO REV. CODE ANN. § 2905.04 (Baldwin)	1974	Child stealing by a parent is a *felony*, if the child is removed from the state, otherwise it is a *misdemeanor*.
OHIO REV. CODE ANN. § 2919.23 (Baldwin)		Interference with a custody decree is a *misdemeanor*.
OKLA. STAT. ANN. tit. 21, § 891 (West)	1910	Child stealing is a *felony*.
OR. REV. STAT. § 163.245	1971	Custodial interference in second degree is a *misdemeanor*.
OR. REV. STAT. § 163.257	1971	Custodial interference in first degree is committed when an actor violates § 163.245 and removes the child from state or causes harm to the child. This offense is a *felony*.
18 PA. CONS. STAT. ANN. § 2904 (Purdon)	1973	Interference with custody by a parent or a third party is a *misdemeanor*, but it is a defense that the child was 14 years old and went of its own volition, or the child was in danger.

Statute	Effective Date	Provisions
P.R. LAWS ANN. tit. 33, § 4178	1974	Kidnapping is a *felony*.
R.I. GEN. LAWS 11-26-1	1956	Kidnapping is a *felony*.
S.C. CODE § 16-17-495	1976	Violation of a custody order by transporting a child out of state is a *felony*; if the child is returned within 7 days it is a *misdemeanor*.
S.D. COMPILED LAWS ANN. § 22-19-9 (1979 Supp.)	1979	Interference with custody is a *misdemeanor*.
TENN. CODE ANN. § 39-2602	1932	Concealment of a child from lawful custodian is a *felony*.
TEX. [PENAL] CODE ANN. tit. 6, § 25.03	1979	Interference with custody is a *felony* if the child is removed from the state, but it is a defense to prosecution if he is returned within 7 days to the state.
UTAH CODE ANN. § 76-5-303	1979	Interference with custody including visitation rights by either a parent or a third party is a *misdemeanor*, but if the child is removed from the state it is a *felony*.
VT. STAT. ANN. tit. 13, § 2401	1971	Kidnapping is a *felony*.

Table of Criminal Statutes— *continued*

Statute	Effective Date	Provisions
VA. CODE § 18.2-47	1979	Abduction of child in violation of a custody order is a *misdemeanor* and actor may also be found in contempt of court.
V.I. CODE ANN. tit. 14, § 1051	1974	Parents are exempted from prosecution for kidnapping their own child.
WASH. REV. CODE ANN. § 9A.40.050	1975	Custodial interference is a *misdemeanor*.
W. VA. CODE § 61-2-14	1933	Parents are exempted from prosecution for kidnapping their own children.
WIS. STAT. ANN. § 946.71 (West)	1978	Interference with custody is a *felony* if the child is removed from the state.
WYO. STAT. § 6-4-203	1977	Interference with custody is a *misdemeanor*.

State Kidnapping and
Custodial Interference Statues

Alabama

Tit. 13A Sec. 6-45. Interference with custody.

(a) A person commits the crime of interference with custody if he knowingly takes or entices:

(1) Any child under the age of 18 from the lawful custody of its parent, guardian or other lawful custodian, or

(2) Any committed person from the lawful custody of its parent, guardian or other lawful custodian. "Committed person" means, in addition to anyone committed under judicial warrant, any neglected, dependent of delinquent child, mentally defective or insane person or any other incompetent person entrusted to another's custody by authority of law.

(b) A person does not commit a crime under this section if:

(1) The actor is a relative of the child, and

(2) The actor's sole purpose is to assume lawful control of the child.

The burden of injecting the issue is on the defendant, but this does not shift the burden of proof.

(c) Interference with custody is a Class A misdemeanor.

(Acts 1977, No. 607, § 2215.)

Alaska

Sec. 11.41.320. Custodial interference in the first degree.

(a) A person commits the crime of custodial interference in the first degree if he violates § 330 of this chapter and causes the victim to be removed from the state.

(b) Custodial interference in the first degree is a class C felony.

(§ 3 ch 166 SLA 1978)

Sec. 11.41.330. Custodial interference in the second degree.

(a) A person commits the crime of custodial interference in the second degree if, being a relative of a child under 18 years of age or a relative of an incompetent person and knowing that he has no legal right to do so, he takes, entices, or keeps that child or incompetent person from his lawful custodian with intent to hold him for a protracted period.

(b) Custodial interference in the second degree is a class A misdemeanor.

(§ 3 ch 166 SLA 1978)

Sec. 11.41.370. Definitions.

In §§ 300 — 370 of this chapter, unless the context requires otherwise,

(1) "lawful custodian" means a parent, guardian, or other person responsible by authority of law for the care, custody, or control of another;

(2) "relative" means a parent, stepparent, ancestor, descendant, sibling, uncle, or aunt, including a relative of the same degree through marriage or adoption;

(3) "restrain" means to restrict a person's movements unlawfully and without consent, so as to interfere substantially with his liberty by moving him from one place to another or by confining him either in the place where the restriction commences or in a place to which he has been moved; a restraint is "without consent" if it is accomplished

(A) by acquiescence of the victim, if the victim is under 16 years of age or is an incompetent person and his lawful custodian has not acquiesced in the movement or confinement; or

(B) by force, threat, or deception.

(§ 3 ch 166 SLA 1978)

Arizona

Sec. 13-1302. Custodial interference; classification.

A. A person commits custodial interference if, knowing or having reason to know that he has no legal right to do so, such person knowingly takes, entices or keeps from lawful custody any child less than eighteen years of age or incompetent, entrusted by authority of law to the custody of another person or institution.

B. Custodial interference in a class 6 felony unless the person taken from lawful custody is returned voluntarily by the defendant without physical injury prior to arrest in which case it is a class 1 misdemeanor.

Added Laws 1977, Ch. 142 § 62, eff. Oct. 1, 1978.

Arkansas

Sec. 41-2411. Interference with custody.

(1) A person commits the offense of interference with custody if, knowing that he has no lawful right to do so, he takes, entices, or keeps any person entrusted by court decree to the custody of another person or to an institution from the lawful custody of that person or institution.

(2) Interference with custody is a class D felony is such person is taken, enticed, or kept without the state of Arkansas. Otherwise, it is a class A misdemeanor.

[Acts 1975, No. 280, § 2411, p. 500.]

California

Chapter 4. Child Abduction.

Heading of Chapter 4 was amended by Stats.
1976, c. 1399, p. 6315, § 8.

Sec. 278. Definition; punishment; return; expenses

(a) Every person, not have a right of custody, who maliciously * * * takes, * * * entices away, detains or conceals any minor child with intent to detain or conceal such child from * * * a parent, or guardian, or other person having the lawful charge of such child * * * shall be punished by imprisonment in the state prison * * * for two, three or four years, a fine of not more than ten thousand dollars ($10,000), or both, or imprisonment in a county jail for a period of not more than one year, a fine of not more than one thousand dollars ($1,000), or both.

(b) A child who has been detained or concealed in violation of subdivision (a) shall be returned to the person having lawful charge of the child. Any expenses incurred in returning the child shall be reimbursed as provided in Section 4605 of the Civil Code. Such costs shall be assesed against any defendant convicted of a violation of this section.

(Added by Stats. 1976, c. 1399, p. 6315, § 10. Ammended by Stats. 1976, c. 1399, p. 6315, § 10.5, operative July 1, 1977.)

Sec. 278.5. Violation of custody decree; punishment; return; expenses.

(a) Every person who in violation of a custody decree takes, retains after the expiration of a visitation period, or conceals the child from his legal custodian, and every person who has custody of a child pursuant to an order, judgment or decree of any court which grants another person rights to custody or visitation of such child, and who detains or conceals such child with the intent to deprive the other person of such right to custody or visitation shall be punished by imprisonment in the state prison for a period of not more than one year and one day or by imprisonment in a county jail for a period of not more than one year, a fine of not more than one thousand dollars ($1,000), or both.

(b) A child who has been detained or concealed in violation of subdivision (a) shall be returned to the person having lawful charge of the child. Any expenses incurred in returning the child shall be reimbursed as provided in Section 4605 of the Civil Code. Such costs shall be assessed against any defendant convicted of a violation of this section.

(Added by Stats. 1976, c. 1399, p. 6315, § 11.)

Colorado

Sec. 18-3-304. Violation of custody.

(1) Any person, including a natural or foster parent, who, knowing that he has no privilege to do so or heedless in that regard, takes or entices any child under the age of eighteen years from the custody of his parents, guardian, or other lawful custodian commits a class 5 felony.

(2) Any parent or other person who violates an order of any district or juvenile court of this state, granting the custody of a child under the age of eighteen years to any person, agency, or institution, with the intent to deprive the lawful custodian of the custody of a child under the age of eighteen years, commits a class 5 felony.

(3) It shall be an affirmative defense either that the offender reasonably believed that his conduct was necessary to preserve the child from danger to his welfare, or that the child, being at the time more than fourteen years old, was taken away at his own instigation without enticement and without purpose to commit a criminal offense with or against the child.

Source: R & RE, L. 71, p. 422, § 1; C.R.S. 1963, § 40-3-304.

Connecticut

Sec. 53a-97. Custodial interference in the first degree: Class D felony.

(a) A person is guilty of custodial interference in the first degree when he commits the crime of custodial interference in the second degree as defined in section 53a-98:

(1) Under circumstances which expose the child or person taken or enticed from lawful custody to a risk that his safety will be endangered or his health materially impaired; or

(2) if he takes or entices the child or person out of this state.

(b) Custodial interference in the first degree is a class D felony.

(1969, P.A. 828, § 99, eff. Oct. 1, 1971.)

Sec. 53a-98. Custodial interference in the second degree: Class A misdemeanor.

(a) A person is guilty of custodial interference in the second degree when:

(1) Being a relative of a child who is less than sixteen years old and intending to hold such child permanently or for a protracted period and knowing that he has no legal right to do so, he takes or entices such child from his lawful custodian; or

(2) knowing that he has no legal right to do so, he takes or entices from lawful custody any incompetent person or any person entrusted by authority of law to the custody of another person or institution.

(b) Custodial interference in the second degree is a class A misdemeanor.

(1969, P.A. 828, § 100, eff. Oct. 1; 1971.)

Delaware

Sec. 785. Interference with custody;
Class A misdemeanor.

A person is guilty of interference with custody when:

(1) Being a relative of a child less than 16 years old, intending to hold the child permanently or for a prolonged period and knowing that he has not legal right to do so, he takes or entices the child from his lawful custodian; or

(2) Knowing that he has no legal right to do so, he takes or entices from lawful custody any incompetent person or other person entrusted by authority of law to the custody of another person or an institution.

Interference with custody is a class A misdemeanor.

(11 Del. C. 1953, § 785; 58 Del. Laws, c. 497, § 1.)

District of Columbia

KIDNAPPING

Sec. 22—2201. Definition and penalty—
Conspiracy.

Whoever shall be guilty of, or of aiding or abetting in, seizing, confining, inveigling, enticing, decoying, kidnapping, abducting, concealing, or carrying away any individual by any means whatsoever, and holding or detaining, or with the intent to hold or detain, such individual for ransom or reward or otherwise, except, in the case of a minor, by a parent thereof, shall, upon conviction thereof, be punished by imprisonment for life or for such term as the court in its discretion may determine. This section shall be held to have been violated if either the seizing, confining, inveigling, enticing, decoying, kidnapping, abducting, concealing, carrying away, holding, or detaining occurs in the District of Columbia. If two or more individuals enter into any agreement or conspiracy to do any act or acts which would constitute a violation of the provisions of this section, and one or more of such individuals do any act to effect the object of such agreement or conspiracy, each such individual shall be deemed to have violated the provisions of this section. Mar. 3, 1901, ch. 854, § 812, 31 Stat. 1322; Feb. 18, 1933, ch. 103, 47 Stat. 858; Nov. 8, 1965, Pub.L. 89–347, § 3, 79 Stat. 1307.

Florida

Sec. 787.03. Interference with custody.

(1) Whoever, without lawful authority, knowingly or recklessly takes or entices any child 17 years of age or under or any incompetent person from the custody of his parent, guardian, or other lawful custodian commits the offense of interference with custody and shall be guilty of a misdemeanor of the first degree, punishable as provided in s. 775.082,

s. 774.083, or s. 775.-084.

(2) It is a defense that:

(a) The defendant reasonably believes that his action was necessary to preserve the child or the incompetent person from danger to his welfare.

(b) The child or incompetent person was taken away at his own instigation without enticement and without purpose to commit a criminal offense with or against the child or incompetent person.

(3) Proof that a child was 17 years of age or under creates the presumption that the defendant knew the child's age or acted in reckless disregard thereof.

Amended by Laws 1977, c. 77–174, § 1, eff. Aug. 2, 1977.

Sec. 787.04. Felony to remove children from state contrary to court order.

(1) It is unlawful for any person, in violation of a court order, to lead, take, entice or remove a child beyond the limits of this state with personal knowledge of the order.

(2) It is unlawful for any person, with criminal intent, to lead, take, entice or remove a child beyond the limits of this state during the pendency of any action or proceeding affecting custody of a child after having received notice as required by law of the pendency of the action or proceeding, without the permission of the court in which the action or proceeding is pending.

(3) It is unlawful for any person, who has carried beyond the limits of this state any child whose custody is involved in any action or proceeding pending in this state, pursuant to the order of the court in which the action or proceeding is pending, or pursuant to the permission of the court, thereafter, to fail to produce the child in the court or deliver the child to the person designated by the court.

(4) Any person convicted of a violation of this law shall be guilty of a felony of the third degree, punishable as provided in § 775.082, § 775.083, or § 775.084.

Georgia

Sec. 26-1312. Interference with custody.

(a) A person commits interference with custody when he:

(1) Knowingly or recklessly takes or entices any committed person away from lawful custody when he is not privileged to do so.

(2) Knowingly brings into this State a committed person who has been committed to the custody of another person who is a resident of another state or nation, without the consent of the person with legal custody.

(3) Knowingly harbors any committed person who has absconded.

(b) (1) Except as provided in paragraph (2) of this subsection, any person violating the provisions of this section is guilty of a misdemeanor and upon conviction shall be punished as for a misdemeanor.

(2) A person convicted of interference with custody by taking a committed person beyond the limits of this State shall be punished by imprisonment for not less than one nor more than five years.

(c) As used in this section:

(1) Person includes a parent of a committed person.

(2) "Committed person" means, in addition to anyone committed or whose custody is awarded under judicial warrant or court order, any orphan, neglected, or delinquent child, mentally defective or insane person, or other dependent or incompetent person entrusted to another's custody by authority of law.

(Acts 1968, pp. 1249, 1283; 1978, p. 1420, eff. July 1, 1978.)

Hawaii

Sec. 707. Extortion.

A person commits extortion if he does any of the following:

(1) Obtains, or exerts control over, the property or services of another with intent to deprive him of the property or services by threatening by word or conduct to:

(a) Cause bodily injury in the future to the person threatened or to any other person; or

(b) Cause damage to property; or

(c) Subject the person threatened or any other person to physical confinement or restraint; or

(d) Commit a penal offense; or

(e) Accuse some person of any offense or cause a penal charge to be instituted against some person; or

(f) Expose a secret or publicize an asserted fact, whether true or false, tending to subject some person to hatred, contempt, or ridicule, or to impair his credit or business repute; or

(g) Reveal any information sought to be concealed by the person threatened or any other person; or

(h) Testify or provide information or withhold testimony or information with respect to another's legal claim or defense; or

(i) Take or withhold action as a public servant, or cause a public servant to take or withhold such action; or

(j) Bring about or continue a strike, boycott, or other similar collective action, to obtain property which is not demanded or received for the benefit of the group which the defendant purports to represent; or

(k) Do any other act which would not in itself substantially benefit the defendant which is calculated to harm substantially some person with respect to his health, safety, business, calling, career, financial condition, reputation, or personal relationships; or

(2) Intentionally compels or induces another person to engage in conduct from which he has a legal right to abstain or to abstain from conduct in which he has a legal right to engage by threatening by word or conduct to do any of the actions set forth in paragraphs (a) through (k) of this section; or

(3) Makes or finances any extortionate extension of credit, or collects any extension of credit by extortionate means.

Idaho

Sec. 18-4501. Kidnapping defined.

Every person who wilfully:

1. Seizes, confines, inveigles or kidnaps another, with intent to cause him, without authority of law, to be secretly confined or imprisoned within this state, or to be sent out of this state, or in any way held to service or kept or detained against his will; or,

2. Leads, takes, entices away or detains a child under the age of sixteen (16) years, with intent to keep a conceal it from its parent, guardian or other person having lawful care or control thereof, or with intent to steal any article upon the person of the child; or,

3. Abducts, entices or by force or fraud unlawfully takes or carries away another at or from a place without the state, or procures, advises, aids or abets such an abduction, enticing, taking or carrying away, and afterwards sends, brings, has or keeps such person, or causes him to be kept or secreted within this state; or,

4. Seizes, confines, inveigles, leads, takes, entices away or kidnaps another against his will to extort money, property or any other thing of value or obtain money, property or reward or any other thing of value for the return or disposition of such person is guilty of kidnapping.

[I.C., § 18-4501, as added by 1972, ch. 336, § 1, p. 844.]

Sec. 18-4503. Second degree kidnapping when not for ransom.

Every other kidnapping committed shall be kidnapping in the second degree.

[I.C., § 18-4503, as added by 1972, ch. 336, § 1, p. 844.]

Illinois

Sec. 10-5. Child Abduction.

(a) Definitions. (1) "Court order," as used in this Section, means an order of an Illinois court having jurisdiction over the person of a child;

(2) "Child," as used in Subsections (b) (1) and (b) (2) means a person under the age of 14 at the time the violation of this Section is alleged to have occurred.

(b) Offense. A person commits child abduction when, with intent to violate a court order awarding custody of a child to another, he or she:

(1) removes the child from Illinois without the consent of the person lawfully having custody of the child; or

(2) conceals the child within Illinois.

(c) Affirmative Defenses. It shall be an affirmative defense that:

(1) at the time the court order awarding custody of the child to another was entered, the defendant had custody of the child pursuant to a valid order of a court having jurisdiction over the person of that child; or

(2) after the court order awarding custody of the child to another was entered, the defendant obtained custody of the child pursuant to the order of a court which had jurisdiction over the person of that child, and which had been advised of the prior court order, and which court specifically found the prior court order to be invalid as a matter of law; or

(3) within 72 hours of the alleged violation of this Section, the defendant submitted the child to the jurisdiction of an Illinois court.

(d) Limitations. Nothing contained in this Section shall be construed to limit the court's civil contempt power.

(e) Penalty. Child abduction is a Class 4 felony.

Laws 1961, p. 1983, § 10–5, added by P.A. 80–1393, § 1, eff. Aug. 22, 1978.

Indiana

Sec. 35-1-55-2 [10-2902]. Child stealing.

Whoever takes, leads, carries, decoys or entices away a child under age of fourteen [14] years, with intent unlawfully to detain or conceal such child from its parents, guardian or other person having the lawful charge or custody of such child, and whoever, with the intent aforesaid, knowingly harbors or conceals any such child so led, taken, carried, decoyed or enticed away, on conviction, shall be fined not less than fifty dollars [$50.00], nor more than one thousand dollars [$1,000], and be imprisoned in the state prison not less than two [2] years nor more than fourteen [14] years.

[Acts 1905, ch. 169, § 359, p. 584.]

Iowa

Sec. 710.6. Violating custodial order.

Any relative of a child who, acting in violation of any order of any court which fixes, permanently or temporarily, the custody of such child in another, takes and removes such child from the state, and conceals the child's whereabouts without the consent of the person having lawful custody, commits a class "D" felony.

Any parent of a child living apart from the other parent who takes and conceals that child from another within the state in violation of a custodial order and without the other parent's consent shall be guilty of a serious misdemeanor.

Any parent of a child living apart from the other parent who conceals that child in violation of a court order granting visitation rights and without the other parent's consent, shall be guilty of a serious misdemeanor.

Acts 1976 (66 G.A.) ch. 1245, ch. 1, § 1006, eff. Jan. 1, 1978.
Amended by Acts 1978 (67 G.A.) ch. 1029, § 49.

Kansas

Sec. 21-3422. Interference with parental custody.

Interference with parental custody is leading, taking, carrying away, decoying or enticing away any child under the age of fourteen (14) years, with the intent to detain or conceal such child from its parent, guardian, or other person having the lawful charge of such child.

Interference with parental custody is a class A misdemeanor. [L. 1969, ch. 180, § 21-3422, July 1, 1970.]

Sec. 21-3422a. Aggravated interference with parental custody.

(1) Aggravated interference with parental custody is hiring someone to commit the crime of interference with parental custody, as defined by K.S.A. 21-3422, or committing interference with parental custody, as defined by K.S.A. 21-3422, when done with the intent to deprive of custody such child's parent, guardian, or other person having the lawful charge or custody of such child, and when:

(a) Committed by a person who has previously been convicted of interference with parental custody, as defined by K.S.A. 21-3422;

(b) committed by a person for hire;

(c) committed by a person who takes the child outside the state without the consent of either the person having custody or the court;

(d) committed by a person who, after lawfully taking the child outside the state while exercising visitation rights, refuses to return the child at the expiration of such rights; or

(e) committed by a person who, at the expiration of visitation rights outside the state, refuses to return or impedes the return of such child.

Aggravated interference with parental custody is a class E felony.

(2) This section shall be a part of and supplemental to the Kansas criminal code.

History: L. 1978, ch. 121, § 1; July 1.

Kentucky

Sec. 509.070. Custodial interference.

(1) A person is guilty of custodial interference when, knowing that he has no legal right to do so, he takes, entices or keeps from lawful custody any incompetent or other person entrusted by authority of law to the custody of another person or to an institution.

(2) It is a defense to custodial interference tha the person taken from lawful custody was returned by the defendant voluntarily and before arrest or the issuance of a warrant for arrest.

(3) Custodial interference is a Class D felony unless the person taken from lawful custody is returned voluntarily by the defendant or unless the defendant is a relative of the victim in which case it is a Class A misdemeanor.

(Enact. Acts 1974, ch. 406, § 79.)

Louisiana

Sec. 45. Simple kidnapping.

A. Simple kidnapping is:

(1) The intentional and forcible seizing and carrying of any person from one place to another without his consent; or

(2) The intentional taking, enticing or decoying away, for an unlawful purpose, of any child not his own and under the age of fourteen years, without the consent of its parent or the person charged with its custody; or

(3) The intentional taking, enticing or decoying away, without the consent of the proper authority, of any person who has been lawfully committed to any orphan, insane, feeble-minded or other similar institution.

(4) The intentional taking, enticing or decoying away and removing from the state, by any parent of his or her child, from the custody of any person to whom custody has been awarded by any court of competent jurisdiction of any state, without the consent of the legal custodian, with, intent to defeat the jurisdiction of the said court over the custody of the child.

(5) The taking, enticing or decoying away and removing from the state, by any person, other than the parent, of a child temporarily placed in his custody by any court of competent jurisdiction in the state, with intent to defeat the jurisdiction of said court over the custody of the child.

B. Whoever commits the crime of simple kidnapping shall be fined not more than two thousand dollars or be imprisoned, with or without hard labor, for not more than five years, or both.

Amended by Acts 1962, No. 344, § 1; Acts 1966, No.253, § 1.

Maine

Sec. 303. Criminal restraint by parent.

1. A person is guilty of criminal restraint by parent if, being the parent of a child under the age of 16, he takes, retains or entices the child from the custody of his other parent, guardian or other lawful custodian,

knowing he has no legal right to do so and with the intent to remove the child from the State or to secrete the child and hold him in a place where he is not likely to be found.

2. Consent by the person taken, enticed or retained is not a defense under this section.

3. A law enforcement officer shall not be held liable for taking physical custody of a child whom he reasonably believes has been taken, retained or enticed in violation of this section and for delivering the child to a person whom he reasonably believes is the child's lawful custodian or to any other suitable person.

4. A law enforcement officer may arrest without a warrant any person who he has probable cause to believe has violated or is violating this section.

5. Criminal restraint by parent is a Class E crime.

Added by 1979, c. 512, § 26.

Maryland

Sec. 2A. Child abduction.

(a) *"Lawful custodian" defined.*—As used in this section, "lawful custodian" means a person authorized, either alone or together with another person or persons, to have custody and exercise control over a child less than 12 years of age at the time and place of an act to which any provision of this section is, or may be alleged to be, applicable. The term shall include any person so authorized:

(1) By an order of a court of competent jurisdiction of this State.

(2) By an order of a court of competent jurisdiction of another state, territory or the District of Columbia. However, when there has been a designation of a lawful custodian by an order of a court of this State and there appears to be conflict between that order and a custody order issued by the court of another state or jurisdiction qualifying some other person as the custodian of the child, the "lawful custodian" is the person appointed by order by a court of this State unless the order of the other state or jurisdiction:

(i) Is later in date than the order of a court of this State; and

(ii) Was issued in proceedings in which the person appointed by a custody order of a court of this State either consented to the custody order entered by the court of the other state or jurisdiction, or participated therein personally as a party.

(b) *Meaning of "relative."* — As used in this section, "relative" means a parent, other ancestor, brother, sister, uncle, or aunt, or one who has at some prior time been a lawful custodian.

(c) *Prohibited acts.* — A relative, who is aware that another person is a lawful custodian of a child, may not:

(1) Abduct, take, or carry away a child under 12 years of age from the lawful custodian;

(2) Detain a child under 12 years of age away from the lawful custodian for more than 48 hours after return is demanded by the lawful custodian;

(3) Harbor or secrete a child under 12 years of age knowing that the physical custody of the child has been obtained or retained in violation of this section; or

(4) Act as an accessory to any of the actions forbidden in this section.

(d) *Penalty.* — A person convicted of violating any provision of this section is guilty of a misdemeanor; and upon conviction, shall be imprisoned for a period not exceeding 30 days, or fined a sum not exceeding $250, or both.

(e) *Determination constituting defense.* — If the court determines that the abducting, detaining, or secreting of a child by a relative was done at a time or times when to do otherwise would have resulted in a clear and present danger to the health, safety, or welfare of the child, and if, within 96 hours of such abducting, detaining, or secreting, the relative submits a petition to a court of competent jurisdiction within this State explaining the circumstances and seeking to revise, amend, or clarify the existing custody order, then this determination shall be a complete defense to any action brought pursuant to this section.

(1978, ch. 435.)

Massachusetts

Sec. 26A. Kidnapping of minor or incompetent by relative; punishment.

Whoever, being a relative of a child less than eighteen years old, without lawful authority, holds or intends to hold such a child permanently or for a protracted period, or takes or entices such a child from his lawful custodian, or takes or entices from lawful custody any incompetent person or other person entrusted by authority of law to the custody of another person or institution shall be punished by imprisonment in the house of correction for not more than one year or by a fine of up to one thousand dollars, or both. Whoever commits any offense described in this section under circumstances which expose the person taken or enticed from lawful custody to a risk which endangers his safety shall be punished by a fine of not more than five thousand dollars, or by imprisonment in the state prison for not more than five years, or by both such fine and imprisonment.

Added by St.1979, c. 485, § 2.

Michigan

Sec. 28.582.

Taking or enticing away child under fourteen years of age; application to parents of adopted child.] Sec. 350.

Any person who shall maliciously, forcibly or fraudulently lead, take or carry away, or decoy or entice away, any child under the age of fourteen [14] years, with intent to detain or conceal such child from its parent or guardian, or from the person or persons who have lawfully adopted said child or from any other person having the lawful charge of said child, shall be guilty of a felony, punishable by imprisonment in the state prison for life or any term of years. In case such child shall have been adopted by a person or persons other than its parents, in accordance with the statute providing for such adoption, then this section shall apply as well to such taking, carrying, decoying or enticing away of such child, by its father or mother, as by any other person.

(CL '48, § 750.350.)

Minnesota

Sec. 609.26. Obtaining or retaining a child.

Subdivision 1. Whoever intentionally takes, detains or fails to return his own child under the age of 18 years in violation of an existing court order which grants another person rights of custody may be sentenced as provided in subdivision 5.

Subd. 2. Whoever details or fails to return a child under the age of 18 years knowing that the physical custody of the child has been obtained or retained by another in violation of subdivision 1 may be sentenced as provided in subdivision 5.

Subd. 3. A person who violates this section may be prosecuted and tried either in the county in which the child was taken, concealed or detained or in the county of lawful residence of the child.

Subd. 4. A child who has been obtained or retained in violation of this section shall be returned to the person having lawful custody of the child. In addition to any sentence imposed, the court may assess any expense incurred in returning the child against any person convicted of violating this section.

Subd. 5 Whoever violates this section may be sentenced as follows:

(1) To imprisonment for not more than 90 days or to payment of a fine of not more than $500, or both, if he voluntarily returns the child within 14 days after he takes, detains or fails to return the child in violation of this section; or

(2) Otherwise to imprisonment for not more than one year and one day or to payment of a fine of $1,000, or both.

Amended by Laws 1967, c. 570, § 1, eff. May 19, 1967; Laws 1979, c. 263, § 1, eff. May 30, 1979.

Mississippi

Sec. 97-3-51. Kidnapping.

Every person who shall, without lawful authority, forcibly seize and confine any other, or shall inveigle or kidnap any other with intent to cause such person to be secretly confined or imprisoned in the state against his will, or to cause such other person to be sent out of this state against his will, or to cause such other person to be deprived of his liberty, or in any way held to service against his will, shall upon conviction, be punished by imprisonment in the penitentiary not exceeding ten years. Upon the trial of any such offense the consent of the person so kidnapped or confined shall not be a defense, unless it appear that such consent was not extorted by threats or duress.

Missouri

Sec. 565.150. Interference with custody.

1. A person commits the crime of interference with custody if, knowing that he has no legal right to do so, he takes or entices from lawful custody any person entrusted by order of a court to the custody of another person or institution.

2. Interference with custody is a class A misdemeanor unless the person taken or enticed away from legal custody is removed from this state, in which case it is a class D felony.

(L.1977, S.B.No.60, p. 662, § 1, eff. Jan. 1, 1979.)

Montana

Sec. 45-5-304. Custodial interference.

(1) A person commits the offense of custodial interference if, knowing that he has no legal right to do so, he takes, entices, or withholds from lawful custody any child, incompetent person, or other person entrusted by authority of law to the custody of another person or institution.

(2) A person convicted of the offense of custodial interference shall be imprisoned in the state prison for any term not to exceed 10 years.

(3) A person who has not left the state does not commit an offense under this section if he voluntarily returns such person to lawful custody prior to arraignment. A person who has left the state does not commit an offense under this section if he voluntarily returns such person to lawful custody prior to arrest.

History: En. 94-5-305 by Sec. 1, Ch. 513, L. 1973; R.C.M. 1947, 94-5-305; amd. Sec. 1, Ch. 274, L. 1979.

Nebraska

Sec. 28-316. Violation of custody; penalty.

(1) Any person, including a natural or foster parent, who, knowing that he has no legal right to do so or, heedless in that regard, takes or entices any child under the age of eighteen years from the custody of its

parent having legal custody, guardian, or other lawful custodian commits the offense of violation of custody.

(2) Except as provided in subsection (3) of this section, violation of custody is a Class II misdemeanor.

(3) Violation of custody in contravention of an order of any district or juvenile court of this state granting the custody of a child under the age of eighteen years to any person, agency, or institution, with the intent to deprive the lawful custodian of the custody of such child, is a Class IV felony.

Source: Laws 1977, LB 38, § 31. Operative date January 1, 1979.

Nevada

Sec. 200.359. Detention, concealment, removal of child from person having lawful custody in violation of court order a misdemeanor.

Every person have a limited right of custody to a child pursuant to an order, judgment or decree of any court, or any parent having no right of custody to the child, who in violation of an order, judgment or decree of any court detains, conceals or removes such child from a parent, guardian or other person having lawful custody is guilty of a misdemeanor.

(Added to NRS by 1975, 1397)

New Hampshire

Sec. 633:1. Kidnapping.

I. A person is guilty of kidnapping if he knowingly confines another under his control with a purpose to:

    (a) Hold him for ransom or as a hostage; or

    (b) Avoid apprehension by a law enforcement official; or

    (c) Terrorize him or some other person; or

    (d) Commit an offense against him.

II. Kidnapping is a class A felony unless the actor voluntarily releases the victim without serious bodily injury and in a safe place prior to trial, in which case it is a class B felony.

History: Source. 1971, 518:1, eff. Nov. 1, 1973.

New Jersey

Sec. 2C:13-4. Interference with Custody.

    a. Custody of children. A person commits an offense if he knowingly takes or entices any child under the age of 18 from the custody of the parent, guardian or other lawful custodian of the child, when he has no privilege to do so, or he does so in violation of a court order. It is an affirmative defense that:

(1) The actor believed that his action was necessary to preserve the child from danger to his welfare; or

(2) The child, being at the time not less than 14 years old, was taken away at his own volition and without purpose to commit a criminal offense with or against the child.

Proof that the child was below the critical age gives rise to a presumption that the actor knew the child's age.

The offense is a crime of the fourth degree if the actor is neither a parent of or person in equivalent relation to the child and if he acted with knowledge that his conduct would cause serious alarm for the child's safety or in reckless disregard of a likelihood of causing such alarm. In all other cases it is a disorderly persons offense.

b. Custody of committed persons. A person is guilty of a crime of the fourth degree if he knowingly takes or entices any committed person away from lawful custody when he is not privileged to do so. "Committed person" means, in addition to anyone committed under judicial warrant, any orphan, neglected or delinquent child, mentally defective or insane person, or other dependent or incompetent person entrusted to another's custody by or through a recognized social agency or otherwise by authority of law.

L.1978, c. 95, § 2C:13–14, eff. Sept. 1, 1979. Amended by L.179, c. 1978, § 25, eff. Sept. 1, 1979.

New Mexico

Sec. 30-4-4. Custodial interference; penalty.

A. Custodial interference consists of the taking from this state or causing to be taken from this state, or enticing to leave this state or causing to be enticed to leave this state, a child who is less than sixteen years of age by a parent with the intention of holding the child permanently or for a protracted period, knowing that he has no legal right to do so.

B. Whoever commits custodial interference is guilty of a fourth degree felony.

History: 1953 Comp., § 40A-4-3.1, enacted by Laws 1977, ch. 58, § 1.

New York

Sec. 135.45. Custodial interference in the second degree.

A person is guilty of custodial interference in the second degree when:

1. Being a relative of a child less than sixteen years old, intending to hold such child permanently or for a protracted period, and knowing that he has no legal right to do so, he takes or entices such child from his lawful custodian; or

2. Knowing that he has no legal right to do so, he takes or entices from lawful custody any incompetent person or other person entrusted by authority of law to the custody of another person or institution.

Custodial interference in the second degree is a class A misdemeanor.

L.1965, c. 1030.

Sec. 135.50.   Custodial interference in the first degree.

A person is guilty of custodial interference in the first degree when he commits the crime of custodial interference in the second degree under circumstances which expose the person taken or enticed from lawful custody to a risk that his safety will be endangered or his health materially impaired.

Custodial interference in the first degree is a class E felony.

L.1965, c. 1030.

North Carolina

**Sec. 14-320.1.   Transporting child outside the State with
intent to violate custody order.**

When any court of competent jurisdiction in this State shall have awarded custody of a child under the age of sixteen years, it shall be a felony for any person with the intent to violate the court order to take or transport, or cause to be taken or transported, any such child from any point within this State to any point outside the limits of this State or to keep any such child outside the limits of this State. Such crime shall be punishable by a fine in the discretion of the court or by imprisonment in the State's prison for not more than three years, in the discretion of the court, or by both such fine and imprisonment. Provided that keeping a child outside the limits of the State in violation of a court order for a period in excess of seventy-two hours shall be prima facie evidence that the person charged intended to violate the order at the time of taking.

(1969, c. 81.)

North Dakota

**Sec. 14-14-22.1.   Removal of child from state in violation of
custody decree — Penalty.**

Any person who intentionally removes, causes the removal of, or detains his or her own child under the age of eighteen years outside North Dakota with the intent to deny another person's rights under an existing custody decree shall be guilty of a class C felony. Detaining the child outside North Dakota in violation of the custody decree for more than seventy-two hours shall be prima facie evidence that the person charged intended to violate the custody decree at the time of removal.

Source: S.L.1979, ch. 198, § 1.

Ohio

Sec. 2905.04.   Child stealing.

(A) No person, by any means, and with purpose to withhold a child under the age of fourteen or mentally incompetent from the legal custody of his parent, guardian, or custodian, shall remove such child from the place where he is found.

(B) It is an affirmative defense to a charge under this section that the actor reasonably believed that his conduct was necessary to preserve the child's health or welfare.

(C) Whoever violates this section is guilty of child stealing, a felony of the second degree. If the offender is a natural or adoptive parent, or a stepparent of the child, but not entitled to legal custody of the child when the offense is committed, child stealing is a misdemeanor of the first degree unless the offender removes the child from this state, in which case child stealing is a felony of the fourth degree.

History: 1972 H 511, eff. 1-1-74.

Sec. 2919.23. Interference with custody.

(A) No person, knowing he is without privilege to do so or being reckless in that regard, shall entice, take, keep, or harbor any of the following persons from his parent, guardian, or custodian:

(1) A child under the age of eighteen, or a mentally or physically handicapped child under the age of twenty-one;

(2) A person committed by law to an institution for delinquent, unruly, neglected, abused, or dependent children;

(3) A person committed by law to an institution for the mentally ill or mentally deficient.

(B) It is an affirmative defense to a charge of enticing or taking under division (A)(1) of this section, that the actor reasonably believed that his conduct was necessary to preserve the child's health or safety. It is an affirmative defense to a charge of keeping or harboring under division (A) of this section, that the actor in good faith gave notice to law enforcement or judicial authorities within a reasonable time after the child or committed person came under his shelter, protection, or influence.

(C) Whoever violates this section is guilty of interference with custody, a misdemeanor of the third degree.

History: 1975 H 85, eff. 11-28-75, 1972 H 511.

Oklahoma

Sec. 891. Child stealing—Punishment.

Whoever maliciously, forcibly or fraudulently takes or entices away any child under the age of twelve years, with intent to detain and conceal such child from its parent, guardian or other person having the lawful charge of such child is punishable by imprisonment in the penitentiary not exceeding ten years, or by imprisonment in a county jail not exceeding one year, or by a fine not exceeding five hundred dollars, or by both such fine and imprisonment.

R.L.1910, § 2435.

Oregon

Sec. 163.245. Custodial interference in the second degree.

(1) A person commits the crime of custodial interference in the second degree if, knowing or having reason to know that he has no legal wright to do so, he takes, entices or keeps a person from his lawful custodian with intent to hold him permanently or for a protracted period.

(2) Custodial interference in the second degree is a Class A misdemeanor. [1971 c.743 §100]

163.250 [Repealed by 1971 c.743 §432]

163.255 [1955 c.530 §1; repealed by 1971 c.743 §432]

Sec. 163.257 Custodial interference in the first degree.

(1) A person commits the crime of custodial interference in the first degree if he violates ORS 163.245 and:

(a) Causes the person taken, enticed or kept from his lawful custodian to be removed from the state; or

(b) Exposes that person to a substantial risk of illness or physical injury.

(2) Custodial interference in the first degree is a Class C felony. [1971 c.743 §101]

163.260 [Amended by 1955 c.366 §1; repealed by 1971 c.743 §432]

163.270 [Amended by 1955 c.371 §1; 1957 c.640 §1; repealed by 1971 c.743 §432]

Pennsylvania

Sec. 2904. Interference with custody of children.

(a) Offense defined.—A person commits an offense if he knowingly or recklessly takes or entices any child under the age 18 years from the custody of its parent, guardian or other lawful custodian, when he has no privilege to do so.

(b) Defenses.—It is a defense that:

(1) the actor believed that his action was necessary to preserve the child from danger to its welfare; or

(2) the child, being at the time not less than 14 years old, was taken away at its own instigation without enticement and without purpose to commit a criminal offense with or against the child; or

(3) the actor is the child's parent or guardian or other lawful custodian and is not acting contrary to an order entered by a court of competent jurisdiction.

(c) Grading.—The offense is a misdemeanor of the second degree unless the actor, not being a parent or person in equivalent relation to the child, acted with knowledge that his conduct would cause serious alarm for the safety of the child, or in reckless disregard of a likelihood of causing such alarm, in which case the offense is a misdemeanor of the first degree.

1972, Dec. 6, P.L. ___, No. 334, § 1, eff. June 6, 1973.

Puerto Rico

Sec. 4178. Kidnapping.

Any person who by force, violence, intimidation, fraud or deceit, steals another person to deprive him of his liberty, shall be punishable by imprisonment for a minimum term of 10 years and a maximum of 40 years.

Penal Code, 1974, § 137.

Rhode Island

Sec. 11-26-1. Penalty for kidnapping.

Whoever, without lawful authority, forceably or secretly confines or imprisons another person within this state against his will, or forceably carries or sends another person out of this state, or forceably seizes or confines or inveigles or kidnaps another person with intent either to cause him to be secretly confined or imprisoned within this state against his will or to cause him to be sent out of this state against his will, shall be guilty of a felony and upon conviction thereof shall be punished by imprisonment for not more than twenty (20) years.

South Carolina

Sec. 16-17-495. Transporting child under sixteen years of age outside State with intent to violate a custody order.

When any court of competent jurisdiction in this State shall have awarded custody of a child under the age of sixteen years, it shall be a felony for any person with the intent to violate the court order to take or transport, or cause to be taken or transported, any such child from any point within this State to any point outside the limits of this State or to keep any such child outside the limits of this State. Such crime shall be punishable by a fine in the discretion of the court or by imprisonment in the State's prison for not more than three years, in the discretion of the court, or by both such fine and imprisonment; *provided,* that keeping a child outside the limits of the State in violation of a court order for a period in excess of seventy-two hours shall be prima facie evidence that the person charged intended to violate the order at the time of taking; *provided,* further, that if the person violating the provisions of this section returns the child to the jurisdiction of the court issuing such order within seven days after so removing the child from this State, such person shall be deemed guilty of a misdemeanor and upon conviction shall be punished as provided herein.

History: 1976 Act No. 592.

South Dakota

Sec. 22-19-9.

Any parent who takes or entices away his unmarried minor child from the custody of the other parent, or any other person having lawful custody, without prior consent is guilty of a Class 1 misdemeanor.

Enacted SL 1979, ch 171, § 7.

Tennessee

Sec. 39-2602. Kidnapping children under sixteen—Penalty.

Every person who unlawfully takes or decoys away any child under the age of sixteen (16) years, with intent to detain or conceal such child from its parents, guardian, or other person having the lawful charge of such child, shall, on conviction, be imprisoned in the penitentiary not less than one (1) year nor more than five (5) years.

[Code 1858, § 4619; Shan., § 6465; mod. Code 1932, § 10793.]

Texas

Sec. 25.03. Interference with Child Custody

(a) A person commits an offense if he takes or retains a child younger than 18 years out of this state when he:

(1) knows that his taking or retention violates the express terms of a judgment or order of a court disposing of the child's custody; or

(2) has not been awarded custody of the child by a court of competent jurisdiction and knows that a suit for divorce, or a civil suit or application for habeas corpus to dispose of the child's custody, has been filed.

(b) It is a defense to prosecution under Subsection (a) (2) of this section that the actor returned the child to this state within seven days after the date of the commission of the offense.

(c) An offense under this section is a felony of the third degree.

Utah

Sec. 76-5-303. Custodial interference.

(1) A person, whether a parent or other, is guilty of custodial interference if, without good cause, he or she takes, entices, conceals, or detains a child under the age of sixteen from his or her parent, guardian, or other lawful custodian

(a) Knowing he or she has no legal right to do so; and

(b) With intent to hold the child for a period substantially longer than the visitation or custody period previously awarded by a court of competent jurisdiction.

(2) A person, whether a parent or other, is guilty of custodial interference if, having actual physical custody of a child under the age of six-

teen pursuant to a judicial award of any court of competent jurisdiction which grants to another person visitation or custody rights, and without good cause he or she conceals or detains the child with intent to deprive the other person of his or her lawful visitation or custody rights.

(3) A person is guilty of custodial interference if without good cause he or she takes, entices, conceals, or detains an incompetent or other person under the age of sixteen who has been committed by authority of law to the custody of another person or institution from the other person or institution, knowing he or she has no legal right to do so.

(4) Custodial interference is a class A misdemeanor unless the child is removed and taken from one state to another, in which case it is a felony of the third degree.

History: C. 1953, 76-5-303, enacted by L. 1973, ch. 196, § 76-5-303; L. 1979, ch. 70, § 1.

Vermont
Sec. 2401. Definition and punishment.
A person who, without legal authority, forcibly or secretly confines or imprisons another person within this state against his will, or forcibly carries or sends such person out of the state, or forcibly seizes or confines or inveigles or kidnaps another person with intent to cause him to be secretly confined or imprisoned in this state against his will, or to cause him to be sent out of this state against his will, or in any way held to service against his will, shall be imprisoned not more than twenty-five years or fined not more than $10,000.00, or both.

Amended 1971, No. 199 (Adj. Sess.), § 15, eff. July 1, 1972.

Virginia
Sec. 18.2-47. Abduction and kidnapping defined; punishment.
Any person, who, by force, intimidation or deception, and without legal justification or excuse, seizes, takes, transports, detains or secretes the person of another, with the intent to deprive such other person of his personal liberty or to withhold or conceal him from any person, authority or institution lawfully entitled to his charge, shall be deemed guilty of "abduction;" but the provisions of this section shall not apply to any law-enforcement officer in the performance of his duty. The terms "abduction" and "kidnapping" shall be synonymous in this Code.

Abduction for which no punishment is otherwise prescribed shall be punished as a Class 5 felony; provided, however, that such offense, if committed by the parent of the person abducted and punishable as contempt of court in any proceeding then pending, shall be a Class 1 misdemeanor in addition to being punishable as contempt of court.

(Code 1950, §§ 18.1-36, 18.1-37; 1960, c. 358; 1975, cc. 14, 15; 1979, c. 663.)

Virgin Islands

Sec. 1051. False imprisonment and kidnapping.

Whoever without lawful authority confines or imprisons another person within this Territory against his will, or confines or inveigles or kidnaps another person, with intent to cause him to be confined or imprisoned in this Territory against his will, or to cause him to be sent out of this Territory against his will; and whoever willfully and knowingly sells, or in any manner transfers, for any term, the services or labor of any other person who has been unlawfully seized, taken, inveigled or kidnapped from this Territory to any other state, territory or country, is guilty of kidnapping and shall be imprisoned for not less than one and not more than 20 years. This action shall not apply in any case when a parent abducts his own child.

Amended May 1, 1974, No. 3560, § 3, Sess. L. 1974, p. 88.

Washington

Sec. 9A.40.050. Custodial interference.

(1) A person is guilty of custodial interference if, knowing that he has no legal right to do so, he takes or entices from lawful custody any incompetent person or other person entrusted by authority of law to the custody of another person or institution.

(2) Custodial interference is a gross misdemeanor.

West Virginia

Sec. 61-2-14. Abduction of female; kidnapping or concealing child; penalties.

If any person take away, or detain against her will, a female person, with intent to marry or defile her, or to cause her to be married or defiled by another person; or take away from any person having lawful charge of her a female child under the age of sixteen years, for the purpose of prostitution or concubinage, he shall be guilty of a felony, and, upon conviction, shall be confined in the penitentiary not less than three nor more than ten years. And if any person, other than the father or mother, illegally, or for any unlawful, improper or immoral purpose other than the purposes stated in section fourteen-(a) [§ 61-2-14a] of this article, seize, take or secrete a child under sixteen years of age, from the person or persons have lawful charge of such child, he shall be guilty of a felony, and upon conviction, shall be confined in the penitentiary not less than one nor more than five years, or, in the discretion of the court, be confined in jail not exceeding one year and be fined not exceeding one thousand dollars.

(Code 1849, c. 191, §§ 14, 16; Code 1860, c. 101, §§ 14, 16, 18; Code 1868, c. 144, §§ 14, 16; 1882, c. 18, §§ 14, 16; 1901, c. 101; 1905, c. 74; Code 1923, c. 144, §§ 14, 16; 1933, 2nd Ex. Sess., c. 70.)

Wisconsin

Sec. 946.71. Interference with custody of child.

Except as provided under ch. 48, whoever intentionally does any of the following is guilty of a Class E felony:

(1) Interferes with the custody * * * of any * * * child under the age of 18 who has been committed or whose legal custody or guardianship has been transferred under ch. 48 to the department of health and social services or to any person, county agency or licensed child welfare agency * * *

(2) Entices away or takes away any child under the age of 18 from the parent or other person have legal custody under an order or judgment in * * * an action for divorce, legal separation, annulment, custody, paternity, guardianship or habeas corpus * * * with intent to take the child out of the state for the purpose of depriving the parent or other person of the custody of the child without the consent of such parent or other person, unless the court which awarded custody has consented that the child be taken out of the state by the person who so takes * * * the child.

(3) Entices away, takes away or withholds for more than 12 hours beyond the court-approved visitation period any child under the age of 14 from a parent or other person having legal custody under an order or judgment in an action for divorce, legal separation, annulment, custody, paternity, guardianship or habeas corpus without the consent of the legal custodian, unless a court has entered an order authorizing the taking or withholding.

(4) Entices away, takes away or withholds for more than 12 hours any child under the age of 14 from the parents, or the child's mother in the case of a child born out of wedlock and not subsequently legitimated, without the consent of the parents or the mother, unless custody has been granted by court order to the person enticing, taking or withholding the child.

Wyoming

Sec. 6-4-203. Involuntary transfer of physical custody of child.

When any parent, living apart from the other parent who by express agreement or court order has the physical custody or control of a child under the age of fourteen (14) years, takes, leads, carries, decoys or entices away the child with the intent to cause a change in the physical custody of the child without the consent of the parent or guardian having physical custody or control of the child or without authorization to do so by a court having appropriate jurisdiction, he shall, upon conviction, be imprisoned in the county jail for a period not exceeding six (6) months, fined not more than five hundred dollars ($500.00), or both.

(Laws 1977, ch. 92, § 1.)

Appendix C

Parental Kidnapping Prevention Act of 1980*

SEC. 6. Sections 6 to 10 of this Act may be cited as the "Parental Kidnapping Prevention Act of 1980."

Findings and Purposes

SEC. 7.(a) The Congress finds that —

(1) there is a large and growing number of cases annually involving disputes between persons claiming rights of custody and visitation of children under the laws, and in the courts, of different States, the District of Columbia, the Commonwealth of Puerto Rico, and the territories and possessions of the United States;

(2) the laws and practices by which the courts of those jurisdictions determine their jurisdiction to decide such disputes, and the effect to be given the decisions of such disputes by the courts of other jurisdictions, are often inconsistent and conflicting;

(3) those characteristics of the law and practice in such cases, along with the limits imposed by a Federal system on the authority of each such jurisdiction to conduct investigations and take other actions outside its own boundaries, contribute to a tendency of parties involved in such disputes to frequently resort to the seizure, restraint, concealment, and interstate transportation of children, the disregard of court orders, excessive relitigation of cases, obtaining of conflicting orders by the courts of various jurisdictions, and interstate travel and communication that is so expensive and time consuming as to disrupt their occupations and commercial activities; and

(4) among the results of those conditions and activities are the failure of the courts of such jursidictions to give full faith and credit to the judicial proceedings of the other jurisdictions, the deprivation of rights of liberty and property without due process of law, burdens on

---

*Pub. L. No. 96-611 §§ 6–10, 94 Stat. 3568 (Parental Kidnapping Prevention Act of 1980) amends Title XVIII of the Social Security Act to provide for medical coverage of pneumococcal vaccine and its administration.

commerce among such jurisdictions and with foreign nations, and harm to the welfare of children and their parents and other custodians.

(b) For those reasons it is necessary to establish a national system for locating parents and children who travel from one such jurisdiction to another and are concealed in connection with such disputes, and to establish national standards under which the courts of such jurisdictions will determine their jurisdiction to decide such disputes and the effect to be given by each such jurisdiction to such decisions by the courts of other such jurisdictions.

(c) The general purposes of sections 6 to 10 of this Act are to —

(1) promote cooperation between State courts to the end that a determination of custody and visitation is rendered in the State which can best decide the case in the interest of the child;

(2) promote and expand the exchange of information and other forms of mutual assistance between States which are concerned with the same child;

(3) facilitate the enforcement of custody and visitation decrees of sister States;

(4) discourage continuing interstate controversies over child custody in the interest of greater stability of home environment and of secure family relationships for the child;

(5) avoid jurisdictional competition and conflict between State courts in matters of child custody and visitation which have in the past resulted in the shifting of children from State to State with harmful effects on their well-being; and

(6) deter interstate abductions and other unilateral removals of children undertaken to obtain custody and visitation awards.

Full Faith and Credit Given to Child Custody Determinations

Sec. 8.(a) Chapter 115 of title 28, United States Code, is amended by adding immediately after section 1738 the following new section:

"§ 1738A. Full faith and credit given to child custody determinations.

"(a) The appropriate authorities of every State shall enforce according to its terms, and shall not modify except as provided in subsection (f) of this section, any child custody determination made consistently with the provisions of this section by a court of another State.

"(b) As used in this section, the term—

"(1) 'child' means a person under the age of eighteen;

"(2) 'contestant' means a person, including a parent, who claims a right to custody or visitation of a child;

"(3) 'custody determination' means a judgment, decree, or other order of a court providing for the custody or visitation of a child, and includes permanent and temporary orders, and initial orders and modifications;

"(4) 'home State' means the State in which, immediately preceding the time involved, the child lived with his parents, a parent, or a person acting as parent, for at least six consecutive months, and in the case of a child less than six months old, the State in which the child lived from birth with any of such persons. Periods of temporary absence of any of such persons are counted as part of the six-month or other period;

"(5) 'modification' and 'modify' refer to a custody determination which modifies, replaces, supersedes, or otherwise is made subsequent to, a prior custody determination concerning the same child, whether made by the same court or not;

"(6) 'person acting as a parent' means a person, other than a parent, who has physical custody of a child and who has either been awarded custody by a court or claims a right to custody;

"(7) 'physical custody' means actual possession and control of a child; and

"(8) 'State' means a State of the United States, the District of Columbia, the Commonwealth of Puerto Rico, or a territory or possession of the United States.

"(c) A child custody determination made by a court of a State is consistent with the provisions of this section only if—

"(1) such court has jurisdiction under the law of such State; and

"(2) one of the following conditions is met:

"(A) such State (i) is the home State of the child on the date of the commencement of the proceeding, or (ii) had been the child's home State within six months before the date of the commencement of the proceeding and the child is absent from such State because of his removal or retention by a contestant or for other reasons, and a contestant continues to live in such State;

"(B)(i) it appears that no other State would have jurisdiction under subparagraph (A), and (ii) it is in the best interest of the child that a court of such State assume jurisdiction because (I) the child and his parents, or the child and at least one contestant, have a significant connection with such State other than mere physical presence in such State, and (II) there is available in such State substantial evidence concerning the child's present or future care, protection, training, and personal relationships;

"(C) the child is physically present in such State and (i) the child has been abandoned, or (ii) it is necessary in an emergency to protect the child because he has been subjected to or threatened with mistreatment or abuse;

"(D)(i) it appears that no other State would have jurisdiction under subparagraph (A), (B), (C), or (E), or another State has declined to exercise jurisdiction on the ground that the State whose jurisdiction is in issue is the more appropriate forum to determine the custody of the child, and (ii) it is in the best interest of the child that such court assume jurisdiction; or

"(E) the court has continuing jurisdiction pursuant to subsection (d) of this section.

"(d) The jurisdiction of a court of a State which has made a child custody determination consistently with the provisions of this section continues as long as the requirement of subsection (c)(1) of this section continues to be met and such State remains the residence of the child or of any contestant.

"(e) Before a child custody determination is made, reasonable notice and opportunity to be heard shall be given to the contestants, any parent whose parental rights have not been previously terminated and any person who has physical custody of a child.

"(f) A court of a State may modify a determination of the custody of the same child made by a court of another State, if—

"(1) it has jurisdiction to make such a child custody determination; and

"(2) the court of the other State no longer has jurisdiction, or it has declined to exercise such jurisdiction to modify such determination.

"(g) A court of a State shall not exercise jurisdiction in any proceeding for a custody determination commenced during the pendency of a proceeding in a court of another State where such court of that other State is exercising jurisdiction consistently with the provisions of this section to make a custody determination."

(b) The table of sections at the beginning of chapter 115 of title 28, United States Code, is amended by inserting after the item relating to section 1738 the following new item:
"1738A. Full faith and credit given to child custody determinations."

(c) In furtherance of the purposes of Section 1738A of title 28, United States Code, as added by subsection (a) of this section, State courts are encouraged to h —

(1) afford priority to proceedings for custody determinations; and
(2) award to the person entitled to custody or visitation pursuant to a custody determination which is consistent with the provisions of such section 1738A, necessary travel expenses, attorneys' fees, costs of private investigations, witness fees or expenses, and other expenses incurred in connection with such custody determination in any case in which—

(A) a contestant has, without the consent of the person entitled to custody or visitation pursuant to a custody determination which is consistent with the provisions of such section 1738A, (i) wrongfully removed the child from the physical custody of such person, or (ii) wrongfully retained the child after a visit or other temporary relinquishment of physical custody; or

(B) the court determines it is appropriate.

Use of Federal Parent Locator Service in Connection with the Enforcement or Determination of Child Custody and in Cases of Parental Kidnapping of a Child

SEC. 9.(a) Section 454 of the Social Security Act is amended—

(1) by striking out "and" at the end of paragraph (15),

(2) by striking out the period at the end of paragraph (16) and inserting in lieu thereof ";and"; and

(3) by inserting after paragraph (16) the following new paragraph:

"(17) in the case of a State which has in effect an agreement with the Secretary entered into pursuant to section 463 for the use of the Parent Locator Service established under section 453, to accept and transmit to the Secretary requests for information authorized under the provisions of the agreement to be furnished by such Service to authorized persons, and to impose and collect (in accordance with regulations of the Secretary) a fee sufficient to cover the costs to the State and to the Secretary incurred by reason of such requests, to transmit to the Secretary from time to time (in accordance with such regulations) so much of the fees collected as are attributable to such costs to the Secretary so incurred, and during the period that such agreement is in effect, otherwise to comply with such agreement and regulations of the Secretary with respect thereto."

(b) Part D of Title IV of the Social Security Act is amended by adding at the end thereof the following new section:

"Use of Federal Parent Locator Service in Connection with the Enforcement or Determination of Child Custody and in Cases of Parental Kidnapping of a Child

"SEC. 463.(a) The Secretary shall enter into an agreement with any State which is able and willing to do so, under which the services of the Parent Locator Service established under section 453 shall be made available to such State for the purpose of determining the whereabouts of any absent parent or child when such information is to be used to locate such parent or child for the purpose of—

"(1) enforcing any State or Federal law with respect to the unlawful taking or restraint of a child; or

"(2) making or enforcing a child custody determination.

"(b) An agreement entered into under this section shall provide that the State agency described in section 454 will, under procedures prescribed by the Secretary in regulations, receive and transmit to the Secretary requests from authorized persons for information as to (or useful in determining) the whereabouts of any absent parent or child when such information is to be used to locate such parent or child for the purpose of—

"(1) enforcing any State or Federal law with respect to the unlawful taking or restraint of a child; or

"(2) making or enforcing a child custody determination.

"(c) Information authorized to be provided by the Secretary under this section shall be subject to the same conditions with respect to disclosure as information authorized to be provided under section 453, and a request for information by the Secretary under this section shall be considered to be a request for information under section 453 which is authorized to be provided under such section. Only information as to the most recent address and place of employment of any absent parent or child shall be provided under this section.

"(d) For purposes of this section—

"(1) the term 'custody determination' means a judgment, decree, or other order of a court providing for this custody or visitation of a child, and includes permanent and temporary orders, and initial orders and modification;

"(2) the term 'authorized person' means—

"(A) any agent or attorney of any State having an agreement under this section, who has the duty or authority under the law of such State to enforce a child custody determination;

"(B) any court having jurisdiction to make or enforce such a child custody determination, or any agent of such court; and

"(C) any agent or attorney of the United States, or of a State having an agreement under this section, who has the duty or authority to investigate, enforce, or bring a prosecution with respect to the unlawful taking or restraint of a child."

(c) Section 455(a) of such Act is amended by adding after parapraph (3) the following: "except that no amount shall be paid to any State on account of amounts expended to carry out an agreement which it has entered into pursuant to section 463."

(d) No agreement entered into under section 463 of the Social Security Act shall become effective before the date on which section 1738A of title 28. United States Code (as added by this title) becomes effective.

Parental Kidnapping

Sec. 10. (a) In view of the findings of the Congress and the purposes of sections 6 to 10 of this Act set forth in section 302, the Congress here-by expressly declares its intent that section 1073 of title 18, Untied States Code, apply to cases involving parental kidnapping and interstate or international flight to avoid prosecution under applicable State felony statutes.

(b) The Attorney General of the United States, not later than 120 days after the date of the enactment of this section (and once every 6 months during the 3-year period following such 120-day period), shall submit a report to the Congress with respect to steps taken to comply with the intent of the Congress set forth in subsection (a). Each such report shall include—

(1) data relating to the number of applications for complaints under section 1073 of title 18, United States Code, in cases involving parental kidnapping;

(2) data relating to the number of complaints issued in such cases; and

(3) such other information as may assist in describing the activities of the Department of Justice in conformance with such intent.

* * *

Bibliography

American Jurisprudence (Second), "Contempt" vol. 17 (1964).

Annotation, "Extraterritorial Effect of Valid Award of Custody of Child of Divorced Parents in Absence of Substantial Change in Circumstances" *American Law Reports (Third),* vol. 34 (1971).

Black's Law Dictionary (4th rev. ed. 1968).

Bodenheimer, Curbing Child Snatching on Three Fronts, State, National and International, and the Uniform Child Custody Jurisdiction Act (May 29, 1980) (unpublished manuscript).

Bodenheimer, "The Hague Draft Convention on International Child Abduction," 14 *Family Law Quarterly* 99 (1981).

Bodenheimer, "Interstate Custody: Initial Jurisdiction and Continuing Jurisdiction under the UCCJA," 14 *Family Law Quarterly* 203 (1981).

Bodenheimer, "Progress under the Uniform Child Custody Jurisidiction Act and Remaining Problems: Punitive Decrees, Joint Custody and Excessive Modifications," 65 *California Law Review* 978 (1977).

Bodenheimer, "The Uniform Child Custody Jurisdiction Act: A Legislative Remedy for Children Caught in the Conflict of Laws," 22 *Vanderbilt Law Review* 1207 (1969).

Clark, *Domestic Relations* (2d ed. 1974).

Clark, *Law of Domestic Relations in the United States* (1968).

Comment, "Child Custody Jurisdiction in Ohio—Implementing the UCCJA," 12 *Akron Law Review* 121 (1978).

Comment, "Jurisdictional Guidelines in Matters of Child Custody: Kansas Adopts the UCCJA," 27 *University of Kansas Law Review* 469 (1979).

Congressional Record, vol. 75; 13,296 (1932).

Congressional Record, vol. 124, S. 498-503, daily ed., Jan. 25, 1978.

Congressional Record, vol. 124, S. 860, daily ed., Jan. 25, 1978.

Coombs, "The 'Snatched' Child is Halfway Home in Congress," 11 *Family Law Quarterly* 407 (1978).

Crouch, "Clearing the Court of Unneeded Custody Disputes," 3 *Family Advocate* 6 (1980).

Crouch, *Interstate Custody Litigation: A Guide to Use and Court Interpretation of the Uniform Child Custody Jurisdiction Act* (1981).

Ehrenzweig, "Interstate Recognition of Custody Decrees," 15 *Michigan Law Review* 345 (1953).

Ehrenzweig and Louisell, *Jurisdiction in a Nutshell* (3d ed. 1973).

Foster and Freed, "A Legislative Beginning to Child-Snatching Prevention," 17 *Trial Magazine* 36 (April, 1981).

Gelles, Research Issues in the Study of Parental Kidnapping (Report prepared for the National Institute of Justice, U.S. Department of Justice, July, 1980).

Graham, "The UCCJA in Idaho: Purposes, Application and Problems," 15 *Idaho Law Review* 305 (1979).

Inker and Perretta, "A Child's Right to Counsel in Custody Cases," 5 *Family Law Quarterly* 108 (1971).

Kleinfeld, "The Balance of Power among Infants, Their Parents and the State," 4 *Family Law Quarterly* 319 (1970).

Leflar, *American Conflicts Law* (3d ed. 1977).

Luxenberg and McLaughlin, "Family Law Issues of the 1980s—Child Snatching," 5 *District Lawyer* 43 (1980).

McClintock, *Principles of Equity* (1948).

McCoy, "Parental Kidnapping," Issue Brief #1B77117, Library of Congress, Congressional Research Service, March 26, 1979.

Middleton, "Legislation Proposed on Parent Kidnapping," 66 *American Bar Association Journal* 1059 (1980).

Note, "The Interstate Child Custody Problem Revisited," 16 *ABA Family Law Newsletter* 1 (1975).

Note, "Legalized Kidnapping of Children by Their Parents," 80 *Dickinson Law Review* 305 (1976).

Note, "New York Adopts the Uniform Child Custody Jursidiction Act," 45 *Brooklyn Law Review* 89 (1978).

Ratner, "Child Custody in a Federal System," 62 *Michigan Law Review* 795 (1964).

Restatement of Conflict of Laws (1934).

Restatement (Second) of Conflict of Laws (1967).

Restatement (Second) of Torts (1977).

Siegel and Hurley, "The Role of the Child's Preference in Custody Proceedings," 11 *Family Law Quarterly* 1 (1977).

Uniform Child Custody Jurisdiction Act, 9 *Uniform Laws Annotated* 116 (1977) (cited as UCCJA) (see Appendix A for the complete text of the Act).

United States Constitution, article IV, section 1.

Table of Cases

Index

THE YOUNGEST MINORITY

LAWYERS IN DEFENSE OF CHILDREN

Sanford N. Katz, Editor

Volumes I and II

Volume I begins with a discussion of the used and misused phrase, "the best interests of the child," and concludes with a bill of rights for children. The volume includes articles on the child in custody disputes, in foster care, the stepchild, the illegitimate, the retarded, the battered, the "stubborn," the child in need of medical treatment, the unemancipated and the juvenile court victim.

Volume II offers solutions for other contemporary juvenile problems. The role of the father in the legal life of the child is examined. Other topics discussed are subsidized adoption for children in special circumstances, the plight of children committed to institutions, the child's preference in custody proceedings, and the reputation rights of children.

These two volumes should be immensely useful to social workers. They should also be of major interest, assistance and guidance to judges, legislators, attorneys and their clients, domestic relations professors and to all those whose lives are involved in the legal lives of children.

Order Form

The Youngest Minority
(513-0009)

	Qty.	Total
Youngest Minority I at $5.00 each	_____	$_____
Youngest Minority II at $5.00 each	_____	_____
Youngest Minority I & II at $8.50 for the set	_____	_____
Total for handling		$ 1.00
Total enclosed		$_____

Name _____

Address _____

City _____

State _____ Zip _____

Please make your check payable to the American Bar Association, and mail it with this order form to *Order Billing 513, American Bar Assn., 1155 E. 60th St., Chicago, IL 60637.*